John Dryden

AN ESSAY OF DRAMATIC POESY

John Dryden

AN ESSAY OF DRAMATIC POESY

[Edited with Introduction, Author's Information, Complete Text, Summary and Analysis and and Criticision]

Aditya Nandwani

B.A. English (Hons), Delhi University;
M.A. (English), IGNOU; Print Journalism (English) YMCA

ANMOL PUBLICATIONS PVT. LTD.

NEW DELHI - 110 002 (INDIA)

ANMOL PUBLICATIONS PVT. LTD.

H.O.: 4374/4B, Ansari Road, Darya Ganj,
New Delhi-110 002 (India)
Ph.: 23278000, 23261597

B.O.: No. 1015, Ist Main Road, BSK IIIrd Stage
IIIrd Phase, IIIrd Block
Bangalore - 560 085 (India)
Visit us at: www.anmolpublications.com

An Essay of Dramatic Poesy

First Published, 2009

PRINTED IN INDIA

Printed at Balaji Offset Press, Delhi.

Contents

Preface

John Dryden, an English poet and dramatist who would dominate literary efforts of The Restoration, was born on August 19, 1631, in Aldwinkle, Northamptonshire, England. He received a classical education at Westminster School and Trinity College, Cambridge, then moved to London in 1657 to commence his career as a professional writer. His first play, The Wild Gallant (1663), was a failure when first presented, but Dryden soon found more success with The Indian Queen (1664) which he co-authored with Sir Robert Howard and which served as his initial attempt to found a new theatrical genre, the heroic tragedy. Although George Villiers' The Rehearsal, a vicious satire of heroic tragedy, brought a quick end to the form, Dryden still managed to produce a number of successful works in this genre including The Indian Emperor (1665) and Secret Love (1667) which mixed heroic tragedy with contemporary comedy.

The young playwright's reputation grew quickly, and in 1668, only ten years after his move to London, Dryden was appointed Poet Laureate of England. (He was later stripped of the title because of religious differences when William and Mary came into power.) That same year, he agreed to write exclusively for Thomas Killigrew's theatrical company and became a shareholder. Both his first offering, Tyrannick Love (1669), and his successful follow-up, The Conquest of Granada by the Spaniards (1670), are examples of heroic tragedy. In 1672, however, perhaps sensing the demise of his short-lived genre, Dryden turned his hand to comedy and produced Marriage A-la-Mode, a brilliant battle of the sexes. Dryden's relationship with Killigrew's company continued until 1678 at which point he broke with the theatre (which was floundering in debt) and offered his latest play, Oedipus, a drama he had co-authored with Nathaniel Lee, to another company.

Author

Chapter 1

Introduction

The age of Elizabeth, memorable for so many reasons in the history of England, was especially brilliant in literature, and, within literature, in the drama. With some falling off in spontaneity, the impulse to great dramatic production lasted till the Long Parliament closed the theaters in 1642; and when they were reopened at the Restoration, in 1660, the stage only too faithfully reflected the debased moral tone of the court society of Charles II.

John Dryden, the great representative figure in the literature of the latter part of the seventeenth century, exemplifies in his work most of the main tendencies of the time. He came into notice with a poem on the death of Cromwell in 1658, and two years later was composing couplets expressing his loyalty to the returned king. He married Lady Elizabeth Howard, the daughter of a royalist house, and for practically all the rest of his life remained an adherent of the Tory Party. In 1663 he began writing for the stage, and during the next thirty years he attempted nearly all the current forms of drama. His"Annus Mirabilis", celebrating the English naval victories over the Dutch, brought him in 1670 the Poet Laureateship. He had, meantime, begun the writing of those admirable critical essays, represented in the present series by his Preface to the"Fables" and his Dedication to the translation of Virgil. In these he shows himself not only a critic of sound and penetrating judgment, but the first master of modern English prose style.

With"Absalom and Achitophel," a satire on the Whig leader, Shaftesbury, Dryden entered a new phase, and achieved what is regarded as"the finest of all political satires." This was followed by"The Medal," again directed against the Whigs, and this by"Mac Flecknoe," a fierce attack on his enemy and rival Shadwell. The Government rewarded his services by a lucrative appointment.

After triumphing in the three fields of drama, criticism, and satire, Dryden appears next as a religious poet in his"Religio Laici," an exposition of the doctrines of the Church of England from a layman's point of view. In the same year that the Catholic James II. ascended the throne, Dryden joined the Roman Church, and two years later defended his new religion in"The Hind and the Panther," an allegorical debate between two animals standing respectively for Catholicism and Anglicanism.

The Revolution of 1688 put an end to Dryden's prosperity; and after a short return to dramatic composition, he turned to translation as a means of supporting himself. He had already done something in this line; and after a series of translations from Juvenal, Persius, and Ovid, he undertook, at the age of sixty-three, the enormous task of turning the entire works of Virgil into English verse. How he succeeded in this, readers of the"Aeneid" in a companion volume of these classics can judge for themselves. Dryden's production closes with the collection of narrative poems called"Fables," published in 1700, in which year he died and was buried in the Poet's Corner in Westminster Abbey.

Dryden lived in an age of reaction against excessive religious idealism, and both his character and his works are marked by the somewhat unheroic traits of such a period. But he was, on the whole, an honest man, open minded, genial, candid, and modest; the wielder of a style, both in verse and prose, unmatched for clearness, vigour, and sanity.

Three types of comedy appeared in England in the time of Dryden-the comedy of humors, the comedy of intrigue, and the comedy of manners-and in all he did work that classed him with the ablest of his contemporaries. He developed the somewhat bombastic type of drama known as the heroic play, and brought it to its height in his"Conquest of Granada"; then, becoming dissatisfied with this form, he cultivated the French classic tragedy on the model of Racine. This he modified by combining with the regularity of the French treatment of dramatic action a richness of characterization in which he showed himself a disciple of Shakespeare, and of this mixed type his best example is"All for Love." Here he has the daring to challenge comparison with his master, and the greatest testimony to his achievement is the fact that, as Professor Noyes has said,"fresh from Shakespeare's'Antony and Cleopatra,' we can still read with intense pleasure Dryden's version of the story."

Chapter 2

Biography of John Dryden

John Dryden was born at the vicarage of Aldwinkle, Northamptonshire, on August 9, 1631, son of Erasmus Dryden and Mary Pickering. His family were Parliamentary supporters with Puritan leanings. He attended Westminster School as a king's scholar under Richard Busby, and was an avid student of the classics. While at Westminster, Dryden published his first verses, an elegy"Upon the Death of Lord Hastings", in Lachrymæ Musarum. He entered Trinity College, Cambridge, in 1650, and took a BA in 1654.

Dryden moved to London around 1657, and first gained notice with his'Heroic Stanzas' on the death of Lord Protector Cromwell. In the Royalist climate of the Restoration, he sensibly wrote Astraea Redux to celebrate the return of King Charles II. For the coronation, Dryden wrote "To His Sacred Majesty, A Panegyric". In 1662, Dryden wrote verses "To My Lord Chancellor" Clarendon, and was elected to the Royal Society. The theatres had been reopened, demand for entertainments was high, and Dryden set to writing plays. In 1663, Dryden married Lady Elizabeth Howard, the sister of his theatrical partner Sir Robert Howard, and the eldest daughter of the Earl of Berkshire. His first play was the prose comedy of humours A Wild Gallant, a wholly unremarkable piece, followed by the tragicomedy The Rival Ladies and The Indian Queen. In 1665, the theatres were closed down because of the plague that raged in London, and the King's court relocated to Oxford. There, Dryden finally established a reputation as a playwright with The Indian Emperor, a heroic drama.

The year 1666 was eventful in English history, including both the naval war with the Dutch, and the Great Fire of London. Dryden commemorated this'year of wonders" in his long poem, Annus Mirabilis, in 1667. This poem secured him the position of Poet Laureate on the death of William D'Avenant in 1668. The same year, he was also given the degree of M. A. by the Archbishop of Canterbury. As a fellow of the Royal Society, he was furthermore made Historiographer Royal in 1670, which brought him an annual income of £200.

In 1668, Dryden began a fruitful period of both critical and dramatic writing. His first major critical work was the Essay of Dramatic Poesy, followed by A Defence of an Essay, and Essay of Heroic Plays. His plays from this period include the comedy Secret Love; the heroic drama Tyrannic Love; the two-part The Conquest of Granada; and the comedy Marriage á la Mode. In 1674, Dryden published a tribute to Milton in the form of a musical adaptation of Paradise Lost, entitled The State of Innocence-it was never performed. The tragedy Aureng-Zebe was Dryden's first play in blank verse, followed by his masterpiece All for Love, based on the story of Anthony and Cleopatra.

The success and fame Dryden enjoyed naturally garnered him enemies. He was ridiculed in Buckingham's The Rehearsal, and brutally beaten in an attack in Rose Alley, Covent Garden, on December 18, 1679. It has been suggested, though never proved, that Lord Rochester had a hand in hiring the ruffians responsible for the attack. Rochester had lampooned Dryden earlier, and had in turn suspected of Dryden for complicity in ridiculing him in Lord Mulgrave's Essay on Satire.

With the the unsuccessful prose comedy "Limberham", the poor adaptation of Troilus and Cressida, and the play "Spanish Friar", Dryden left his career as dramatist for a time and turned his attention to satire. His political satire on Monmouth and Shaftesbury, Absalom and Achitophel, appeared in 1681. It is one of the great English satires, and it brought him further favor with Charles II, who was pleased at this attack against the Whigs during the Exclusion Crisis. Dryden dutifully wrote the Second Part of Absalom and Achitophel in collaboration with Nahum Tate, as well as another attack on Shaftesbury's supporters, The Medal. These naturally provoked counterattacks, including Thomas Shadwell's The Medal of John Bayes. Dryden in turn responded Mac Flecknoe, full of ridicule for Shadwell, perhaps his most entertaining poem, pirated in 1682, and officially printed in 1684.

Dryden also had a keen interest in theology, and this resulted first in the publication of Religio Laici. This work, the title of which translates as "A Layman's Faith", was a long religious poem arguing Christianity over Deism, the Bible as the guide to salvation, and the Anglican Church over the Catholic Church. This period saw some of Dryden's best poems, the Pindaric ode "Threnodia Augustalis" at the death of Charles II, the beautiful lyrical ode "To the Pious Memory... of Mrs Anne Killigrew" written to commemorate a painter who drowned in the Thames, and "A Song for Saint Cecilia's Day". Dryden had long grappled with religious uncertainty, and converted into Roman Catholicism in 1686, the year after the ascension to the throne of King James II, a Catholic. In 1687, Dryden published The Hind and the Panther, an allegorical fable criticizing the Anglican church. Dryden suffered for this almost immediately. The Revolution of 1688, which placed the Protestant William III on the throne, caused him to be deprived of his laureateship, and what was worse, he was replaced by his old enemy, Shadwell.

Dryden returned to the theatre. He wrote the libretto to Purcell's opera King Arthur; a tragicomedy, Don Sebastian; a comedy of errors, Amphitryon; and Cleomenes: the Spartan Hero. Dryden's Love Triumphant, the prologue of which announced it as his last play, was a failure. Dryden turned to writing translations, including the satires of Perseus and Juvenal and Virgil's Aeneid. He also wrote more poetry, including "An Ode, on the death of Mr Henry Purcell" commemorating the composer, a second ode for St. Cecilia's Day,"Alexander's Feast", which was later incorporated into his Fables Ancient and Modern, paraphrases of Ovid, Boccaccio, and Chaucer. Dryden died on April 30, 1700, soon after the publication of the Fables, of inflammation caused by gout. He was buried in Westminster Abbey. Dryden was a good playwright and poet, a fine translator, a solid critic, and an excellent satirist whose works are still worthy of much admiration.

Early Life

Dryden was born in the village rectory of Aldwincle near Oundle in Northamptonshire, where his maternal grandfather was Rector of All Saints. He was the eldest of fourteen children born to Erasmus Dryden and wife Mary Pickering, paternal grandson of Sir Erasmus Dryden, 1st Baronet and wife Frances Wilkes, Puritan landowning gentry who supported the Puritan cause and Parliament. He was also a second cousin once removed of Jonathan Swift. As a boy Dryden lived in the nearby village of Titchmarsh where it is also likely that he received his first education. In 1644 he was sent to Westminster School as a King's Scholar where his headmaster was Dr Richard Busby, a charismatic teacher and severe disciplinarian. Recently enough re-founded by Elizabeth I, Westminster during this period embraced a very different religious and political spirit encouraging royalism and high Anglicanism. Whatever Dryden's response to this was, he clearly respected the Headmaster and would later send two of his own sons to school at Westminster. Many years after his death a house at Westminster was founded in his name.

As a humanist grammar school, Westminster maintained a curriculum which trained pupils in the art of rhetoric and the presentation of arguments for both sides of a given issue. This is a skill which would remain with Dryden and influence his later writing and thinking, as much of it displays these dialectical patterns. The Westminster curriculum also included weekly translation assignments which developed Dryden's capacity for assimilation. This was also to be exhibited in his later works. His years at Westminster were not uneventful, and his first published poem, an elegy with a strong royalist feel on the death of his schoolmate Henry, Lord Hastings from smallpox, alludes to the execution of King Charles I, which took place on 30 January 1649.

In 1650 Dryden went up to Trinity College, Cambridge where he would have experienced a return to the religious and political ethos of his childhood. The Master of Trinity was a Puritan preacher by the name of Thomas Hill who had been a rector in Dryden's home village. Though there is little specific information on Dryden's undergraduate years, he would have followed the standard curriculum of classics, rhetoric, and mathematics. In 1654 he obtained his BA, graduating top of the list for Trinity that year. In June of the same year Dryden's father died, leaving him some land which generated a little income, but not enough to live on.

Arriving in London during The Protectorate, Dryden obtained work with Cromwell's Secretary of State, John Thurloe. This appointment may have been the result of influence exercised on his behalf by the Lord Chamberlain Sir Gilbert Pickering, Dryden's cousin. Dryden was present on 23 November 1658 at Cromwell's funeral where he processed with the Puritan poets John Milton and Andrew Marvell. Shortly thereafter he published his first important poem, Heroique Stanzas, a eulogy on Cromwell's death which is cautious and prudent in its emotional display. In 1660 Dryden celebrated the Restoration of the monarchy and the return of Charles II with Astraea Redux, an authentic royalist panegyric. In this work the interregnum is illustrated as a time of anarchy, and Charles is seen as the restorer of peace and order.

Later Life and Career

After the Restoration, Dryden quickly established himself as the leading poet and literary critic of his day and he transferred his allegiances to the new government. Along with Astraea Redux, Dryden welcomed the new regime with two more panegyrics; To His Sacred Majesty: A Panegyric on his Coronation, and To My Lord Chancellor. These poems suggest that Dryden was looking to court a possible patron, but he was to instead make a living in writing for publishers, not for the aristocracy, and thus ultimately for the reading public. These, and his other nondramatic poems, are occasional-that is, they celebrate public events. Thus they are written for the nation rather than the self, and the Poet Laureate (as he would later become) is obliged to write a certain number of these per annum. In November 1662 Dryden was proposed for membership in the Royal Society, and he was elected an early fellow. However, Dryden was inactive in Society affairs and in 1666 was expelled for non-payment of his dues.

On December 1, 1663 Dryden married the royalist sister of Sir Robert Howard-Lady Elizabeth. Dryden's works occasionally contain outbursts against the married state but also celebrations of the same. Thus, little is known of the intimate side of his marriage. Lady Elizabeth however, was to bear him three sons and outlive him.

With the reopening of the theatres after the Puritan ban, Dryden busied himself with the composition of plays. His first play, The Wild Gallant appeared in 1663 and was not successful, but he was to have more success, and from 1668 on he was contracted to produce three plays a year for the King's Company in which he was also to become a shareholder. During the 1660s and 70s theatrical writing was to be his main source of income. He led the way in Restoration comedy, his best known work being Marriage A-la-Mode, as well as heroic tragedy and regular tragedy, in which his greatest success was All for Love. Dryden was never satisfied with his theatrical writings and frequently suggested that his talents were wasted on unworthy audiences. He thus was making a bid for poetic fame off-stage. In 1667, around the same time his dramatic career began, he published Annus Mirabilis, a lengthy historical poem which described the events of 1666; the English defeat of the Dutch naval fleet and the Great Fire of London. It was a modern epic in pentameter quatrains that established him as the preeminent poet of his generation, and was crucial in his attaining the posts of Poet Laureate and historiographer royal.

When the Great Plague closed the theatres in 1665 Dryden retreated to Wiltshire where he wrote Of Dramatick Poesie, arguably the best of his unsystematic prefaces and essays. Dryden constantly defended his own literary practice, and Of Dramatick Poesie, the longest of his critical works, takes the form of a dialogue in which four characters-each based on a prominent contemporary, with Dryden himself as'Neander'-debate the merits of classical, French and English drama. The greater part of his critical works introduce problems which he is eager to discuss, and show the work of a writer of independent mind who feels strongly about his own ideas, ideas which demonstrate the incredible breadth of his reading. He felt strongly about the relation of the poet to tradition and the creative process, and his best heroic play"Aureng-zebe" has a prologue which denounces the use of rhyme in serious drama. His play All for Love, was written in blank verse, and was to immediately follow Aureng-Zebe.

Dryden's greatest achievements were in satiric verse: the mock-heroic MacFlecknoe, a more personal product of his Laureate years, was a lampoon circulated in manuscript and an attack on the playwright Thomas Shadwell. It is not a belittling form of satire, but rather one which makes his object great in ways which are unexpected, transferring the ridiculous into poetry. This line of satire continued with Absalom and Achitophel and The Medal. His other major works from this period are the religious poems Religio Laici, written from the position of a member of the Church of England; his 1683 edition of Plutarchs Lives Translated From the Greek by Several Hands in which he introduced the word biography to English readers; and The Hind and the Panther, which celebrates his conversion to Roman Catholicism.

When in 1688 James was deposed, Dryden's refusal to take the oaths of allegiance to the new government left him out of favour at court. Thomas Shadwell succeeded him as Poet Laureate, and he was forced to give up his public offices and live by the proceeds of his pen. Dryden translated works by Horace, Juvenal, Ovid, Lucretius, and Theocritus, a task which he found far more satisfying than writing for the stage. In 1694 he began work on what would be his most ambitious and defining work as translator, The Works of Virgil, which was published by subscription. The publication of the translation of Virgil was a national event and brought Dryden the sum of ?1,400. His final translations appeared in the volume Fables Ancient and Modern, a series of episodes from Homer, Ovid, and Boccaccio, as well as modernized adaptations from Geoffrey Chaucer interspersed with Dryden's own poems. The Preface to Fables is considered to be both a major work of criticism and one of the finest essays in English. As a critic and translator he was essential in making accessible to the reading English public literary works in the classical languages.

Dryden died in 1700 and is buried in Westminster Abbey. He was the subject of various poetic eulogies, such as Luctus Brittannici: or the Tears of the British Muses; for the Death of John Dryden, Esq. (London, 1700), and The Nine Muses.

Reputation and Influence

Dryden was the dominant literary figure and influence of his age.He established the heroic couplet as the standard meter of English poetry, by writing successful satires, religious pieces, fables, epigrams, compliments, prologues, and plays in it; he also introduced the alexandrine and triplet into the form. In his poems, translations, and criticism, he established a poetic diction appropriate to the heroic couplet-Auden referred to him as"the master of the middle style"-that was a model for his contemporaries and for much of the 18th century. The considerable loss felt by the English literary community at his death was evident from the elegies which it inspired. Dryden's heroic couplet became the dominant poetic form of the 18th century. The most influential poet of the 18th century, Alexander Pope, was heavily influenced by Dryden, and often borrowed from him; other writers were equally influenced by Dryden and Pope. Pope famously praised Dryden's versification in his imitation of Horace's Epistle II.i:"Dryden taught to join/The varying pause, the full resounding line,/The long majestic march, and energy divine." Samuel Johnson summed up the general attitude with his remark that"the veneration with which his name is pronounced by every cultivator of English literature, is paid to him as he refined the language, improved the sentiments, and tuned the numbers of English poetry." His poems were very widely read, and are often quoted, for instance, in Tom Jones and Johnson's essays.

Johnson also noted, however, that"He is, therefore, with all his variety of excellence, not often pathetic; and had so little sensibility of the power of effusions purely natural, that he did not esteem them in others. Simplicity gave him no pleasure." The 18th century did not mind this too much, but in later ages, this was increasingly considered a fault.

One of the first attacks on Dryden's reputation was by Wordsworth, who complained that Dryden's descriptions of natural objects in his translations from Virgil were much inferior to the originals. However, several of Wordsworth's contemporaries, such as George Crabbe, Lord Byron, and Walter Scott (who edited Dryden's works), were still keen admirers of Dryden. Besides, Wordsworth did admire many of Dryden's poems, and his famous"Intimations of Immortality" ode owes something stylistically to Dryden's"Alexander's Feast." John Keats admired the"Fables," and imitated them in his poem Lamia. Later 19th century writers had little use for verse satire, Pope, or Dryden; Matthew Arnold famously dismissed them as"classics of our prose." He did have a committed admirer in George Saintsbury, and was a prominent figure in quotation books such as Bartlett's, but the next major poet to take an interest in Dryden was T. S. Eliot, who wrote that he was'the ancestor of nearly all that is best in the poetry of the eighteenth century', and that'we cannot fully enjoy or rightly estimate a hundred years of English poetry unless we fully enjoy Dryden.' However, in the same essay, Eliot accused Dryden of having a"commonplace mind." Critical interest in Dryden has increased recently, but, as a relatively straightforward writer (William Empson, another modern admirer of Dryden, compared his"flat" use of language with Donne's interest in the"echoes and recesses of words") his work has not occasioned as much interest as Andrew Marvell's or John

Donne's or Pope's.

Poetic Style

What Dryden achieved in his poetry was not the emotional excitement we find in the Romantic poets of the early nineteenth century, nor the intellectual complexities of the metaphysical poets. His subject-matter was often factual, and he aimed at expressing his thoughts in the most precise and concentrated way possible. Although he uses formal poetic structures such as heroic stanzas and heroic couplets, he tried to achieve the rhythms of speech. However, he knew that different subjects need different kinds of verse, and in his preface to Religio Laici he wrote:"...the expressions of a poem designed purely for instruction ought to be plain and natural, yet majestic...The florid, elevated and figurative way is for the passions; for (these) are begotten in the soul by showing the objects out of their true proportion....A man is to be cheated into passion, but to be reasoned into truth."

Chapter 3

Major Works

Astraea Redux, 1660
The Indian Emperor, 1665
Annus Mirabilis, 1667
The Enchanted Island (comedy), 1667, an adaptation with William D'Avenant of Shakespeare's The Tempest
An Essay of Dramatick Poesie, 1668
An Evening's Love (comedy), 1669
Tyrannick Love (tragedy), 1669
The Conquest of Granada, 1670
Marriage A-la-Mode, 1672
Aureng-zebe, 1675
All for Love, 1678
Oedipus (heroic drama), 1679, an adaptation with Nathaniel Lee of Sophocles' Oedipus
Absalom and Achitophel, 1681
MacFlecknoe, 1682
The Medal, 1682
Religio Laici, 1682
The Hind and the Panther, 1687
Amphitryon, 1690
Don Sebastian, 1690
Amboyna, or the Cruelties of the Dutch to the English Merchants, 1673
The Works of Virgil, 1697
Fables, Ancient and Modern, 1700

Chapter 4

Dryden as Critic

Dryden was the major literary figure in both literature and criticism of during the Restoration and later 17th century, and the most influential critic of the whole century. Criticism during the Jacobean age and the Commonwhealth will fail to justly appraise or even recognize the great works of the age. It is an undeveloped genre, and the information about literature often consists of a"roll-call" of authors, a bare list of names and works with some laudatory comment appended to them. There is not even a single detailed study or commentary of a literary work. Dryden will do much to change this situation; his success is also the success of criticism in English letters.

Being a writer as well as a critic, Dryden always wrote criticism to some practical end concerning his own works. Much of his critical work is to be found in prefaces to his own works. Besides, he was a professional writer. He was not a nobleman writing for his pleasure: he had to live from his work and in the age he wrote in this meant that he had to find some patron or other to take him under his protection. He had to flatter, and this explains not only the nature of his writing, but also sometimes that of his criticism.

Sometimes his reasoning is flawed by this need to flatter. As in the critics we have studied up to now, we find in Dryden an interest in the general issues of criticism rather than in a close reading of particular texts (although he will provide one of the first of such readings, that of Jonson's The Silent Woman). He wants to rely on both authority and common sense, and often seems at a loss when the two seem to go against each other. We call Dryden a neoclassical critic, just as Boileau, although in fact there are wide differences between them. Dryden meditates on the neoclassical rules, which he feels to be right in the main, but then he also wants to find a critical justification for the great tradition of English poetry, which lay beyond those rules. It is to his credit that he thought over the principles of French neo-Classicism and did not apply them mechanically to the English letters. According to T.S. Eliot, Dryden's great work consists not so much in the originality of his principles as in having realized the need to affirm the native tradition, as opposed to the overwhelming French influence. His best-known work, the Essay of Dramatic Poesy, partly reflects this tension in Dryden's commitments.

Its dialogue form has often been criticised as inconclusive, but actually, as in most dialogues, there is a spokesman more weighty than the others. Dryden carries about his task with efficiency, stating his own ideas but leaving some leeway for difference of opinion. Neander's overall statement on the rules is that they can add to the perfection of a work, but that they will not improve a work which does not already contain some degree of perfection or genius in it. And we may find writers like Shakespeare, Dryden believes, who did not follow the rules but are nevertheless obviously superior to any"regular" writer. Shakespeare disconcerts Dryden, who recognises his superiority but is more at ease with Ben Jonson.

In Dryden, then, we find a"liberal" neoclassicist, although he is most coherent when he is dealing with that which can be understood and reduced to rule. His relaxation is to a great extent both a refusal to believe in the universal application in the neoclassic principles and an inability to provide new and more comprehensive principles. Because his most cogent statement on the rules (following Rapin) is that if the rules be well considered, we shall find them to be made only to reduce nature into method... they are founded upon good sense and sound reason, rather than on authority.

Dryden is not a great analyst of texts nor an important literary historian, but some of his works are significant steps in the development of both directions in criticism. Dryden's importance as a critic comes from his place in history at the start of the long neoclassical era, whose principles he helped determine; he contributed a great deal to raise the standards of criticism and to define the role of the discipline. As he says himself they wholly mistake the nature of criticism who thinks its business is principally to find fault. Criticism, as it was first instituted by Aristotle, was meant a standard of judging well; the chiefest part of which is to observe those excellencies which should delight a reasonable reader. And of course his ideas also give us insights into his own work.

The Poet and the Creative Process

The way the work is"moulded to shape" is through"fancy moving the sleeping images of things towards the light, there to be distinguished and then either chosen or rejected by the judgement." In Dryden, and indeed in all the 18th-century critics after him, fancy is sometimes synonymous with imagination and sometimes identified as a special kind of imagination."Wit" is also used to refer to this faculty. Fancy and imagination will become different concepts in Coleridge. So we have two opposite principles at work in the writer's mind: fancy and judgement (cf. the different accounts of the creative process in Sidney, Bacon, and Hobbes). We may note that fancy is subordinate to judgement, although it seems to be assigned a more relevant role than in Hobbes' theory. Fancy is synthetic, while judgement is analytic, as Hobbes had said and Locke will reaffirm.

Of course, Dryden has to give fancy its due in the composition of a work. But it is something he mistrusts. It is too lawless, and there is a danger that it may get out of hand. Strictures placed during the process of composition, such as the rules or the use of rhyme, are a good means to restrict the impulse of fancy and allow judgement to become dominant. While writing,"fancy, memory and judgement are then extended in the rack". Writing is a painstaking activity, one which demands the utmost of the writer's capabilities. In the preface to his poem Annus Mirabilis, Dryden gave an account of the phases of the creative process, which we can profitably compare with the inventio, dispositio and elocutio of classical rhetoric. To compose an epic poem, he says, a poet needs wit."Wit" in the eighteenth century did not suggest the gift of the quick repartee or the bon mot, as it does today; rather, it stood for the creative faculty of the human mind, above all the aspect defined by Hobbes as"fancy," the ability to see the resemblances between different objects. Dryden defines wit as imagination, as the ability to find the right memory or the right metaphor we are looking for:

But to proceed from wit in the general notion of it to the proper wit of an heroic or historical poem, I judge it chiefly to consist in the delightful imaging of persons, actions, passions, or things... it is some lively and apt description, dressed in such a colors of speech, that it sets before your eyes the absent object, as perfectly and more delightfully than nature. So then, the first happiness of the poet's imagination is properly invention or finding the thought; the second is fancy, or the variation, deriving or molding of that thought, as the judgment represents it proper to the subject; the third is elocution, or the art of clothing and adorning that thought so found and varied, in apt, significant and sounding words: the quickness of the imagination is seen in the invention, the fertility in the fancy, and the accuracy in the expression.

Writers in dramatic style, such as Ovid and all playwrights, must excel in invention and fancy; those speaking in his own voice, like Virgil, must cultivate their expression. So, there are different creative faculties in the human mind, and each kind of work may demand a special development of one or other. Dryden feels at times the need to specialise: he wrote works in practically all genres except the novel, but he seems to think that each writer excels in a particular kind of writing. He complains that the Ancients were either tragedians or comedians, and that it is easier to attain perfection in this way, writing only the kind of thing one does best. This natural gift has to be controlled by technique. The good writer must be a born genius (here Dryden refers us to Longinus), and he must know the emotions he is depicting. But he must not be carried away by them because probably the audience would not follow him. Dryden believes that poetry is an art for witty men, and not for madmen. Passion would blur the differences between characters, and it is judgment which keeps them separate. We can compare this analytical labour of the judgment to Hobbes once again. Dryden's interest in the successful objectification of the poet's emotions is an interesting prefiguration of later aesthetic theories (e.g. Schopenhauer's). Of course we have the classical models to guide us. To copy their ways is not a fault, rather a virtue. In the Essay of Dramatic Poesy we find this phrase as a commendation of Ben Jonson:"He was not only a professed imitator of Horace, but a learned plagiary of all the others".

But true imitation must be original and improve the models. Dryden believes that poetry has a historical development, and he wishes"that poetry may not go backward, when all other arts and sciences are advancing." We may profit from the models and the experience of the ancients and try to go beyond them. All great writers have borrowed from others, without their being less original for it. He traces the Homeric influence in Virgil, for instance. The neoclassical era is not particularly sensitive to originality and invention, but nevertheless Dryden believes that other things being equal, originality is to be preferred to good imitation, and is a greater proof of genius.

One word on the subject of progress in literature: Dryden, as many other critics of his time, seems to believe in a cyclical alternance of barbarian ages with ages of refinement and progress. They believe themselves to be in the equivalent of the Roman Empire. Shakespeare is Dryden's Homer, and Jonson is his Virgil. He does not seem to believe that the heights of the classical age can be reached again; even the language is too unstable for great works and inferior to Greek. Like Pope, Dryden believed that writing in English is like writing on sand, compared to the writing on marble of the Ancients.

Prosody and Diction

Rhyme is for Dryden something more than a mere ornament. It is a way of consciously controlling the process of composition: because of the superior attention it requires, rhyme demands a greater consciousness on the part of the poet, and less abandonment to the inspiration of his fancy. Rhyme bounds and circumscribes the fancy.... The fancy then gives leisure to the judgment to come in, which, seeing so heavy a tax imposed, is ready to cut off all unnecessary expenses".

Rhyme, then, is not mere"embroidery of sense," it is a means of clarifying the thought. We shall see that Dryden initially favored the use of rhyme in plays when the appropriateness of this convention coming from France is being debated. Verse is right; it is only unnatural when it is forced. Rhyme is superior to blank verse, which Dryden believed was invented by Shakespeare. Paradoxically, he recognizes that it is blank verse which is the tradition natural to English. However, Dryden's statement on rhyme does not end here. We may note that he accepts blank verse in the less serious types of plays. And in later years, he was to modify his views, and he came to recognize that blank verse was a suitable vehicle for serious drama. In the prologue to Aureng-Zebe, he admits to growing"weary of his long-loved mistress, rhyme" and recognizes Shakespeare's superiority. And in the preface to All for Love, an imitation of Shakespeare's Antony and Cleopatra, he admits that blank verse is more suitable for a Shakespearean imitation, even if it is a tragedy.

Maybe the neoclassical preference for the heroic couplet is the reason for this change: couplets of alexandrines, the staple of French classical drama, are all right for the French language, but the English heroic couplet does not lend itself so easily to the portrayal of conversation. It is best fit to long series of meditative or essayistic verses, and it is here where it will triumph; English drama reverts to blank verse and then to prose.

Dryden also writes a miniature history of modern prosody. Although he is a bit patronizing on Chaucer, he is readier than most people in his age to recognize his genius. However, at the time Chaucer's language was still unknown (Dryden laughs at the first news of a reconstruction of Chaucer's regular metrics in the preface to his translation), so

Dryden does not recognize his merits as a versifier, and considers Waller and Denham (who are minor poets from our point of view) to be the first great versifiers of the English language. Waller is the inventor of the couplet: he"first showed us to conclude the sense most commonly in diptychs". Dryden will insist on the connection between form and sense: in this way form will impose itself directly on sense. Couplets and quatrains must contain a unit of sense. On the other hand, he opposes the strict equality of syllables in all lines, a reasonable thing to do, since stressing certain weak syllables and making them count for measure is unnatural to English.

Dryden opposes Aristotle in believing that the soul of a play is not to be found in its plot, but rather in its author's language, in diction and thought. Dryden wants a literature written in a pure language, one which is free from neologism and pedantry alike. However, he accepts coinages from Latin. Like Swift whose complaints will be much the same, he longs for an academy with an authority to decide on linguistic matters.

We find in the age of Dryden a growing reaction against the Ramist conception of rhetoric. If rhetoric is just an addition of ornamental words, it is better to do away with it. The Cartesian and the empiricist ideas coincide here. Fancy will seen as something which plays with words, while judgment defines the real relationships between things. One of the most notable phenomena of the age is the definition of the language of science in opposition to rhetoric. The Royal Society inspires the works of John Wilkins (Essay towards a Real Character and a Philosophical Language, 1668) and Thomas Sprat, who advocates a"mathematical plainness" in style: one word, one thing. These ideas will be satirized in Swift's Gulliver's Travels, where the wise men in Laputa carry with them all the objects they want to speak about and merely point to them. For Locke, the most influential philosopher during the eighteenth century, eloquence misleads judgment, instead of directing it. All these writers mistrust literature, poetry, rhetoric, which they consider empty words. There is a growing emphasis on reason which will be felt in literary theory as well.

Character and Plot

Dryden discusses character and plot as technical difficulties faced by the writer, sometimes working one against the other. This conception is very characteristic of British criticism. We can compare it with E. M. Forster's account in Aspects of the Novel, which describes how the plot seems to lead the writer in one direction and the characters in a different one. For both Forster and Dryden, it is the poet's art to respect both the decorum of the characters and the causally necessary, natural solution to the plot. The writer, Dryden says, is like a god to his characters, having prescience and power of determination. But it is difficult to use them in a way altogether convincing, working as a whole.

We may note that decorum and rule are for Dryden a means of giving formal integrity to the work: that is, they are not only content, but form as well; their aim is not to depict the world as it is, but to give unity to the work. Dryden, like many later critics, is conscious of two different tendencies present in a work: although he does not use these terms, we might call them the mimetic tendency (the relationship between an element in the work and reality) and the structural tendency (the coherence of the work imposing its own conventions, the concern for formal integrity).

He opposes the strongly conventionalized characters and plots of Roman comedies, asking for a wider imitation of nature, although he also appreciates the advantages of patterning and of structural simplicity in current French plays, and he believes some of Shakespeare's plays to be"ridiculously cramped" with incident. But the interest of the plot and the characters is also to be found in variety and not simply in a well-defined structure. In variety we recognize real life, and this is one of the advantages of the English approach to dramatic art.

The story itself is the least important part of a poet's work, the one which lends it most easily to imitation. It is a material which must be worked on, finding suitable characters and style. Aristotle, Dryden points out, placed plot first of all elements in a play as the basis on which the others are built, and not as the most important one to determine the quality of a play. For Dryden, it is the characters' language which is the most important element in a play.

Dryden repeats Aristotle's theory on the unity of action, but understanding it in a wider sense than many neoclassical critics. There can be unity in a play with two lines of action, if they are causally linked. Dryden introduces in English criticism the criterion of unity used by Corneille, the contrast between the suspense of the partial actions and the final repose of the mind of the audience when the whole of the action is completed. He demands that beginning, middle and end follow each other in a necessary way: a fable ought to have a beginning, middle, and an end, all just and natural, so that that part which is the middle, could not naturally be the beginning or end, and so of the rest: all are depending on one another, like the links of a curious chain.

This does not happen, he says, in Spanish plots; as in perspective, so in tragedy there must be a point of sight in which all the lines terminate; otherwise the eye wanders, and the work is false ("Grounds" 167). It is the moral that directs the whole action of the play to one centre.

Dryden also repeats Aristotle's doctrine on characters. Manners must be apparent (shown in action and discourse), suitable, resembling, and constant. Characters derive from manners, but they must be a suitable composite of manners, and not be grounded on a single trait. We may compare this conception, once again, to E. M. Forster's well-known opposition between flat and round characters (Aspects of the Novel).

The Essay of Dramatic Poesy

In 1663, a Frenchman called Sorbière published a book on England, in which he made fun of the state of both the science and the arts in that country. Thomas Sprat, of the Royal Society, answered back with a treatise on the new science which was being developed in England. Dryden wrote his Essay of Dramatic Poesy, a meditation on the nature and conventions of drama which was an answer to Sorbière (who had criticized English drama for not following the unities) as well as to French dramatic theory and practice in general. It is a defence of the English theatrical ways, presenting them at least as an alternative to the classical and the French styles.

Something can be said for them, and not just against them, and we may well think that Meander's arguments for English drama are the strongest. However, it is not clear which is the drama Dryden is defending, because he answers Sorbière's attack against current English theatre with an appeal to Ben Jonson and Shakespeare, the writers of the"last age", fifty years his predecessors. Dryden's comments on earlier playwrights are important not only in themselves, but also because they are at the start of a tradition of valuation of English literature,"dearest moments in the history of national self-appreciation" for Sampson. Dryden set the rules for Shakespearean criticism for the next century and a half; and if his admiration for Ben Jonson seems excessive to us now, we still use many of his views of the differences between both writers, in whom he saw an entirely different force at work. For us, there is little doubt that French drama in Dryden's time was superior to whatever was being written in England and to anything written for the English stage for centuries afterwards; Molière, Corneille and Racine are far better playwrights than the Restoration comedians (Congreve, Vanbrugh, Sedley, Wycherley) and they are above Dryden himself as a tragedian.

In any case, Dryden expounds in a fair enough way the reasons for and against the dramatic practice of both countries, as well as of that of the Ancients, and re-states the classical doctrine on drama. Dryden retains openness to contrary argument which almost approaches skepticism, although it would be more accurate to define his views as probabilistic rather than skeptic (Wimsatt and Brooks 193). Dryden was accused of inconclusiveness, and he retorted with the Defence of an Essay of Dramatic Poesy, and there he alludes to the Aristotelian difference between demonstrative and probabilistic arguments: the latter Aristotle had said to be proper to rhetoric. It is up to the talent of each fictional speaker to convince us of the rightness of his opinions. They are Cities, Eugenics, Siliceous, and Meander. Although Meander is generally recognized as Dryden's spokesman and as the more cogent speaker of all, all are allowed to have their say, and the dialogue is not brought to a conclusion through the victory of Meander's argument: we leave the four friends still debating the issues. And in the Defence of the Essay of Dramatic Poesy,

Dryden says that his argument is not demonstrative but probabilistic: it is up to the reader to decide which of the speakers he will side with. Crites defends and extreme Classicist position, although he is not blind to the merits of modern versification. Siliceous and Eugenics accept the same Classical premises as Crites, but say that modern poets have profited from the experience and imitation of the Classics and follow rules more exactly. Siliceous adds that the rules have been best followed by French drama, which is to be regarded as the model. Meander insists on the need of liveliness-which he feels is lacking in Classical and French plays-rather than plain verisimilitude. He approves as well of Corneille's phrase,"il est facile aux speculatifs d'estre severes," and he is concerned with the excessive rigidity that critical principles, divorced of actual dramatic practice, tend to impose on drama.

The Dramatic Unities of Time and Place

The three unities, Dryden observes, ought to be followed in all regular plays. But he is tolerant enough with plays which are moderately irregular.

In the Essay of Dramatic Poesy, Crites repeats the account of the unities given by Corneille (without his qualifications on the difficulty of the enterprise). The unities aim at verisimilitude; the space and time of representation must be as close as possible to those of the feigned action. Any distortion must be supposed to fall between the acts, plots have to begin"in medias rest", narration must be restricted to events simultaneous with the action if possible, etc.

In time we find that the coincidence of times works all right in dealing with the precipitate events at the conclusion of a play, but makes the complication seem artificial or else rely too much on narrative. Dryden follows Corneille in showing how the unities of space and time are mutually related and regularity in one favors regularity in the other. This may be helped through the"liaison des scenes." Place (and time, too) remains the same inside each act, and that you may know it to be the same, the stage is so supplied with persons that it is never empty all the time.

But the view of the question give by Crites is much qualified in the debate by the advocates of the moderns. The disadvantages of regularity are pointed out: there is a danger of narrowness and monotony. The"liaison des scenes" is only possible in French plays because their plots contain little action and their scenes are very long. This also demands an excessive use of monologue, which is unnatural. One main end of theatre, delight, is not sufficiently attended to in Greek or French plays.

Rhyme and Verisimilitude

Dryden held an interesting debate with his brother-in-law, Sir Robert Howard, on the property of rhyme in plays and its relationship to verisimilitude. Howard opposed the use of rhyme, which he believed to break the illusion of reality which any play ought to produce. Dryden defended the use of rhyme. He believes that the end of a play is not so much to give a faithful imitation of human life as to give a heightened image of reality. Rhyme works in that way: it guides the attention and gives greater tightness to speeches. Besides, Dryden says, blank verse (which was proposed by Howard as a substitute for rhyme) is not"natural," either. Howard based his attack on rhyme on the principle that if a play is to trick our minds into a fictive reality, then the use of rhyme worked against that, because men do not speak in rhyme; we will not believe that it is the character who is actually speaking. Dryden's answer is categorical: we are never tricked in a play into believing that we are facing a real scene; and it is the author, not the characters, whom we consider to be speaking in the last analysis. In the Essay of Dramatic Poesy, even Crites acknowledges that dramatic verisimilitude deceives us because we desire to be deceived, and that we know all the time that we are being deceived. We will have to keep this in mind when we discuss the definition of the audience's role as a"willing suspension of disbelief" in nineteenth-century criticism.

Howard was also against following of the three unities, also for the sake of verisimilitude: he believed that too much use must be made of coincidence to concentrate an action in so restricted a space and time. Paradoxically, Dryden holds the opposite: the unities produce an effect of verisimilitude.

Actually, Dryden's position is not incoherent; only, verisimilitude as such is not the only thing at stake here. Howard, we may note, is for a relaxation of the formalities of theatre: no rhyme, no rules, whereas Dryden appreciates the value which they have in the making of a work of art, because of the tightness they impose on experience, the concentration, the dramatic intensity, the heightened attention of the audience. Dryden sees that the essence of art is more than just imitation of real life. Drama is not trompe-l'il, that extreme of mimetic trickery. Verisimilitude is all right, it is relevant to the question, but we need something more than just verisimilitude, something which rhyme and a concentrated action help to shape. A tragedy is always natural as a tragedy:

The plot, the characters, the wit, the descriptions, are all exalted above the level of common converse, as high as the imagination of the poet can carry them with proportion to versatility.

Verse, then, is natural to tragedy, even if it is not natural to life: Verse,'tis true, is not the effect of sudden thought; but this hinders not that sudden thought may be represented in verse.

Delight and Instruction

In his definition of a play in the Essay of Dramatic Poesy, Dryden says it is "a just and lively image of human nature, representing its passions and humors, and the changes of fortune to which it is subject, for the delight and instruction of mankind."

So, once again we meet a version of the Horatian" "productive delight." Elsewhere Dryden writes: "these two ends may be thus distinguished. The chief end of the poet is to please, for his immediate reputation depends on it. The great end of the poet is to instruct, which is performed by making pleasure the vehicle of that instruction; for poetry is an art, and all arts are made to profit."

But in later pronouncements, Dryden asserts that

"delight is the chief, if not the only end of poesy; instruction can be admitted but in the second place, for poesy only instructs as it delights, or that instruction is the end of tragedy, but in comedy it is not so; for the chief end of it is divertissement and delight, and that so much, that it is disputed... whether instruction be any part of its employment."

Dryden does not believe comedy to be grounded on any serious principle such as moral instruction. Here Dryden sides with Heinsius in declaring that comedy has amusement and delight as its only aim, far from the serious concerns of tragedy. Comedy works not on the best impulses of the audience, but on the worst, making them laugh. The pleasure coming from comedy is a"malicious pleasure"; comedy may instruct, but it is a secondary purpose: its main duty is to please. But he often changed opinions on this subject, alternately stressing or playing down the responsibilities and moral requirements of drama. In this sense he is not the typical neoclassical critic. The general attitude towards comedy is that it ought to provide moral instruction. Sidney and Jonson had even defended comedy without laughter. Others defend, of course, laughter, such as Molière and Pope. Dryden affirms that Ben Jonson did not require creative wit, being satisfied with humour. He believes that as far as wit is concerned, modern playwrights are superior to Jonson. His characters are funny, but not witty. They do not make us laugh willingly: we laugh at them. They are at once more realistic, and more approximate to real conversation. Dryden distinguishes between a comedy of wit and a comedy of humors, and he prefers a mixture of the two.

In A Discourse Concerning the Original and Progress of Satire, written in his old age, Dryden asserts that pleasure is only a secondary end to poetry. It is only a means to the real end, which is instruction. Conversely, the aim of the poet is to please, but not everything that pleases is good. Dryden believes that the quality of a work is inherent to it, that it comes from its having certain qualities; he mistrusts to some extent the judgment of the audience. The dramatist must not be a slave to the taste of the audience.

So we find in Dryden all the gamut of combinations between the poles of delight and instruction. Instruction comes unconsciously from the admiration produced by the events in the plot. The soul of the spectator is wound insensibly into the practice of that which it admires.

In the late 1670s, Dryden receives strong influence from the French critics Boileau, Rapin and Le Bossu, and also from the extreme classicism of another Englishman, Rymer. In his Tragedies of the Last Age, Thomas Rymer had introduced the term"poetic justice" and had insisted that it had to be respected in all plays. Many were ready to agree with him for a long time, such as Dennis, and Addison, who still exaggerate the concept. Rymer launched some silly attacks on Shakespeare, criticizing him for his moral faults and his ignorance of the unities. Dryden had a respect for Rymer which we cannot understand today: but then we must not forget that Dryden himself was a great rewriter and"improver" of Shakespearean plays (All for Love, The Tempest, Troilus and Cressida, etc.). But Dryden, while accepting poetic justice, is not an extreme advocate of it. And he makes some interesting observations on the conflicts it arises in tragedy, when it runs against sympathy. The aim of tragedy is to instruct by example. Dryden proposes love as the most suitable theme to move the pity of the audience, a subject which"was almost unknown to the Ancients." The poet must labour to arouse pity for the criminal, and not for the victim, and terror must come from the punishment of the criminal we pity: this idea introduces some complexity beyond the simplicity of poetic justice.

We may note that the favourite theatrical emotions of the Neoclassic age, when a new ethics of benevolence is developing, are poetic justice, pity, melodrama, the pleasure of compassion of injured innocence. All are in direct opposition to Aristotle's catharsis and his basic requirements for tragedy. Now a sentimentalized version of catharsis is fashionable: it is understood to be the abating of pride and anger through fear and pity. The stage is ready for the development of sentimental drama and bourgeois tragedy or melodrama (George Lillo, The London Merchant, 1731; Richard Steele, The Conscious Lovers, 1722).

Satire

Dryden wrote a long essay on satire: A Discourse Concerning the Original and Progress of Satire. He follows Horace and the French critic Dacier, who had undertaken a similar enterprise before.

Satire is a kind of poetry, without a series of action, invented for the purging of our minds; in which human vices, ignorance and error, and all things besides, which are produced from them, in every man, are severely reprehended; partly dramatically, partly simply; but for the most time figuratively and occult.... It ought only to treat of one subject; to be confined to a particular theme, or, at least, to one principally. Satire is not libel or slander: it is concerned with the castigation of universal vice through its manifestation in individuals (cf. A's comedy vs. lampoon or poetry vs. history). Nevertheless, satires will still be concerned with attack to particular persons on concrete occasions.

Dryden traces the independent development of satire in Greece and Rome, the similar restrictions placed by law upon it, the influence on Roman satire not of Greek satire, but of Greek Old Comedy. He classifies the types of satire, following those previous writers, according to the poet who first developed them. We have then Menippean (or Varronian) satire, which mixes verse with prose and serious philosophical matters with pleasantries, parodies and obscenity. The term became popular once more with Northop Frye's Anatomy of Criticism. Frye expands the term to include works of intellectual or philosophical parody and disquisition such as Rabelais' Gargantua and Pantagruel, Burton's Anatomy of

Melancholy, Montesquieu's Lettres persanes, Voltaire's Candide, Swift's Tale of a Tub and Gulliver. The other main styles in satire were developed by Persius, who writes invective and insults against vice rather than satire, and above all by Horace and Juvenal. Horace is more profitable, and Juvenal more delightful. Also, they castigate different things: Horace folly, Juvenal vice. Horace's instructions are more general:

Horace had found out the skill of Virgil, to hide his sentences to give you the virtue of them without showing them in their full extent, which is the ostentation of a poet, and not his art".

However, Dryden finds that Horace's wit is insipid, and that Juvenal is sharper. Horace specialises in fine mockery, Juvenal is more direct and pungent. Dryden's conclusion is that although Horatian satire is the best kind of satire, both in tone and in objects, Horace has carried it to less perfection than Juvenal, who writes more successfully an inferior kind of satire.

Chapter 5

Complete Text

To the Right Honourable
CHARLES LORD BUCKHURST.
My Lord,

As I was lately reviewing my loose Papers, amongst the rest I found this Essay, the writing of which in this rude and indigested manner wherein your Lordship now sees it, serv'd as an amusement to me in the Country, when the violence of the last Plague had driven me from the Town. Seeing then our Theaters shut up, I was engag'd in these kind of thoughts with the same delight with which men think upon their absent Mistresses: I confess I find many things in this discourse which I do not now approve; my judgment being a little alter'd since the writing of it, but whether for the better or the worse I know not: Neither indeed is it much material in an Essay, where all I have said is problematical. For the way of writing Playes in verse, which I have seemed to favour, I have since that time laid the Practice of it aside, till I have more leisure, because I find it troublesome and slow.

But I am no way alter'd from my opinion of it, at least with any reasons which have oppos'd it. For your Lordship may easily observe that none are very violent against it, but those who either have not attempted it, or who have succeeded ill in their attempt. 'Tis enough for me to have your Lordships example for my excuse in that little which I have done in it; and I am sure my Adversaries can bring no such Arguments against Verse, as the fourth Act of Pompey will furnish me with, in its defence. Yet, my Lord, you must suffer me a little to complain of you, that you too soon withdraw from us a contentment, of which we expected the continuance, because you gave it us so early. 'Tis a revolt without occasion from your Party, where your merits had already rais'd you to the highest commands, and where you have not the excuse of other men that you have been ill us'd, and therefore laid down Armes. I know no other quarrel you can have to Verse, then that which Spurina had to his beauty, when he tore and mangled the features of his Face, onely because they pleas'd too well the lookers on. It was an honour which seem'd to wait for you, to lead out a new Colony of Writers from the Mother Nation: and upon the first spreading of your Ensignes there had been many in a readiness to have follow'd so fortunate a Leader; if not all, yet the better part of Writers.

Pars, indocili melior grege; mollis & expes
Inominata perprimat cubila.

I am almost of opinion, that we should force you to accept of the command, as sometimes the Prætorian Bands have compell'd their Captains to receive the Empire. The Court, which is the best and surest judge of writing, has generally allow'd of Verse; and in the Town it has found favourers of Wit and Quality. As for your own particular, My Lord, you have yet youth, and time enough to give part of it to the divertisement of the Publick, before you enter into the serious and more unpleasant business of the world. That which the French Poet said of the Temple of Love, may be as well apply'd to the Temple of the Muses. The words, as near as I can remember them, were these:

La jeunesse a mauvaise grace.
N' ayant pas adoré dans le temple d'Amour:
Il faut qu'il entre, & pour le sage
Si ce nest son vray sejour
C'est un giste sur son passage.

I leave the words to work their effect upon your Lordship in their own Language, because no other can so well express the nobleness of the thought; And wish you may be soon call'd to bear a part in the affairs of the Nation, where I know the world expects you, and wonders why you have been so long forgotten; there being no person amongst our young Nobility, on whom the eyes of all men are so much bent. But in the mean time your Lordship may imitate the course of Nature, who gives us the flower before the fruit: that I may speak to you in the language of the Muses, which I have taken from an excellent Poem to the King.

As Nature, when she fruit designes, thinks fit
By beauteous blossoms to proceed to it;
And while she does accomplish all the Spring,
Birds to her secret operations sing.

I confess I have no greater reason, in addressing this Essay to your Lordship, then that it might awaken in you the desire of writing something, in whatever kind it be, which might be an honour to our Age and Country. And me thinks it might have the same effect upon you, which Homer tells us the sight of the Greeks and Trojans before the Fleet, had on the spirit of Achilles, who though he had resolved not to ingage, yet found a martial warmth to steal upon him, at the sight of Blows, the sound of Trumpets, and the cries of fighting Men. For my own part, if in treating of this subject I sometimes dissent from the opinion of better Wits, I declare it is not so much to combat their opinions, as to defend my own, which were first made publick. Sometimes, like a Schollar in an Fencing-School I put forth my self, and show my own ill play, on purpose to be better taught. Sometimes I stand desperately to my Armes, like the Foot when deserted by their Horse, not in hope to overcome, but onely to yield on more honourable termes.

And yet, my Lord, this war of opinions, you well know, has fallen out among the Writers of all Ages, and sometimes betwixt Friends. Onely it has been prosecuted by some, like Pedants, with violence of words, and manag'd by others like Gentlemen, with candour and ciuility. Even Tully had a Controversie with his dear Atticus; and in one of his Dialogues makes him sustain the part of an Enemy of Philosophy, who in his Letters is his confident of State, and made privy to the most weighty affairs of the Roman Senate. And the same respect which was paid by Tully to Atticus, we find return'd to him afterwards by Cæsar on a like occasion, who answering his Book in praise of Cato, made it not so much his business to condemn Cato, as to praise Cicero. But that I may decline some part of the encounter with my Adversaries, whom I am neither willing to combate, nor well able to resist; I will give your Lordship the Relation of a Dispute betwixt some of our Wits upon this subject, in which they did not onely speak to Playes in Verse, but mingled, in the freedom of Discourse, some thing of the Ancient, many of the Modern wayes of writing, comparing those with these, and the Wits of our Nation with those of others: 'tis true they differ'd in their opinions, as 'tis probable they would: neither do I take upon me to reconcile, but to relate them: and that as Tacitus professes of himself, Sine studio partium aut ira: without Passion or Interest; leaving your Lordship to decide it in favour of which part you shall judge most reasonable, and withall, to pardon the many errours of,

Your Lordships most obedient humble Servant,

JOHN DRYDEN.

TO THE READER.

The drift of the ensuing Discourse was chiefly to vindicate the honour of our English Writers, from the censure of those who unjustly prefer the French before them. This I intimate, least any should think me so exceeding vain, as to teach others an Art which they understand much better than my self. But if this incorrect Essay, written in the Country without the help of Books, or advice of Friends, shall find any acceptance in the world, I promise to my self a better success of the second part, wherein the Vertues and Faults of the English Poets, who have written either in this, the Epique, or the Lyrique way, will be more fully treated of, and their several styles impartially imitated.

AN

ESSAY

OF

Dramatick Poesie.

It was that memorable day, in the first Summer of the late War, when our Navy ingag'd the Dutch: a day wherein the two most mighty and best appointed Fleets which any age had ever seen, disputed the command of the greater half of the

Globe, the commerce of Nations, and the riches of the Universe. While these vast floating bodies, on either side, mov'd against each other in parallel lines, and our Country men, under the happy conduct of his Royal Highness, went breaking, by little and little, into the line of the Enemies; the noise of the Cannon from both Navies reach'd our ears about the City: so that all men, being alarm'd with it, and in a dreadful suspence of the event, which we knew was then deciding, every one went following the sound as his fancy led him; and leaving the Town almost empty, some took towards the Park, some cross the River, others down it; all seeking the noise in the depth of silence. Amongst the rest, it was the fortune of *Eugenius, Crites, Lisideius* and *Neander*, to be in company together: three of them persons whom their witt and Quality have made known to all the Town: and whom I have chose to hide under these borrowed names, that they may not suffer by so ill a relation as I am going to make of their discourse.

Taking then a Barge which a servant of *Lisideus* had provided for them, they made haste to shoot the Bridge, and left behind them that great fall of waters which hindred them from hearing what they desired: after which, having disiingag'd themselves from many Vessels which rode at Anchor in the *Thames*, and almost blockt up the passage towards *Greenwich*, they order'd the Watermen to let fall their Oares more gently; and then every one favouring his own curiosity with a strict silence, it was not long ere they perceiv'd the Air break about them like the noise of distant Thunder, or of Swallows in a Chimney: those little undulations of sound, though almost vanishing before they reach'd them, yet still seeming to retain somewhat of their first horrour which they had betwixt the Fleets: after they had attentively listned till such time as the sound by little and little went from them; *Eugenius* lifting up his head, and taking notice of it, was the first who congratulated to the rest that happy Omen of our Nations Victory: adding, we had but this to desire in confirmation of it, that we might hear no more of that noise which was now leaving the English Coast. When the rest had concur'd in the same opinion, *Crites*, a person of a sharp judgment, and somewhat too delicate a taste in wit, which the world have mistaken in him for ill nature, said, smiling to us, that if the concernment of this battel had not been so exceeding great, he could scarce have wish'd the Victory at the price he knew must pay for it, in being subject to the reading and hearing of so many ill verses as he was sure would be made upon it; adding, that no Argument could scape some of those eternal Rhimers, who watch a Battel with more diligence then the Ravens and birds of Prey; and the worst of them surest to be first in upon the quarry, while the better able, either out of modesty writ not at all, or set that due value upon their Poems, as to let them be often call'd for and long expected! there are some of those impertinent people you speak of, answer'd *Lisideius,* who to my knowledg, are already so provided, either way, that they can produce not onely a Panegirick upon the Victory, but, if need be, a funeral elegy upon the Duke: and after they have crown'd his valour with many Lawrels, at last deplore the odds under which he fell, concluding that his courage deserv'd a better destiny.

All the company smil'd at the conceipt of *Lisideius,* but *Crites,* more eager then before, began to make particular exceptions against some Writers, and said the publick Magistrate ought to send betimes to forbid them; and that it concern'd the peace and quiet of all honest people, that ill Poets should be as well silenc'd as seditious Preachers. In my opinion, replyed *Eugenius,* you pursue your point too far; for as to my own particular, I am so great a lover of Poesie, that I could wish them all rewarded who attempt but to do well; at least I would not have them worse us'd then *Sylla* the Dictator did one of their brethren heretofore: *Quem in concione vidimus* (says *Tully* speaking of him) *cum ei libellum malus poeta de populo subjecisset, quod epigramma in eum fecisset tantummodo alternis versibus longiuculis, statim ex iis rebus quæ tunc vendebat jubere ei præmium tribui, sub ea conditione ne quid postea scriberet.*

I could wish with all my heart, replied *Crites,* that many whom we know were as bountifully thank'd upon the same condition, that they would never trouble us again. For amongst others, I have a mortal apprehension of two Poets, whom this victory with the help of both her wings will never be able to escape; 'tis easie to guess whom you intend, said *Lisideius*; and without naming them, I ask you if one of them does not perpetually pay us with clenches upon words and a certain clownish kind of raillery? if now and then he does not offer at a Catecresis or Clevelandism, wresting and torturing a word into another meaning: In fine, if he be not one of those whom the French would call *un mauvais buffon*; one that is so much a well-willer to the Satire, that he spares no man; and though he cannot strike a blow to hurt any, yet ought to be punish'd for the malice of the action, as our Witches are justly hang'd because they think themselves so; and suffer deservedly for believing they did mischief, because they meant it.

You have described him, said *Crites*, so exactly, that I am affraid to come after you with my other extremity of Poetry: He is one of those who having had some advantage of education and converse, knows better then the other what a Poet should be, but puts it into practice more unluckily then any man; his stile and matter are every where alike; he is the most calm, peaceable Writer you ever read: he never disquiets your passions with the least concernment, but still leaves you in as even a temper as he found you; he is a very Leveller in Poetry, he creeps along with ten little words in every line, and helps out his Numbers with *For to*, and *Vnto*, and all the pretty Expletives he can find, till he draggs them to the end of another line; while the Sense is left tir'd half way behind it; he doubly starves all his Verses, first for want of thought, and then of expression; his Poetry neither has wit in it, nor seems to have it; like him in *Martiall*:

Pauper videri Cinna vult, & est pauper: He affects plainness, to cover his want of imagination: when he writes the serious way, the highest flight of his fancy is some miserable *Antithesis*, or seeming contradiction; and in the Comick he is still reaching at some thin conceit, the ghost of a Jest, and that too flies before him, never to be caught; these Swallows which we see before us on the *Thames*, are just resemblance of his wit: you may observe how near the water they stoop, how many proffers they make to dip, and yet how seldome they touch it:

and when they do, 'tis but the surface: they skim over it but to catch a gnat, and then mount into the ayr and leave it. Well Gentlemen, said *Eugenius*, you may speak your pleasure of these Authors; but though I and some few more about the Town may give you a peaceable hearing, yet, assure your selves, there are multitudes who would think you malicious and them injur'd: especially him who you first described; he is the very *Withers* of the City: they have bought more Editions of his Works then would serve to lay under all the Pies at the Lord Mayor's *Christmass*.

When his famous Poem first came out in the year 1660, I have seen them reading it in the midst of Change-time; many so vehement they were at it, that they lost their bargain by the Candles ends: but what will you say, if he has been received amongst the great Ones? I can assure you he is, this day, the envy of a great person, who is Lord in the Art of Quibbling; and who does not take it well, that any man should intrude so far into his Province. All I would wish replied *Crites*, is, that they who love his Writings, may still admire him, and his fellow Poet: *qui Bavium non odit, &c.* is curse sufficient. And farther, added *Lisideius*, I believe there is no man who writes well, but would think himself very hardly dealt with, if their Admirers should praise any thing of his: *Nam quos contemnimus eorum quoque laudes contemnimus*. There are so few who write well in this Age, said *Crites*, that me-thinks any praises should be wellcome; then neither rise to the dignity of the last Age, nor to any of the Ancients; and we may cry out of the Writers of this time, with more reason than *Petronius* of his, *Pace vestra liceat dixisse, primi omnium eloquentiam perdidistis*: you have debauched the true old Poetry so far, that Nature, which is the soul of it, is not in any of your Writings.

If your quarrel (said *Eugenius*) to those who now write, be grounded onely upon your reverence to Antiquity, there is no man more ready to adore those great Greeks and Romans than I am: but on the other side, I cannot think so contemptibly of the Age I live in, or so dishonourably of my own Countrey, as not to judge we equal the Ancients in most kinds of Poesie, and in some surpass them; neither know I any reason why I may not be as zealous for the Reputation of our Age, as we find the Ancients themselves in reference to those who lived before them. For you hear your *Horace* saying,

Indignor quidquam reprehendi, non quia crassé
Compositum, illepidève putetur, sed quia nuper.
And after,
Si meliora dies, ut vina, poemata reddit,
Scire velim pretium chartis quotus arroget annus?

But I see I am ingaging in a wide dispute, where the arguments are not like to reach close on either side; for Poesie is of so large extent, and so many both of the Ancients and Moderns have done well in all kinds of it, that, in citing one against the other, we shall take up more time this Evening, than each mans occasions will allow him: therefore I would ask *Crites* to what part of Poesie he would confine his Arguments, and whether he would defend the general cause of the Ancients against the Moderns, or oppose any Age of the Moderns against this of ours?

Crites a little while considering upon this Demand, told *Eugenius* he approv'd his Propositions, and, if he pleased, he would limit their Dispute to *Dramatique Poesie*; in which he thought it not difficult to prove, either that the Antients were superiour to the Moderns, or the last Age to this of ours.

Eugenius was somewhat surpriz'd, when he heard *Crites* make choice of that Subject; For ought I see, said he, I have undertaken a harder Province than I imagin'd; for though I never judg'd the Plays of the Greek or Roman Poets comparable to ours; yet on the other side those we now see acted, come short of many which were written in the last Age: but my comfort is if we are orecome, it will be onely by our own Countreymen: and if we yield to them in this one part of Poesie, we more surpass them in all the other; for in the Epique or Lyrique way it will be hard for them to show us one such amongst them, as we have many now living, or who lately were so. They can produce nothing so courtly writ, or which expresses so much the Conversation of a Gentleman, as Sir *John Suckling*; nothing so even, sweet, and flowing as Mr. *Waller*; nothing so Majestique, so correct as Sir *John Denham*; nothing so elevated, so copious, and full of spirit, as Mr *Cowley*; as for the Italian, French, and Spanish Plays, I can make it evident that those who now write, surpass them; and that the *Drama* is wholly ours.

All of them were thus far of *Eugenius* his opinion, that the sweetness of English Verse was never understood or practis'd by our Fathers; even *Crites* himself did not much oppose it: and every one was willing to acknowledge how much our Poesie is improv'd, by the happiness of some Writers yet living; who first taught us to mould our thoughts into easie and significant words; to retrench the superfluities of expression, and to make our Rime so properly a part of the Verse, that it should never mis-lead the sence, but it self be led and govern'd by it. *Eugenius* was going to continue this Discourse, when *Lisideius* told him it was necessary, before they proceeded further, to take a standing measure of their Controversie; for how was it possible to be decided who writ the best Plays, before we know what a Play should be? but, this once agreed on by both Parties, each might have recourse to it, either to prove his own advantages, or discover the failings of his Adversary.

He had no sooner said this, but all desir'd the favour of him to give the definition of a Play; and they were the more importunate, because neither *Aristotle*, nor *Horace*, nor any other, who writ of that Subject, had ever done it.

Lisideius, after some modest denials, at last confess'd he had a rude Notion of it; indeed rather a Description then a Definition: but which serv'd to guide him in his private thoughts, when he was to make a judgment of what others writ: that he conceiv'd a Play ought to be, *A just and lively Image of Humane Nature, representing its Passions and Humours, and the Changes of Fortune to which it is subject; for the Delight and Instruction of Mankind*.

This Definition, though *Crites* rais'd a Logical Objection against it; that it was onely *a genre & fine*, and so not altogether perfect; was yet well received by the rest: and after they had given order to the Water-men to turn their Barge, and row softly, that they might take the cool of the Evening in their return; *Crites*, being desired by the Company to begin, spoke on behalf of the Ancients, in this manner:

If Confidence presage a Victory, *Eugenius*, in his own opinion, has already triumphed over the Ancients; nothing seems more easie to him, than to overcome those whom it is our greatest praise to have imitated well: for we do not onely build upon their foundation; but by their modells. *Dramatique Poesie* had time enough, reckoning from *Thespis* (who first invented it) to *Aristophanes*, to be born, to grow up, and to flourish in Maturity. It has been observed of Arts and Sciences, that in one and the same Century they have arriv'd to a great perfection; and no wonder, since every Age has a kind of Universal Genius, which inclines those that live in it to some particular Studies: the Work then being push'd on by many hands, must of necessity go forward.

Is it not evident, in these last hundred years (when the Study of Philosophy has been the business of all the *Virtuosi* in *Christendome*) that almost a new Nature has been revealed to us? that more errours of the School have been detected, more useful Experiments in Philosophy have been made, more Noble Secrets in Opticks, Medicine, Anatomy, Astronomy, discover'd, than in all those credulous and doting Ages from *Aristotle* to us? so true it is that nothing spreads more fast than Science, when rightly and generally cultivated.

Add to this the more than common emulation that was in those times of writing well; which though it be found in all Ages and all Persons that pretend to the same Reputation; yet Poesie being then in more esteem than now it is, had greater Honours decreed to the Professors of it; and consequently the Rivalship was more high between them; they had Judges ordain'd to decide their Merit, and Prizes to reward it: and Historians have been diligent to record of *Eschylus, Euripides, Sophocles, Lycophron*, and the rest of them, both who they were that vanquish'd in these Wars of the Theater, and how often they were crown'd: while the Asian Kings, and Grecian Common-wealths scarce afforded them a Nobler Subject then the unmanly Luxuries of a Debauch'd Court, or giddy Intrigues of a Factious City. *Alit æmulatio ingenia* (says

Paterculus) & nunc invidia, nunc admiratio incitationem accendit: Emulation is the Spur of Wit, and sometimes Envy, sometimes Admiration quickens our Endeavours.

But now since the Rewards of Honour are taken away, that Vertuous Emulation is turn'd into direct Malice; yet so slothful, that it contents it self to condemn and cry down others, without attempting to do better: 'Tis a Reputation too unprofitable, to take the necessary pains for it; yet wishing they had it, is incitement enough to hinder others from it. And this, in short, *Eugenius*, is the reason, why you have now so few good Poets; and so many severe Judges: Certainly, to imitate the Antients well, much labour and long study is required: which pains, I have already shown, our Poets would want incouragement to take, if yet they had ability to go through with it. Those Ancients have been faithful Imitators and wise Observers of that Nature, which is so torn and ill represented in our Plays, they have handed down to us a perfect resemblance of her; which we, like ill Copyers, neglecting to look on, have rendred monstrous and disfigur'd.

But, that you may know how much you are indebted to those your Masters, and be ashamed to have so ill requited them: I must remember you that all the Rules by which we practise the *Drama* at this day, either such as relate to the justness and symmetry of the Plot; or the Episodical Ornaments, such as Descriptions, Narrations, and other Beauties, which are not essential to the Play; were delivered to us from the Observations that *Aristotle* made, of those Poets, which either liv'd before him, or were his Contemporaries: we have added nothing of our own, except we have the confidence to say our wit is better; which none boast of in our Age, but such as understand not theirs. Of that Book which *Aristotle* has left us *peri tês Poiêtikês*, *Horace* his Art of Poetry is an excellent Comment, and, I believe, restores to us that Second Book of his concerning Comedy, which is wanting in him.

Out of these two has been extracted the Famous Rules which the French call, *Des Trois Vnitez*, or, The Three Unities, which ought to be observ'd in every Regular Play; namely, of Time, Place, and Action.

The unity of Time they comprehend in 24 hours, the compass of a Natural Day; or as near it as can be contriv'd: and the reason of it is obvious to every one, that the time of the feigned action, or fable of the Play, should be proportion'd as near as can be to the duration of that time in which it is represented; since therefore all Playes are acted on the Theater in a space of time much within the compass of 24 hours, that Play is to be thought the nearest imitation of Nature, whose Plot or Action is confin'd within that time; and, by the same Rule which concludes this general proportion of time, it follows, that all the parts of it are to be equally subdivided; as namely, that one act take not up the suppos'd time of half a day; which is out of proportion to the rest: since the other four are then to be straightned within the compas of the remaining half; for it is unnatural that one Act, which being spoke or written, is not longer than the rest, should be suppos'd longer by the Audience; 'tis therefore the Poets duty, to take care that no Act should be imagin'd to exceed the time in which it is represented on the Stage, and that the intervalls and inequalities of time be suppos'd to fall out between the Acts.

This Rule of Time how well it has been observ'd by the Antients, most of their Playes will witness; you see them in their Tragedies (wherein to follow this Rule, is certainly most difficult) from the very beginning of their Playes, falling close into that part of the Story which they intend for the action or principal object of it; leaving the former part to be delivered by Narration: so that they set the Audience, as it were, at the Post where the Race is to be concluded: and, saving them the tedious expectation of seeing the Poet set out and ride the beginning of the Course, you behold him not, till he is in sight of the Goal, and just upon you.

For the Second Unity, which is that of place, the Antients meant by it, That the Scene ought to be continu'd through the Play, in the same place where it was laid in the beginning: for the Stage, on which it is represented, being but one and the same place, it is unnatural to conceive it many; and those far distant from one another. I will not deny but by the variation of painted Scenes, the Fancy (which in these cases will contribute to its own deceit) may sometimes imagine it several places, with some appearance of probability; yet it still carries the greater likelihood of truth, if those places be suppos'd so near each other, as in the same Town or City; which may all be comprehended under the larger Denomination of one place: for a greater distance will bear no proportion to the shortness of time, which is allotted in the acting, to pass from one of them to another; for the Observation of this, next to the Antients, the French are to be most commended. They tie themselves so strictly to the unity of place, that you never see in any of their Plays a Scene chang'd in the middle of the Act: if the Act begins in a Garden, a Street, or Chamber, 'tis ended in the same place; and that you may know it to be the same, the Stage is so supplied with persons that it is never empty all the time: he that enters the second has business with him who was on before; and before the second quits the Stage, a third appears who has business with him.

This *Corneil* calls *La Liaison des Scenes*, the continuity or joyning of the Scenes; and 'tis a good mark of a well contriv'd Play when all the Persons are known to each other, and every one of them has some affairs with all the rest.

As for the third Unity which is that of Action, the Ancients meant no other by it then what the Logicians do by their *Finis*, the end or scope of an action: that which is the first in Intention, and last in Execution: now the Poet is to aim at one great and compleat action, to the carrying on of which all things in his Play, even the very obstacles, are to be subservient; and the reason of this is as evident as any of the former.

For two Actions equally labour'd and driven on by the Writer, would destroy the unity of the Poem; it would be no longer one Play, but two: not but that there may be many actions in a Play, as *Ben. Johnson* has observ'd in his discoveries; but they must be all subservient to the great one, which our language happily expresses in the name of under-plots: such as in *Terences Eunuch* is the difference and reconcilement of *Thais* and *Phædria*, which is not the chief business of the Play, but promotes; the marriage of *Chærea* and *Chreme's* Sister, principally intended by the Poet. There ought to be one action, sayes *Corneile,* that is one compleat action which leaves the mind of the Audience in a full repose: But this cannot be brought to pas but by many other imperfect ones which conduce to it, and hold the Audience in a delightful suspence of what will be.

If by these Rules (to omit many other drawn from the Precepts and Practice of the Ancients) we should judge our modern Playes; 'tis probable, that few of them would endure the tryal: that which should be the business of a day, takes up in some of them an age; instead of one action they are the Epitomes of a mans life; and for one spot of ground (which the Stage should represent) we are sometimes in more Countries then the Map can show us.

But if we will allow the Ancients to have contriv'd well, we must acknowledge them to have writ better; questionless we are depriv'd of a great stock of wit in the loss of *Menander* among the Greek Poets, and of *Cæcilius, Affranius* and *Varius,* among the Romans: we may guess of *Menanders* Excellency by the Plays of *Terence,* who translated some of his, and yet wanted so much of him that he was call'd C. *Cæsar* the Half-*Menander,* and of *Varius,* by the Testimonies of *Horace Martial,* and *Velleus Paterculus*: 'Tis probable that these, could they be recover'd, would decide the controversie; but so long as *Aristophanes* in the old Comedy, and *Plautus* in the new are extant; while the Tragedies of *Eurypides, Sophocles,* and *Seneca* are to be had, I can never see one of those Plays which are now written, but it encreases my admiration of the Ancients; and yet I must acknowledge further, that to admire them as we ought, we should understand them better than we do. Doubtless many things appear flat to us, whose wit depended upon some custome or story which never came to our knowledge, or perhaps upon some Criticism in their language, which being so long dead, and onely remaining in their Books, 'tis not possible they should make us know it perfectly.

To read *Macrobius,* explaining the propriety and elegancy of many words in *Virgil,* which I had before pass'd over without consideration, as common things, is enough to assure me that I ought to think the same of *Terence*; and that in the purity of his style (which *Tully* so much valued that he ever carried his works about him) there is yet left in him great room for admiration, if I knew but where to place it. In the mean time I must desire you to take notice, that the greatest man of the last age (*Ben. Johnson*) was willing to give place to them in all things: He was not onely a professed Imitator of *Horace*, but a learned Plagiary of all the others; you track him every where in their Snow: If *Horace, Lucan, Petronius Arbiter, Seneca*, and *Juvenal*, had their own from him, there are few serious thoughts which are new in him; you will pardon me therefore if I presume he lov'd their fashion when he wore their cloaths. But since I have otherwise a great veneration for him, and you, *Eugenius*, prefer him above all other Poets, I will use no farther argument to you then his example: I will produce Father *Ben.* to you, dress'd in all the ornaments and colours of the Ancients, you will need no other guide to our Party if you follow him; and whether you consider the bad Plays of our Age, or regard the good ones of the last, both the best and worst of the Modern Poets will equally instruct you to esteem the Ancients.

Crites had no sooner left speaking, but *Eugenius* who waited with some impatience for it, thus began: I have observ'd in your Speech that the former part of it is convincing as to what the Moderns have profitted by the rules of the Ancients, but in the latter you are careful to conceal how much they have excell'd them: we own all the helps we have from them, and want neither veneration nor gratitude while we acknowledge that to overcome them we must make use of the advantages we have receiv'd from them; but to these assistances we have joyned our own industry; for (had we sate down with a dull imitation of them) we might then have lost somewhat of the old perfection, but never acquir'd any that was new. We draw not therefore after their lines, but those of Nature; and having the life before us, besides the experience of all they knew, it is no wonder if we hit some airs and features which they have miss'd: I deny not what you urge of Arts and Sciences, that they have flourish'd in some ages more then others; but your instance in Philosophy makes for me: for if Natural Causes be more known now then in the time of

Aristotle, because more studied, it follows that Poesie and other Arts may with the same pains arrive still neerer to perfection, and, that granted, it will rest for you to prove that they wrought more perfect images of humane life then we; which, seeing in your Discourse you have avoided to make good, it shall now be my task to show you some part of their defects, and some few Excellencies of the Moderns; and I think there is none among us can imagine I do it enviously, or with purpose to detract from them; for what interest of Fame or Profit can the living lose by the reputation of the dead? on the other side, it is a great truth which *Velleius Paterculus* affirms, *Audita visis libentius laudemus; & præsentia invidia, præterita admiratione prosequimur; & his nos obrui, illis instrui credimus*: That praise or censure is certainly the most sincere which unbrib'd posterity shall give us.

Be pleased then in the first place to take notice, that the Greek Poesie, which *Crites* has affirm'd to have arriv'd to perfection in the Reign of the old Comedy, was so far from it, that the distinction of it into Acts was not known to them; or if it were, it is yet so darkly deliver'd to us that we can not make it out.

All we know of it is from the singing of their Chorus, and that too is so uncertain that in some of their Playes we have reason to conjecture they sung more then five times: *Aristotle* indeed divides the integral parts of a Play into four: First, The *Protasis* or entrance, which gives light onely to the Characters of the persons, and proceeds very little into any part of the action: 2ly, The *Epitasis*, or working up of the Plot where the Play grows warmer: the design or action of it is drawing on, and you see something promising that it will come to pass: Thirdly, the *Catastasis*, or Counterturn, which destroys that expectation, imbroyles the action in new difficulties, and leaves you far distant from that hope in which it found you, as you may have observ'd in a violent stream resisted by a narrow passage; it runs round to an eddy, and carries back the waters with more swiftness then it brought them on: Lastly, the *Catastrophe*, which the Grecians call'd *lysis*, the French *le denouement*, and we the discovery or unravelling of the Plot:

there you see all things setling again upon their first foundations, and the obstacles which hindred the design or action of the Play once remov'd, it ends with that resemblance of truth and nature, that the audience are satisfied with the conduct of it. Thus this great man deliver'd to us the image of a Play, and I must confess it is so lively that from thence much light has been deriv'd to the forming it more perfectly into Acts and Scenes; but what Poet first limited to five the number of the Acts I know not; onely we see it so firmly establish'd in the time of *Horace*, that he gives it for a rule in Comedy; *Neu brevior quinto, neu sit productior actu*: So that you see the Grecians cannot be said to have consummated this Art; writing rather by Entrances then by Acts, and having rather a general indigested notion of a Play, then knowing how and where to bestow the particular graces of it.

But since the Spaniards at this day allow but three Acts, which they call *Tornadas*, to a Play; and the Italians in many of theirs follow them, when I condemn the Antients, I declare it is not altogether because they have not five Acts to every Play, but because they have not confin'd themselves to one certain number; 'tis building an House without a Modell: and when the succeeded in such undertakings, they ought to have sacrific'd to Fortune, not to the Muses.

Next, for the Plot, which *Aristotle* call'd *to mythos* and often *Tôn pragmatôn synthesis*, and from him the Romans *Fabula*, it has already been judiciously observ'd by a late Writer, that in their Tragedies it was onely some Tale deriv'd from *Thebes* or *Troy*, or at lest some thing that happen'd in those two Ages; which was worn so thred bare by the Pens of all the Epique Poets, and even by Tradition it self of the Talkative Greeklings (as *Ben Johnson* calls them) that before it came upon the Stage, it was already known to all the Audience: and the people so soon as ever they heard the Name of *Oedipus*, knew as well as the Poet, that he had kill'd his Father by mistake, and committed Incest with his Mother, before the Play; that they were now to hear of a great Plague, an Oracle, and the Ghost of *Laius*: so that they sate with a yawning kind of expectation, till he was to come with his eyes pull'd out, and speak a hundred or two of Verses in a Tragick tone, in complaint of his misfortunes. But one *Oedipus, Hercules,* or *Medea,* had been tollerable; poor people they scap'd not so good cheap: they had still the *Chapon Bouillé* set before them, till their appetites were cloy'd with the same dish, and the Novelty being gone, the pleasure vanish'd: so that one main end of *Dramatique Poesie* in its Definition, which was to cause Delight, as of consequence destroy'd.

In their Comedies, the Romans generally borrow'd their Plots from the Greek Poets; and theirs was commonly a little Girle stollen or wandred from her Parents, brought back unknown to the same City, there got with child by some lewd young fellow; who, by the help of his servant, cheats his father, and when her time comes, to cry *Juno Lucina fer opem;* one or other sees a little Box or Cabinet which was carried away with her, and so discovers her to her friends, if some God do not prevent it, by coming down in a Machine, and take the thanks of it to himself.

By the Plot you may gues much of the Characters of the Persons. An Old Father that would willingly before he dies, see his Son well married; his Debauch'd Son, kind in his Nature to his Wench, but miserably in want of Money; a Servant or Slave, who has so much wit to strike in with him, and help to dupe his Father, a Braggadochio Captain, a Parasite, and a Lady of Pleasure.

As for the poor honest Maid, whom all the Story is built upon, and who ought to be one of the principal Actors in the Play, she is commonly a Mute in it: She has the breeding of the Old *Elizabeth* way, for Maids to be seen and not to be heard; and it is enough you know she is willing to be married, when the Fifth Act requires it.

These are Plots built after the Italian Mode of Houses, you see thorow them all at once; the Characters are indeed the Imitations of Nature, but so narrow as if they had imitated onely an Eye or an Hand, and did not dare to venture on the lines of a Face, or the Proportion of a Body.

But in how straight a compass soever they have bounded their Plots and Characters, we will pass it by, if they have regularly pursued them, and perfectly observ'd those three Unities of Time, Place, and Action: the knowledge of which you say is deriv'd to us from them. But in the first place give me leave to tell you, that the Unity of Place, how ever it might be practised by them, was never any of their Rules: We neither find it in *Aristotle, Horace,* of any who have written of it, till in our age the French Poets first made it a Precept of the Stage. The unity of time, even *Terence* himself (who was the best and the most regular of them) has neglected: His *Heautontimoroumenos* or Self-Punisher takes up visibly two dayes; therefore sayes *Scaliger,* the two first Acts concluding the first day, were acted over-night; the three last on the ensuing day: and *Eurypides,* in trying himself to one day, has committed an absurdity never to be forgiven him: for in one of his Tragedies he has made *Theseus* go from *Athens* to *Thebes,* which was about 40 English miles, under the walls of it to give battel, and appear victorious in the next Act; and yet from the time of his departure to the return of the *Nuntius,* who gives the relation of his Victory, *Æthra* and the Chorus have but 36 Verses; that is not for every Mile a Verse.

The like errour is as evident in *Terence* his Eunuch, when *Laches,* the old man, enters in a mistake the house of *Thais,* where betwixt his Exit and the entrance of *Pythias,* who comes to give an ample relation of the Garboyles he has rais'd within, *Parmeno* who was left upon the Stage, has not above five lines to speak: *C'est bien employé un temps si court,* sayes the French Poet, who furnish'd me with one of the observations; And almost all their Tragedies will afford us examples of the like nature.

'Tis true, they have kept the continuity, or as you call'd it *Liaison des Scenes* somewhat better: two do not perpetually come in together, talk, and go out together; and other two succeed them, and do the same throughout the Act, which the English call by the name of single Scenes; but the reason is, because they have seldom above two or three Scenes, properly so call'd, in every act; for it is to be accounted a new Scene, not every time the Stage is empty, but every person who enters, though to others, makes it so: because he introduces a new business: Now the Plots of their Plays being narrow, and the persons few, one of their Acts was written in a less compass then one of our well wrought Scenes, and yet they are often deficient even in this: To go no further then *Terence*, you find in the Eunuch *Antipho* entring single in the midst of the third Act, after *Chremes* and Py*thias* were gone off: In the same Play you have likewise *Dorias* beginning the fourth Act alone; and after she has made a relation of what was done at the Souldiers entertainment (which by the way was very inartificial to do, because she was presum'd to speak directly to the Audience, and to acquaint them with what was necessary to be known, but yet should have been so contriv'd by the Poet as to have been told by persons of the *Drama* to one another, and so by them to have come to the knowledge of the people) she quits the Stage, and *Phædria* enters next, alone likewise: He also gives you an account of himself, and of his returning from the Country in *Monologue*, his *Adelphi* or Brothers, *Syrus* and *Demea* enter; after the Scene was broken by the departure of *Sostrata*, *Geta* and *Cathara*; and indeed you can scarce look into any of his Comedies, where you will not presently discover the same interruption.

But as they have fail'd both in laying of their Plots, and managing of them, swerving from the Rules of their own Art, by mis-representing Nature to us, in which they have ill satified one intention of a Play, which was delight, so in the instructive part they have err'd worse: instead of punishing Vice and rewarding Virtue, they have often shown a Prosperous Wickedness, and Unhappy Piety: They have set before us a bloudy image of revenge in *Medea*, and given her Dragons to convey her safe from punishment. A *Priam* and *Astyanax* murder'd, and *Cassandra* ravish'd, and the lust and murder ending in the victory of him that acted them: In short, there is no indecorum in any of our modern Playes, which if I would excuse, I could not shaddow with some Authority from the Ancients.

And one farther note of them let me leave you: Tragedies and Comedies were not writ then as they are now, promiscuously, by the same person; but he who found his genius bending to the one, never attempted the other way. This is so plain, that I need not instance to you, that *Aristophanes, Plautus, Terence,* never any of them writ a Tragedy; *Æschylus, Eurypides, Sophocles* and *Seneca,* never medled with Comedy; the Sock and Buskin were not worn by the same Poet: having then so much care to excel in one kind, very little is to be pardon'd them if they miscarried in it; and this would lead me to the consideration of their wit, had not *Crites* given me sufficient warning not to be too bold in my judgment of it; because the languages being dead, and many of the Customes and little accidents on which it depended, lost to us, we are not competent judges of it.

But though I grant that here and there we may miss the application of a Proverb or a Custom, yet a thing well said will be wit in all Languages; and though it may lose something in the Translation, yet, to him who reads it in the Original, 'tis still the samc; He has an Idea of its excellency, though it cannot pass from his mind into any other expression or words then those in which he finds it. When *Phædria* — in the Eunuch had a command from his Mistress to be absent two dayes; and encouraging himself to go through with it, said; *Tandem ego non illa caream, si opus sit, vel totum triduum?* Parmeno to mock the softness of his Master, lifting up his hands and eyes, cryes out as it were in admiration; *Hui! universum triduum!* the elegancy of which *universum,* though it cannot be rendred in our language, yet leaves an impression of the wit upon our souls: but this happens seldom in him, in *Plautus* oftner; who is infinitely too bold in his Metaphors and coyning words; out of which many times his wit is nothing, which questionless was one reason why *Horace* falls upon him so severely in those Verses:

Sed Proavi nostri Plautinos & numeros, &
Laudavere sales, nimium patienter utrumque
Ne dicam stolidè.

For *Horace* himself was cautious to obtrude a new word upon his Readers, and makes custom and common use the best measure of receiving it into our writings.

Multa renascentur quæ nunc cecidere, cadentque

Quæ nunc sunt in honore vocabula, si volet usus,
Quem penes, arbitrium est, & jus, & norma loquendi.

The not observing this Rule is that which the world has blam'd in our Satyrist *Cleveland*; to express a thing hard and unnaturally, is his new way of Elocution: 'Tis true, no Poet but may sometimes use a *Catachresis*; *Virgil* does it;

Mistaque ridenti Colocasia fundet Acantho.
In his Eclogue of Pollio, and in his 7th Æneid.
— Miratur & undæ,
Miratur nemus, insuetum fulgentia longe,
Scuta virum fiuvio, pictasque innare carinas.
And Ovid once so modestly, that he askes leave to do it:
Si verbo audacia detur Haud metuam summi dixisse
Palatia coeli.

Calling the Court of *Jupiter* by the name of *Augustus* his Pallace, though in another place he is more bold, where he sayes, *Et longas visent Capitolia pompas*. But to do this alwayes, and never be able to write a line without it, though it may be admir'd by some few Pedants, will not pass upon those who know that wit is best convey'd to us in the most easie language; and is most to be admir'd when a great thought comes drest in words so commonly receiv'd that it is understood by the meanest apprehensiions, as the best meat is the most easily digested: but we cannot read a verse of *Cleveland's* without making a face at it, as if every word were a Pill to swallow: he gives us many times a hard Nut to break our Teeth, without a Kernel for our pains. So that there is this difference betwixt his *Satyres* and Doctor *Donns*, That the one gives us deep thought in common language, though rough cadence; the other gives us common thoughts in abstruse words: 'tis true, in some places his wit is independent of his words, as in that of the Rebel *Scot*:

Had Cain been Scot God would have chang'd his doom;
Not forc'd him wander, but confin'd him home.

Si sic, omnia dixisset! This is wit in all languages: 'tis like Mercury, never to be lost or kill'd; and so that other;

For Beauty like White-powder makes no noise,
And yet the silent Hypocrite destroyes.

You see the last line is highly Metaphorical, but it is so soft and gentle, that it does not shock us as we read it.

But, to return from whence I have digress'd, to the consideration of the Ancients Writing and their Wit, (of which by this time you will grant us in some measure to be fit judges,) Though I see many excellent thoughts in *Seneca*, yet he, of them who had a Genius most proper for the Stage, was *Ovid*; he had a way of writing so fit to stir up a pleasing admiration and concernment, which are the objects of a Tragedy, and to show the various movements of a Soul combating betwixt two different Passions, that, had he live'd in our age, or in his own could have writ with our advantages, no man but must have yielded to him; and therefore I am confident the *Medea* is none of his: for, though I esteem it for the gravity and sentiousness of it, which he himself concludes to be suitable to a Tragedy, *Omme genus scripti gravitate Tragoedia vincit*, yet it moves not my soul enough to judge that he, who in the Epique way wrote things so near the *Drama*, as the Story of *Myrrha*, of *Caunus* and *Biblis*, and the rest, should stir up no more concernment where he most endeavour'd it.

The Master piece of *Seneca* I hold to be that Scene in the *Troades*, where *Vlysses* is seeking for *Astyanax* to kill him; There you see the tenderness of a Mother, so represented in Andromache, that it raises compassion to a high degree in the Reader, and bears the nearest resemblance of any thing in their Tragedies to the excellent Scenes of Passion in *Shakespeare*, or in *Fletcher*: for Love-Scenes you will find few among them, their Tragique Poets dealt not with that soft passion, but with Lust, Cruelty, Revenge, Ambition, and those bloody actions they produc'd; which were more capable of raising horrour then compassion in an audience: leaving love untoucht, whose gentleness would have temper'd them, which is the most frequent of all the passions, and which being the private concernment of every person, is sooth'd by viewing its own image in a publick entertainment.

Among their Comedies, we find a Scene or two of tenderness, and that where you would least expect it, in *Plautus*; but to speak generally, their Lovers say little, when they see each other, but *anima mea, vita mea; zôê kai psychê,* as the women in *Juvenal*'s time us'd to cry out in the fury of their kindness: then indeed to speak sense were an offence. Any sudden gust of passion (as an extasie of love in an unexpected meeting) cannot better be express'd than in a word and a sigh, breaking one another. Nature is dumb on such occasions, and to make her speak, would be to represent her unlike her self. But there are a thousand other concernments of Lovers, as jealousies, complaints, contrivances and the like, where not to open their minds at large to each other, were to be wanting to their own love, and to the expectation of the Audience, who watch the movements of their minds, as much as the changes of their fortunes. For the imaging of the first is properly the work of a Poet, the latter he borrows of the Historian.

Eugenius was proceeding in that part of his Discourse, when *Crites* interrupted him. I see, said he, *Eugenius* and I are never like to have this Question decided betwixt us; for he maintains the Moderns have acquir'd a new perfection in writing, I can onely grant they have alter'd the mode of it. *Homer* describ'd his Heroes men of great appetites, lovers of beef broild upon the coals, and good fellows; contrary to the practice of the French Romances, whose Heroes neither eat, nor drink, nor sleep, for love. *Virgil* makes *Æneas* a bold Avower of his own virtues,

Sum pius Æneas fama super æthera notus;

which in the civility of our Poets is the Character of a Fanfaron or Hector: for with us the Knight takes occasion to walk out, or sleep, to avoid the vanity of telling his own Story, which the trusty Squire is ever to perform for him. So in their Love Scenes, of which *Eugenius* spoke last, the Ancients were more hearty; we more talkative: they writ love as it was then the mode to make it, and I will grant thus much to *Eugenius*, that perhaps one of their Poets, had he liv'd in our Age,

Si foret hoc nostrum fato delapsus in avum (as *Horace* says of *Lucilius*) he had alter'd many things; not that they were not as natural before, but that he might accommodate himself to the Age he liv'd in: yet in the mean time we are not to conclude any thing rashly against those great men; but preserve to them the dignity of Masters, and give that honour to their memories, (Quos libitina sacravit;) part of which we expect may be paid to us in future times.

This moderation of *Crites*, as it was pleasing to all the company, so it put an end to that dispute; which, *Eugenius*, who seem'd to have the better of the Argument, would urge no farther: but *Lisideius* after he had acknowledg'd himself of *Eugenius* his opinion concerning the Ancients; yet told him he had forborn, till his Discourse were ended, to ask him why he prefer'd the English Plays above those of other Nations? and whether we ought not to submit our Stage to the exactness of our next Neighbours?

Though, said *Eugenius*, I am at all times ready to defend the honour of my Countrey against the French, and to maintain, we are as well able to vanquish them with our Pens as our Ancestors have been with their swords; yet, if you please, added he, looking upon *Neander*, I will commit this cause to my friend's management; his opinion of our Plays is the same with mine: and besides, there is no reason, that *Crites* and I, who have now left the Stage, should re-enter so suddenly upon it; which is against the Laws of Comedie.

If the Question had been stated, replied *Lysideius*, who had writ best, the French or English forty years ago, I should have been of your opinion, and adjudg'd the honour to our own Nation; but since that time, (said he, turning towards *Neander*) we have been so long together bad Englishmen, that we had not leisure to be good Poets; *Beaumont*, *Fletcher*, and *Johnson* (who were onely capable of bringing us to that degree of perfection which we have) were just then leaving the world; as if in an Age of so much horror, wit and those milder studies of humanity, had no farther business among us. But the Muses, who ever follow Peace, went to plant in another Countrey; it was then that the great Cardinal of *Richlieu* began to take them into his protection; and that, by his encouragement, *Corneil* and some other Frenchmen reform'd their Theatre, (which before was as much below ours as it now surpasses it and the rest of *Europe*;) but because *Crites*, in his Discourse for the Ancients, has prevented me, by touching upon many Rules of the Stage, which the Moderns have borrow'd from them; I shall onely, in short, demand of you, whether you are not convinc'd that of all Nations the French have best observ'd them? In the unity of time you find them so scrupulous, that it yet remains a dispute among their Poets, whether the artificial day of twelve hours more or less, be not meant by *Aristotle,* rather than the natural one of twenty four; and consequently whether all Plays ought not to be reduc'd into that compass? This I can testifie, that in all their *Drama*'s writ within these last 20 years and upwards, I have not observ'd any that have extended the time to thirty hours: in the unity of place they are full as scrupulous, for many of their Criticks limit it to that very spot of ground where the Play is suppos'd to begin; none of them exceed the compass of the same Town or City. The unity of Action in all their Plays is yet more conspicuous, for they do not burden them with under-plots, as the English do; which is the reason why many Scenes of our Tragi-comedies carry on a design that is nothing of kinne to the main Plot; and that we see two distinct webbs in a Play; like those in ill wrought stuffs; and two actions, that is, two Plays carried on together, to the confounding of the Audience; who, before they are warm in their concernments for one part, are diverted to another; and by that means espouse the interest of neither. From hence likewise it arises that the one half of our Actors are not known to the other. They keep their distances as if they were *Mountagues* and *Capulets,* and seldom begin an acquaintance till the last Scene of the Fifth Act, when they are all to meet upon the Stage.

There is no Theatre in the world has any thing so absurd as the English Tragi-comedie, 'tis a *Drama* of our own invention, and the fashion of it is enough to proclaim it so; here a course of mirth, there another of sadness and passion; a third of honour, and fourth a Duel: Thus in two hours and a half we run through all the fits of *Bedlam*. The French affords you as much variety on the same day, but they do it not so unseasonably, or *mal a propos* as we: Our Poets present you the Play and the farce together; and our Stages still retain somewhat of the Original civility of the Red-Bull;

Atque ursum & pugiles media inter carmina poscunt: The end of Tragedies or serious Playes, sayes *Aristotle,* is to beget admiration, compassion, or concernement; but are not mirth and compassion things incompatible? and is it not evident that the Poet must of necessity destroy the former by intermingling of the latter? that is, he must ruine the sole end and object of his Tragedy to introduce somewhat that is forced in, and is not of the body of it: Would you not think that Physician mad, who having prescribed a Purge, should immediatly order you to take restringents upon it?

But to leave our Playes, and return to theirs, I have noted one great advantage they have had in the Plotting of their Tragedies; that is, they are always grounded upon some known History: accarding to that of *Horace, Ex noto fictum carmen sequar;* and in that they have so imitated the Ancients that they have supass'd them. For the Ancients, as was observ'd before, took for the foundation of their Playes some Poetical Fiction, such as under that consideration could move but little concernment in the Audience, because they already knew the event of it. But the French goes farther;

Atque ita mentitur; sic veris falsæ remiscet, Primo ne medium, medio ne discrepet imum: He so interweaves Truth with probable Fiction, that he puts a pleasing Fallacy upon us; mends the intrigues of Fate, and dispenses with the severity of History, to reward that vertue which has been rendred to us there unfortunate. Sometimes the story has left the sucess so doubtful, that the Writer is free, by the priviledge of a Poet, to take that which of two or more relations will best sute with his design: As for example, the death of *Cyrus,* whom *Justin* and some others report to have perish'd in the *Scythian* war, but *Xenophon* affirms to have died in his bed of extream old age. Nay more, when the event is past dispute, even then we are willing to be deceiv'd, and the Poet, if he contrives it with appearance of truth; has all the audience of his Party; at least during the time his Play is acting: so naturally we are kind to vertue, when our own interest is not in question, that we take it up as the general concernment of Mankind. On the other side, if you consider the Historical Playes of *Shakespeare,* they are rather so many Chronicles of Kings, or the business many times of thirty or forty years, crampt into a representation of two hours and a half, which is not to imitate or paint Nature, but rather to draw her in miniature, to take her in little; to look upon her through the wrong end of a Perspective, and receive her Images not onely much less, but infinitely more imperfect then the life: this instead of making a Play delightful, renders it ridiculous.

Quodcunque ostendis mihi sic, incredulus odi: For the Spirit of man cannot be satisfied but with truth, or at least verisimility; and a Poem is to contain, if not *ta etyma,* yet *etymoisin omoia,* as one of the Greek Poets has expres'd it.

Another thing in which the French differ from us and from the Spaniards, is, that they do not embaras, or cumber themselves with too much Plot: they onely represent so much of a Story as will constitute one whole and great action sufficient for a Play; we, who undertake more, do but multiply adventures; which, not being produc'd from one another, as effects from causes, but barely following, constitute many actions in the Drama, and consequently make it many Playes.

But by pursuing close one argument, which is not cloy'd with many turns, the French have gain'd more liberty for verse, in which they write: they have leisure to dwell upon a subject which deserves it; and to represent the passions (which we have acknowledg'd to be the Poets work) without being hurried from one thing to another, as we are in the Playes of *Calderon,* which we have seen lately upon our Theaters, under the name of Spanish Plotts. I have taken notice but of one Tragedy of ours, whose Plot has that uniformity and unity of design in it which I have commended in the French; and that is *Rollo,* or rather, under the name of *Rollo,* The Story of *Bassianus* and *Geta* in *Herodian,* there indeed the Plot is neither large nor intricate, but just enough to fill the minds of the Audience, not to cloy them. Besides, you see it founded upon the truth of History, onely the time of the action is not reduceable to the strictness of the Rules; and you see in some places a little farce mingled, which is below the dignity of the other parts; and in this all our Poets are extreamly peccant, even *Ben Johnson* himself in *Sejanus* and *Catiline* has given us this Oleo of a Play; this unnatural mixture of Comedy and Tragedy, which to me sounds just as ridiculously as the History of *David* with the merry humours of *Golias*. In *Sejanus* you may take notice of the Scene betwixt *Livia* and the Physician, which is a pleasant Satyre upon the artificial helps of beauty: In *Catiline* you may see the Parliament of Women; the little envies of them to one another; and all that passes betwixt *Curio* and *Fulvia*: Scenes admirable in their kind, but of an ill mingle with the rest.

But I return again to French Writers; who, as I have said, do not burden themselves too much with Plot, which has been reproach'd to them by an *ingenious person* of our Nation as a fault, for he says they commonly make but one person considerable in a Play; they dwell upon him, and his concernments, while the rest of the persons are onely subservient to set him off. If he intends this by it, that there is one person in the Play who is of greater dignity then the rest, he must tax, not onely theirs, but those of the Ancients, and which he would be loth to do, the best of ours; for 'tis impossible but that one person must be more conspicuous in it then any other, and consequently the greatest share in the action must devolve on him. We see it so in the management of all affairs; even in the most equal Aristocracy, the ballance cannot be so justly poys'd, but some one will be superiour to the rest; either in parts, fortune, interest, or the consideration of some glorious exploit; which will reduce the greatest part of business into his hands.

But, if he would have us to imagine that in exalting of one character the rest of them are neglected, and that all of them have not some share or other in the action of the Play, I desire him to produce any of *Corneilles* Tragedies, wherein every person (like so many servants in a well govern'd Family) has not some employment, and who is not necessary to the carrying on of the Plot, or at least to your understanding it.

There are indeed some protatick persons in the Ancients, whom they make use of in their Playes, either to hear, or give the Relation: but the French avoid this with great address, making their narrations onely to, or by such who are some way interested in the main design. And now I am speaking of Relations, I cannot take a fitter opportunity to add this in favour of the French, that they often use them with better judgment and more *a propos* then the English do. Not that I commend narrations in general, but there are two sorts of them; one of those things which are antecedent to the Play, and are related to make the conduct of it more clear to us, but, 'tis a fault to choose such subjects for the Stage which will inforce us upon that Rock; because we see they are seldome listned to by the Audience, and that is many times the ruin of the Play: for, being once let pass without attention, the Audience can never recover themselves to understand the Plot; and indeed it is somewhat unreasonable that they should be put to so much trouble, as, that to comprehend what passes in their sight, they must have recourse to what was done, perhaps, ten or twenty years ago.

But there is another sort of Relations, that is, of things hapning in the Action of the Play, and suppos'd to be done behind the Scenes: and this is many times both convenient and beautiful: for, by it, the French avoid the tumult, which we are subject to in *England*, by representing Duells, Battells, and the like; which renders our Stage too like the Theaters, where they fight Prizes. For what is more ridiculous then to represent an Army with a Drum and five men behind it; all which, the Heroe of the other side is to drive in before him, or to see a Duel fought, and one slain with two or three thrusts of the foyles, which we know are so blunted, that we might give a man an hour to kill another in good earnest with them.

I have observ'd that in all our Tragedies, the Audience cannot forbear laughing when the Actors are to die; 'tis the most Comick part of the whole Play. All *passions* may be lively represented on the Stage, if to the well-writing of them the Actor supplies a good commanded voice, and limbs that move easily, and without stifness; but there are many *actions* which can never be imitated to a just height: dying especially is a thing which none but a Roman Gladiator could naturally perform upon the Stage when he did not imitate or represent, but naturally do it; and therefore it is better to omit the representation of it.

The words of a good Writer which describe it lively, will make a deeper impression of belief in us then all the Actor can perswade us to, when he seems to fall dead before us; as a Poet in the description of a beautiful Garden, or a Meadow, will please our imagination more then the place it self can please our sight. When we see death represented we are convinc'd it is but Fiction; but when we hear it related, our eyes (the strongest witnesses) are wanting, which might have undeceiv'd us; and we are all willing to favour the sleight when the Poet does not too grosly impose upon us. They therefore who imagine these relations would make no concernment in the Audience, are deceiv'd, by confounding them with the other, which are of things antecedent to the Play; those are made often in cold blood (as I may say) to the audience; but these are warm'd with our concernments, which are before awaken'd in the Play. What the Philosophers say of motion, that when it is once begun it continues of it self, and will do so to Eternity without some stop put to it, is clearly true on this occasion; the soul being already mov'd with the Characters and Fortunes of those imaginary persons, continues going of its own accord, and we are no more weary to hear what becomes of them when they are not on the Stage, then we are to listen to the news of an absent Mistress. But it is objected, That if one part of the Play may be related, then why not all? I answer, Some parts of the action are more fit to be represented, some to be related. *Corneille* sayes judiciously, that the Poet is not oblig'd to expose to view all particular actions which conduce to the principal: he ought to select such of them to be seen which will appear with the greatest beauty; either by the magnificence of the show, or the vehemence of passions which they produce, or some other charm which they have in them, and let the rest arrive to the audience by narration. 'Tis a great mistake in us to believe the French present no part of the action upon the Stage: every alteration or crossing of a design, every new sprung passion, and turn of it, is a part of the action, and much the noblest, except we conceive nothing to be action till they come to blows; as if the painting of the Heroes mind were not more properly the Poets work then the strength of his body. Nor does this any thing contradict the opinion of *Horace*, where he tells us,

Segnius irritant animos demissa per aurem
Quam quæ sunt oculis subjecta fidelibus. —
For he sayes immediately after,
— — — — Non tamen intus
Digna geri promes in scenam, multaq; tolles
Ex oculis, quæ mox narret facundia præsens.
Among which many he recounts some.
Nec pueros coram populo Medea trucidet,
Aut in avem Progne mutetur, Cadmus in anguem, &c.

That is, those actions which by reason of their cruelty will cause aversion in us, or by reason of their impossibility unbelief, ought either wholly to be avoided by a Poet, or onely deliver'd by narration. To which, we may have leave to add such as to avoid tumult, (as was before hinted) or to reduce the Plot into a more reasonable compass of time, or for defect of Beauty in them, are rather to be related then presented to the eye. Examples of all these kinds are frequent, not onely among all the Ancients, but in the best receiv'd of our English Poets. We find *Ben. Johnson* using them in his Magnetick Lady, where one comes out from Dinner, and relates the quarrels and disorders of it to save the undecent appearing of them on the Stage, and to abreviate the Story: and this in express imitation of *Terence*, who had done the same before him in his Eunuch, where *Pythias* makes the like relation of what had happen'd within at the Souldiers entertainment. The relations likewise of *Sejanus's* death, and the prodigies before it are remakable, the one of which was hid from sight to avoid the horrour and tumult of the representation; the other to shun the introducing of things impossible to be believ'd. In that excellent Play the King and no King, *Fletcher* goes yet farther; for the whole unravelling of the Plot is done by narration in the fifth Act, after the manner of the Ancients; and it moves great concernment in the Audience, though it be onely a relation of what was done many years before the Play. I could multiply other instances, but these are sufficient to prove that there is no errour in choosing a subject which requires this sort of narrations; in the ill managing of them, there may.

But I find I have been too long in this discourse since the French have many other excellencies not common to use, as that you never see any of their Playes end with a conversion, or simple change of will, which is the ordinary way our Poets use to end theirs. It shows little art in the conclusion of a Dramatick Poem, when they who have hinder'd the felicity during the four Acts, desist from it in the fifth without some powerful cause to take them off; and though I deny not but such reasons may be found, yet it is a path that is cautiously to be trod, and the Poet is to be sure he convinces the Audience that the motive is strong enough. As for example, the conversion of the Usurer in the Scornful Lady, seems to me a little forc'd; for being an Usurer, which implies a lover of Money to the highest degree of covetousness, (and such the Poet has represented him) the account he gives for the sudden change is, that he has been dup'd by the wilde young fellow, which in reason might render him more wary another time, and make him punish himself with harder fare and courser cloaths to get it up again: but that he should look upon it as a judgment, and so repent, we may expect to hear of in a Sermon, but I should never indure it in a Play.

I pass by this; neither will I insist upon the care they take, that no person after his first entrance shall ever appear, but the business which brings him upon the Stage shall be evident: which, if observ'd, must needs render all the events in the Play more natural; for there you see the probability of every accident,in the cause that produc'd it; and that which appears chance in the Play, will seem so reasonable to you, that you will there find it almost necessary; so that in the exits of their Actors you have a clear account of their purpose and design in the next entrance: (though, if the Scene be well wrought, the event will commonly deceive you) for there is nothing so absurd, sayes *Corneille*, as for an Actor to leave the Stage, onely because he has no more to say.

I should now speak of the beauty of their Rhime, and the

just reason I have to prefer that way of writing in the Tragedies before ours in Blanck verse; but because it is partly receiv'd by us, and therefore not altogether peculiar to them, I will say no more of it in relation to their Playes. For our own I doubt not but it will exceedingly beautifie them, and I can see but one reason why it should not generally obtain, that is, because our Poets write so ill in it. This indeed may prove a more prevailing argument then all others which are us'd to destroy it, and therefore I am onely troubled when great and judicious Poets, and those who acknowledg'd such, have writ or spoke against it; as for others they are to be answer'd by that one sentence of an ancient Authour,

Sed ut primo ad consequendos eos quos priores ducimus accendimur, ita ubi aut præteriri, aut æquari eos posse desperavimus, studium cum spe senescit: quod, scilicet, assequi non potest, sequi desinit; præteritoque, eo in quo eminere no possumus, aliquid in quo nitamur conquirimus.

Lisideius concluded in this manner; and *Neander* after a little pause thus answer'd him. I shall grant *Lisideius*, without much dispute, a great part of what he has urg'd against us, for I acknowledg the French contrive their Plots more regularly, observe the Laws of Comedy, and decorum of the Stage (to speak generally) with more exactness then the English. Farther I deny not but he has tax'd us justly in some irregularities of ours which he has mention'd; yet, after all, I am of opinion that neither our faults nor their virtues are considerable enough to place them above us.

For the lively imitation of Nature being in the definition of a Play, those which best fulfil that law ought to be esteem'd superiour to the others. 'Tis true, those beauties of the French-poesie are such as will raise perfection higher where it is, but are not sufficient to give it where it is not: they are indeed the Beauties of a Statue, but not of a Man, because not animated with the Soul of Poesie, which is imitation of humour and passions: and this *Lisideius* himself, or any other, however byassed to their Party, cannot but acknowledg, if he will either compare the humours of our Comedies, or the Characters of our serious Playes with theirs. He that will look upon theirs which have been written till these last ten years or thereabouts, will find it an hard matter to pick out two or three passable humours amongst them. *Corneille* himself, their Arch-Poet, what has he produc'd except *the Lier*, and you know how it was cry'd up in *France*; but when it came upon the English Stage, though well translated, and that part of *Dorant* acted to so much advantage by Mr. *Hart*, as I am confident it never receiv'd in its own Country, the most favourable to it would not put in competition with many of *Fletchers* or *Ben. Johnsons*. In the rest of *Corneilles* Comedies you have little humour; he tells you himself his way is first to show two Lovers in good intelligence with each other; in the working up of the Play to embroyle them by some mistake, and in the latter end to clear it up.

But of late years *de Moliere*, the younger *Corneille*, *Quinault*, and some others, have been imitating of afar off the quick turns and graces of the English Stage. They have mix'd their serious Playes with mirth, like our Tragicomedies since the death of Cardinal *Richlieu*, which *Lisideius* and many others not observing, have commended that in them for a virtue which they themselves no longer practice. Most of their new Playes are like some of ours, deriv'd from the Spanish Novells. There is scarce one of them without a vail, and a trusty *Diego*, who drolls much after the rate of the *Adventures*. But their humours, if I may grace them with that name, are so thin sown that never above one of them come up in any Play: I dare take upon me to find more variety of them in some one Play of *Ben. Johnsons* then in all theirs together: as he who has seen the Alchymist, the silent Woman, or *Bertholmew*-Fair, cannot but acknowledge with me.

I grant the French have performed what was possible on the groundwork of the Spanish Playes; what was pleasant before they have made regular; but there is not above one good Play to be writ upon all those Plots; they are too much alike to please often, which we need not the experience of our own Stage to justifie. As for their new way of mingling mirth with serious Plot I do not with *Lysideius* condemn the thing, though I cannot approve their manner of doing it: He tells us we cannot so speedily recollect our selves after a Scene of great passion and concernment as to pass to another of mirth and humour, and to enjoy it with any relish: but why should he imagine the soul of man more heavy than his Sences? Does not the eye pass from an unpleasant object to a pleasant in a much shorter time then is requir'd to this? and does not the unpleasantness of the first commend the beauty of the latter? The old Rule of Logick might have convinc'd him, that contraries when plac'd near, set off each other. A continued gravity keeps the spirit too much bent; we must refresh it sometimes, as we bait upon a journey, that we may go on with greater ease.

A Scene of mirth mix'd with Tragedy has the same effect upon us which our musick has betwixt the Acts, and that we find a relief to us from the best Plots and language of the Stage, if the discourses have been long. I must therefore have stronger arguments ere I am convinc'd, that compassion and mirth in the same subject destroy each other; and in the mean time cannot but conclude, to the honour of our Nation, that we have invented, increas'd and perfected a more pleasant way of writing for the Stage then was ever known to the Ancients or Moderns of any Nation, which is Tragicomedie.

And this leads me to wonder why *Lisideius* and many others should cry up the barrenness of the French Plots above the variety and copiousness of the English. Their Plots are single, they carry on one design which is push'd forward by all the Actors, every Scene in the Play contributing and moving towards it: Ours, besides the main design, have under plots or by-concernments, of less considerable Persons, and Intrigues, which are carried on with the motion of the main Plot: just as they say the Orb of the fix'd Stars, and those of the Planets, though they have motions of their own, are whirl'd about by the motion of the *primum mobile,* in which they are contain'd: that similitude expresses much of the English Stage: for if contrary motions may be found in Nature to agree; if a Planet can go East and West at the same time; one way by virtue of his own motion, the other by the force of the first mover; it will not be difficult to imagine how the under Plot, which is onely different, not contrary to the great design, may naturally be conducted along with it.

Eugenius has already shown us, from the confession of the French Poets, that the Unity of Action is sufficiently preserv'd if all the imperfect actions of the Play are conducing to the main design: but when those petty intrigues of a Play are so ill order'd that they have no coherence with the other, I must grant *Lisideius* has reason to tax that want of due connexion; for Coordination in a Play is as dangerous and unnatural as in a State. In the mean time he must acknowledge our variety, if well order'd, will afford a greater pleasure to the audience.

As for his other argument, that by pursuing one single Theme they gain an advantage to express and work up the passions, I wish any example he could bring from them would make it good: for I confess their verses are to me the coldest I have ever read: Neither indeed is it possible for them, in the way they take, so to express passion, as that the effects of it should appear in the concernment of an Audience: their Speeches being so many declamations, which tire us with length; so that instead of perswading us to grieve for their imaginary Heroes, we are concern'd for our own trouble, as we are in the tedious visits of bad company; we are in pain till they are gone. When the French Stage came to be reform'd by Cardinal *Richelieu*, those long Harangues were introduc'd, to comply with the gravity of a Churchman. Look upon the *Cinna* and the *Pompey*, they are not so properly to be called Playes, as long discourses of reason of State: and *Polieucte* in matters in Religion is as solemn as the long stops upon our Organs. Since that time it is grown into a custome, and their Actors speak by the Hour-glass, as our Parsons do; nay, they account it the grace of their parts: and think themselves disparag'd by the Poet, if they may not twice or thrice in a Play entertain the Audience with a Speech of an hundred or two hundred lines. I deny not but this may sute well enough with the French; for as we, who are a more sullen people, come to be diverted at our Playes; they who are of an ayery and gay temper come thither to make themselves more serious: And this I conceive to be one reason why Comedy is more pleasing to us, and Tragedies to them. But to speak generally, it cannot be deny'd that short Speeches and Replies are more apt to move the passions, and beget concernment in us then the other: for it is unnatural for any one in a gust of passion to speak long together, or for another in the same condition, to suffer him, without interruption.

Grief and Passion are like floods rais'd in little Brooks by a sudden rain; they are quickly up, and if the concernment be powr'd unexpectedly in upon us, it overflows us: But a long sobre shower gives them leisure to run out as they came in, without troubling the ordinary current. As for Comedy, Repartee is one of its chiefest graces; they greatest pleasure of the Audience is a chase of wit kept up on both sides, and swiftly manag'd. And this our forefathers, if not we, have had in *Fletchers* Playes, to a much higher degree of perfection then the French Poets can arrive at.

There is another part of *Lisideius* his Discourse, in which he has rather excus'd our neighbours then commended them; that is, for aiming onely to make one person considerable in their Playes. 'Tis very true what he has urged, that one character in all Playes, even without the Poets care, will have advantage of all the others; and that the design of the whole *Drama* will chiefly depend on it. But this hinders not that there may be more shining characters in the Play: many persons of a second magnitude, nay, some so very near, so almost equal to the first, that greatness may be oppos'd to greatness, and all the persons be made considerable, not onely by their quality, but their action. 'Tis evident that the more the persons are, the greater will be the variety, of the Plot. If then the parts are manag'd so regularly that the beauty of the whole be kept intire, and that the variety become not a perplex'd and confus'd mass of accidents, you will find it infinitely pleasing to be led in a labyrinth of design, where you see some of your way before you, yet discern not the end till you arrive at it. And that all this is practicable, I can produce for examples many of our English Playes: as the Maids Tragedy, the Alchymist, the Silent Woman; I was going to have named the Fox, but that the unity of design seems not exactly observ'd in it; for there appears two actions in the Play; the first naturally ending with the fourth Act; the second forc'd from it in the fifth: which yet is the less to be condemn'd in him, because the disguise of *Volpone,* though it suited not with his character as a crafty or covetous person, agreed well enough with that of a voluptuary: and by it the Poet gain'd the end he aym'd at, the punishment of Vice, and the reward of Virtue, which that disguise produc'd. So that to judge equally of it, it was an excellent fifth Act, but not so naturally proceeding from the former.

But to leave this, and pass to the latter part of *Lisideius* his discourse, which concerns relations, I must acknowledge with him, that the French have reason when they hide that part of the action which would occasion too much tumult upon the Stage, and choose rather to have it made known by the narration to the Audience. Farther I think it very convenient, for the reasons he has given, that all incredible actions were remov'd; but, whither custome has so insinuated it self into our Country-men, or nature has so form'd them to fierceness, I know not; but they will scarcely suffer combats & other objects of horrour to be taken from them. And indeed, the indecency of tumults is all which can be objected against fighting: For why may not our imagination as well suffer it self to be deluded with the probability of it, as with any other thing in the Play? For my part, I can with as great ease perswade my self that the blowes which are struck are given in good earnest, as I can, that they who strike them are Kings or Princes, or those persons which they represent.

For objects of incredibility I would be satisfied from *Lisideius,* whether we have any so remov'd from all appearance of truth as are those of *Corneilles Andromede*? A Play which has been frequented the most of any he has writ? If the *Perseus,* or the Son of an Heathen God, the *Pegasus* and the Monster were not capable to choak a strong belief, let him blame any representation of ours hereafter. Those indeed were objects of [illegible] the reason is the same as to the probability: for he [illegible] a Ballette or Masque, but a Play, which is to [illegible]th. But for death, that it ought not to be represented, I have besides the Arguments alledg'd by *Lisideius*, the authority of *Ben. Johnson*, who has forborn it in his Tragedies; for both the death of *Sejanus* and *Catiline* are related: though in the latter I cannot but observe one irregularity of that great Poet: he has remov'd the Scene in the same Act, from *Rome* to *Catiline's* Army, and from thence again to *Rome*; and besides has allow'd a very inconsiderable time, after *Catilines* Speech, for the striking of the battle, and the return of *Petreius*, who is to relate the event of it to the Senate: which I should not animadvert upon him, who was otherwise a painful observer of *to prepon*, or the decorum of the Stage, if he had not us'd extream severity in his judgment upon the incomparable *Shakespeare* for the same fault.

To conclude on this subject of Relations, if we are to be blam'd for showing too much of the action, the French are as faulty for discovering too little of it: a mean betwixt both should be observed by every judicious Writer, so as the audience may neither be left unsatisfied by not seeing what is beautiful, or shock'd by beholding what is either incredible or undecent. I hope I have already prov'd in this discourse, that though we are not altogether so punctual as the French, in observing the lawes of Comedy; yet our errours are so few, and little, and those things wherein we excel them so considerable, that we ought of right to be prefer'd before them. But what will *Lisideius* say if they themselves acknowledge they are too strictly ti'd up by those lawes, for breaking which he has blam'd the *English*? I will alledge *Corneille's* words, as I find them in the end of his Discourse of the three Unities; *Il est facile aux speculatifs d'estre severes, &c.*

"'Tis easie for speculative persons to judge severely; but if they would produce to publick view ten or twelve pieces of this nature, they would perhaps give more latitude to the Rules then I have done, when by experience they had known how much we are bound up and constrain'd by them, and how many beauties of the Stage they banish'd from it." To illustrate a little what he has said, by their servile observations of the unities of time and place, and integrity of Scenes, they have brought upon themselves that dearth of Plot, and narrowness of Imagination, which may be observ'd in all their Playes. How many beautifull accidents might naturally happen in two or three dayes, which cannot arrive with any probability in the compass of 24 hours? There is time to be allowed also for maturity of design, which amongst great and prudent persons, such as are often represented in Tragedy, cannot, with any likelihood of truth, be brought to pass at so short a warning. Farther, by tying themselves strictly to the unity of place, and unbroken Scenes, they are forc'd many times to omit some beauties which cannot be shown where the Act began; but might, if the Scene were interrupted, and the Stage clear'd for the persons to enter in another place; and therefore the French Poets are often forc'd upon absurdities: for if the Act begins in a chamber all the persons in the Play must have some business or other to come thither, or else they are not to be shown that Act, and sometimes their characters are very unfitting to appear there; As, suppose it were the Kings Bed-chamber, yet the meanest man in the Tragedy must come and dispatch his busines rather then in the Lobby or Court-yard (which is fitter for him) for fear the Stage should be clear'd, and the Scenes broken.

Many times they fall by it into a greater inconvenience; for they keep their Scenes unbroken, and yet change the place; as in one of their newest Playes, where the Act begins in the Street. There a Gentleman is to meet his Friend; he sees him with his man, coming out from his Fathers house; they talk together, and the first goes out: the second, who is a Lover, has made an appointment with his Mistress; she appears at the window, and then we are to imagine the Scene lies under it. This Gentleman is call'd away, and leaves his servant with his Mistress: presently her Father is heard from within; the young Lady is affraid the Servingman should be discover'd, and thrusts him in through a door which is suppos'd to be her Closet. After this, the Father enters to the Daughter, and now the Scene is in a House: for he is seeking from one room to another for this poor *Philipin*, or French *Diego*, who is heard from within, drolling and breaking many a miserable conceit upon his sad condition. In this ridiculous manner the Play goes on, the Stage being never empty all the while: so that the Street, the Window, the two Houses, and the Closet, are made to walk about, and the Persons to stand still. Now what I beseech you is more easie than to write a regular French Play, or more difficult then to write an irregular English one, like those of *Fletcher*, or of *Shakespeare*.

If they content themselves as *Corneille* did, with some flat design, which, like an ill Riddle, is found out e're if be half propos'd; such Plots we can make every way regular as easily as they: but when e're they endeavour to rise up to any quick turns and counterturns of Plot, as some of them have attempted, since *Corneilles* Playes have been less in vogue, you see they write as irregularly as we, though they cover it more speciously. Hence the reason is perspicuous, why no French Playes, when translated, have, or ever can succeed upon the English Stage. For, if you consider the Plots, our own are fuller of variety, if the writing ours are more quick and fuller of spirit: and therefore 'tis a strange mistake in those who decry the way of writing Playes in Verse, as if the English therein imitated the French. We have borrow'd nothing from them; our Plots are weav'd in English Loomes: we endeavour therein to follow the variety and greatness of characters which are deriv'd to us from *Shakespeare* and *Fletcher*: the copiousness and well-knitting of the intrigues we have from *Johnson*, and for the Verse it self we have English Presidents of elder date then any of *Corneilles*'s Playes: (not to name our old Comedies before *Shakespeare*, which were all writ in verse of six feet, or *Alexandrin's*, such as the French now use) I can show in *Shakespeare*, many Scenes of rhyme together, and the like in *Ben. Johnsons* Tragedies: In *Catiline* and *Sejanus* sometimes thirty or forty lines; I mean besides the Chorus, or the Monologues, which by the way, show'd *Ben.* no enemy to this way of writing, especially if you look upon his sad Shepherd which goes sometimes upon rhyme, sometimes upon blanck Verse, like an Horse who eases himself upon Trot and Amble. You find him likewise commending *Fletcher's* Pastoral of the Faithful Shepherdess; which is for the most part Rhyme, though not refin'd to that purity to which it hath since been brought: And these examples are enough to clear us from a servile imitation of the French. But to return from whence I have digress'd, I dare boldly affirm these two things of the English *Drama*: First, That we have many Playes of ours as regular as any of theirs; and which, besides, have more variety of Plot and Characters: And secondly, that in most of the irregular Playes of *Shakespeare* or *Fletcher* (for *Ben. Johnson's* are for the most part regular) there is a more masculine fancy and greater spirit in all the writing, then there is in any of the French. I could produce even in *Shakespeare's* and *Fletcher's* Works, some Playes which are almost exactly form'd; as the Merry Wives of *Windsor*, and the Scornful Lady: but because (generally speaking) *Shakespeare*, who writ first, did not perfectly observe the Laws of Comedy, and *Fletcher*, who came nearer to perfection, yet through carelessness made many faults; I will take the pattern of a perfect Play from *Ben. Johnson*, who was a careful and learned observer of the Dramatique Lawes, and from all his Comedies I shall select *The Silent Woman*; of which I will make a short Examen, according to those Rules which the French observe.

As *Neander* was beginning to examine the Silent Woman, *Eugenius*, looking earnestly upon him; I beseech you *Neander*, said he, gratifie the company and me in particular so far, as before you speak of the Play, to give us a Character of the Authour; and tell us franckly your opinion, whether you do not think all Writers, both French and English, ought to give place to him?

I fear, replied *Neander*, That in obeying your commands I shall draw a little envy upon my self. Besides, in performing them, it will be first necessary to speak somewhat of *Shakespeare* and *Fletcher*, his Rivalls in Poesie; and one of them, in my opinion, at least his equal, perhaps his superiour.

To begin then with *Shakespeare*; he was the man who of all Modern, and perhaps Ancient Poets, had the largest and most comprehensive soul. All the Images of Nature were still present to him, and he drew them not laboriously, but luckily: when he describes any thing, you more than see it, you feel it too. Those who accuse him to have wanted learning, give him the greater commendation: he was naturally learn'd; he needed not the spectacles of Books to read Nature; he look'd inwards, and found her there. I cannot say he is every where alike; were he so, I should do him injury to compare him with the greatest of Mankind. He is many times flat, insipid; his Comick wit degenerating into clenches; his serious swelling into Bombast. But he is alwayes great, when some great occasion is presented to him: no man can say he ever had a fit subject for his wit, and did not then raise himself as high above the rest of the Poets,

Quantum lent a solent, inter viberna cupressi: The consideration of this made Mr. *Hales* of *Eaton* say, That there was no subject of which any Poet ever writ, but he would produce it much better treated of in *Shakespeare*; and however others are now generally prefer'd before him, yet the Age wherein he liv'd, which had contemporaries with him, *Fletcher* and *Johnson* never equall'd them to him in their esteem: And in the last Kings Court, when *Ben's* reputation was at highest, Sir *John Suckling*, and with him the greater part of the Courtiers, set our *Shakespeare* far above him.

Beaumont and *Fletcher* of whom I am next to speak, had with the advantage of *Shakespeare*'s wit, which was their precedent, great natural gifts, improv'd by study. *Beaumont* especially being so accurate a judge of Playes, that *Ben. Johnson* while he liv'd, submitted all his Writings to his Censure, and 'tis thought, us'd his judgement in correcting, if not contriving all his Plots. What value he had for him, appears by the Verses he writ to him; and therefore I need speak no farther of it. The first Play which brought *Fletcher* and him in esteem was their *Philaster*: for before that, they had written two or three very unsuccessfully: as the like is reported of *Ben. Johnson*, before he writ *Every Man in his Humour*. Their Plots were generally more regular then *Shakespeare's*, especially those which were made before *Beaumont's* death; and they understood and imitated the conversation of Gentlemen much better; whose wilde debaucheries, and quickness of wit in reparties, no Poet can ever paint as they have done. This Humour of which *Ben. Johnson* deriv'd from particular persons, they made it not their business to describe: they represented all the passions very lively, but above all, Love. I am apt to believe the English Language in them arriv'd to its highest perfection; what words have since been taken in, are rather superfluous then necessary. Their Playes are now the most pleasant and frequent entertainments of the Stage; two of theirs being acted through the year for one of *Shakespeare's* or *Johnsons*: the reason is, because there is a certain gayety in their Comedies, and Pathos in their more serious Playes, which suits generally with all mens humours. *Shakespeares* language is likewise a little obsolete, and *Ben. Johnson's* wit comes short of theirs.

As for *Johnson*, to whose Character I am now arriv'd, if we look upon him while he was himself, (for his last Playes were but his dotages) I think him the most learned and judicious Writer which any Theater ever had. He was a most severe Judge of himself as well as others. One cannot say he wanted wit, but rather that he was frugal of it. In his works you find little to retrench or alter. Wit and Language, and Humour also in some measure we had before him; but something of Art was wanting to the *Drama* till he came. He manag'd his strength to more advantage then any who preceded him. You seldome find him making Love in any of his Scenes, or endeavouring to move the Passions; his genius was too sullen and saturnine to do it gracefully, especially when he knew he came after those who had performed both to such an height. Humour was his proper Sphere, and in that he delighted most to represent Mechanick people.

He was deeply conversant in the Ancients, both Greek and Latine, and he borrow'd boldly from them: there is scarce a Poet or Historian among the Roman Authours of those times whom he has not translated in *Sejanus* and *Catiline*. But he has done his Robberies so openly, that one may see he fears not to be taxed by any Law. He invades Authours like a Monarch, and what would be theft in other Poets, is onely victory in him. With the spoils of these Writers he so represents old *Rome* to us, in its Rites, Ceremonies and Customs, that if one of their Poets had written either of his Tragedies, we had seen less of it then in him. If there was any fault in his Language, 'twas that he weav'd it too closely and laboriously in his serious Playes; perhaps too, he did a little to much Romanize our Tongue, leaving the words which he translated almost as much Latine as he found them: wherein though he learnedly followed the Idiom of their language, he did not enough comply with ours. If I would compare him with *Shakespeare*, I must acknowledge him the more correct Poet, but *Shakespeare* the greater wit. *Shakespeare* was the *Homer*, or Father of our Dramatick Poets; *Johnson* was the *Virgil*, the pattern of elaborate writing; I admire him, but I love *Shakespeare*. To conclude of him, as he has given us the most correct Playes, so in the precepts which he has laid down in his Discoveries, we have as many and profitable Rules for perfecting the Stage as any wherewith the French can furnish us.

Having thus spoken of the Authour, I proceed to the examination of his Comedy, The Silent Woman.

Examen of the Silent Woman: To begin first with the length of the Action, it is so far from exceeding the compass of a Natural day, that it takes not up an Artificial one. 'Tis all included in the limits of three hours and an half, which is not more than is requir'd for the presentment on the Stage. A beauty perhaps not much observ'd; if it had, we should not have look'd upon the Spanish Translation of five hours with so much wonder. The Scene of it is laid in *London*; the latitude of place is almost as little as you can imagine: for it lies all within the compass of two Houses, and after the first Act, in one. The continuity of Scenes is observ'd more than in any of our Playes, excepting his own Fox and Alchymist. They are not broken above twice or thrice at most in the whole Comedy, and in the two best of *Corneille's* Playes, the *Cid* and *Cinna*, they are interrupted once apiece. The action of the Play is intirely one; the end or aim of which is the setling of *Morose*'s Estate on *Dauphine*.

The Intrigue of it is the greatest and most noble of any pure unmix'd Comedy in any Language: you see it in many persons of various characters and humours, and all delightful: As first, *Morose*, or an old Man, to whom all noise but his own talking is offensive. Some who would be thought Criticks, say this humour of his is forc'd: but to remove that objection, we may consider him first to be naturally of a delicate hearing, as many are to whom all sharp sounds are unpleasant; and secondly, we may attribute much of it to the peevishness of his Age, or the wayward authority of an old man in his own house, where he may make himself obeyed; and this the Poet seems to allude to in his name *Morose*. Besides this, I am assur'd from diverse persons, that *Ben. Johnson* was actually acquainted with such a man, one altogether as ridiculous as he is here represented. Others say it is not enough to find one man of such an humour; it must be common to more, and the more common the more natural.

To prove this, they instance in the best of Comical Characters, *Falstaff*: There are many men resembling him; Old, Fat, Merry, Cowardly, Drunken, Amorous, Vain, and Lying: But to convince these people, I need but tell them, that humour is the ridiculous extravagance of conversation, wherein one man differs from all others. If then it be common, or communicated to many, how differs it from other mens? or what indeed causes it to be ridiculous so much as the singularity of it? As for *Falstaffe*, he is not properly one humour, but a Miscellany of Humours or Images, drawn from so many several men; that wherein he is singular in his wit, or those things he sayes, *præter expectatum*, unexpected by the Audience; his quick evasions when you imagine him surpriz'd, which as they are extreamly diverting of themselves, so receive a great addition from his person; for the very sight of such an unwieldy old debauch'd fellow is a Comedy alone.

And here having a place so proper for it I cannot but enlarge somewhat upon this subject of humour into which I am fallen. The Ancients had little of it in their Comedies; for the *to geloion*, of the Old Comedy, of which *Aristophanes* was chief, was not so much to imitate a man, as to make the people laugh at some odd conceit, which had commonly somewhat of unnatural or obscene in it. Thus when you see *Socrates* brought upon the Stage, you are not to imagine him made ridiculous by the imitation of his actions, but rather by making him perform something very unlike himself: something so childish and absurd, as by comparing it with the gravity of the true *Socrates*, makes a ridiculous object for the Spectators. In their new Comedy which succeeded, the Poets fought indeed to express the *êthos*, as in their Tragedies the *pathos* of Mankind. But this *êthos* contain'd onely the general Characters of men and manners; as old men, Lovers, Servingmen, Courtizans, Parasites, and such other persons as we see in their Comedies; all which they made alike: that is, one old man or Father; one Lover, one Courtizan so like another, as if the first of them had begot the rest of every sort: *Ex homine hunc natum dicas*. The same custome they observ'd likewise in their Tragedies.

As for the *French*, though they have the word *humeur* among them, yet they have small use of it in their Comedies, or Farces; they being but ill imitations of the *ridiculum*, or that which stirr'd up laughter in the old Comedy. But among the *English* 'tis otherwise: where by humour is meant some extravagant habit, passion, or affection; particular (as I said before) to some one person: by the oddness of which, he is immediately distinguish'd from the rest of men; which being lively and naturally represented, most frequently begets that malicious pleasure in the Audience which is testified by laughter: as all things which are deviations from common customes are ever the aptest to produce it: though by the way this laughter is onely accidental, as the person represented is Fantastick or Bizarre; but pleasure is essential to it, as the imitation of what is natural. The description of these humours, drawn from the knowledge and observation of particular persons, was the peculiar genius and talent of *Ben. Johnson*; To whose Play I now return.

Besides *Morose*, there are at least 9 or 10 different Characters and humours in the *Silent Woman*, all which persons have several concernments of their own, yet are all us'd by the Poet, to the conducting of the main design to perfection. I shall not waste time in commending the writing of this Play, but I will give you my opinion, that there is more wit and acuteness of Fancy in it then in any of *Ben. Johnson's*. Besides, that he has here describ'd the conversation of Gentlemen in the persons of *True-Wit*, and his Friends, with more gayety, ayre and freedom, then in the rest of his Comedies. For the contrivance of the Plot 'tis extream elaborate, and yet withal easie; for the *lysis*, or untying of it, 'tis so admirable, that when it is done, no one of the Audience would think the Poet could have miss'd it; and yet it was conceald so much before the last Scene, that any other way would sooner have enter'd into your thoughts. But I dare not take upon me to commend the Fabrick of it, because it is altogether so full of Art, that I must unravel every Scene in it to commend it as I ought. And this excellent contrivance is still the more to be admir'd, because 'tis Comedy where the persons are onely of common rank, and their business private, not elevated by passions or high concernments as in serious Playes. Here every one is a proper Judge of all he sees; nothing is represented but that with which he daily converses: so that by consequence all faults lie open to discovery, and few are pardonable. 'Tis this which *Horace* has judiciously observed:

Creditur ex medio quia res arcessit habere
Sudoris minimum, sed habet Comedia tanto
Plus oneris, quanto veniæ minus. — —

But our Poet, who was not ignorant of these difficulties, had prevail'd himself of all advantages; as he who designes a large leap takes his rise from the highest ground. One of these advantages is that which *Corneille* has laid down as the greatest which can arrive to any Poem, and which he himself could never compass above thrice in all his Playes, *viz.* the making choice of some signal and long expected day, whereon the action of the Play is to depend. This day was that design'd by *Dauphine* for the setling of his Uncles Estate upon him; which to compass he contrives to marry him: that the marriage had been plotted by him long beforehand is made evident by what he tells *Truwit* in the second Act, that in one moment he had destroy'd what he had been raising many months.

There is another artifice of the Poet, which I cannot here omit, because by the frequent practice of it in his Comedies, he has left it to us almost as a Rule, that is, when he has any Character or humour wherein he would show a *Coup de*

Maistre, or his highest skill; he recommends it to your observation by a pleasant description of it before the person first appears. Thus, in *Bartholomew Fair* he gives you the Pictures of *Numps* and *Cokes*, and in this those of *Daw*, *Lasocle*, *Morose*, and the *Collegiate Ladies*; all which you hear describ'd before you see them. So that before they come upon the Stage you have a longing expectation of them, which prepares you to receive them favourably; and when they are there, even from their first appearance you are so far acquainted with them, that nothing of their humour is lost to you.

I will observe yet one thing further of this admirable Plot; the business of it rises in every Act. The second is greater then the first; the third then the second, and so forward to the fifth. There too you see, till the very last Scene, new difficulties arising to obstruct the action of the Play; and when the Audience is brought into despair that the business can naturally be effected, then, and not before, the discovery is made. But that the Poet might entertain you with more variety all this while, he reserves some new Characters to show you, which he opens not till the second and third Act. In the second, *Morose*, *Daw*, the *Barber* and *Otter*; in the third the *Collegiat Ladies*: All which he moves afterwards in by-walks, or under-Plots, as diversions to the main design, least it should grow tedious, though they are still naturally joyn'd with it, and somewhere or other subservient to it. Thus, like a skilful Chest-player, by little and little he draws out his men, and makes his pawns of use to his greater persons.

If this Comedy, and some others of his, were translated into French Prose (which would now be no wonder to them, since *Moliere* has lately given them Playes out of Verse which have not displeas'd them) I believe the controversie would soon be decided betwixt the two Nations, even making them the Judges. But we need not call our Hero's to our ayde; Be it spoken to the honour of the English, our Nation can never want in any Age such who are able to dispute the Empire of Wit with any people in the Universe. And though the fury of a Civil War, and Power, for twenty years together, abandon'd to a barbarous race of men, Enemies of all good Learning, had buried the Muses under the ruines of Monarchy; yet with the restoration of our happiness, we see reviv'd Poesie lifting up its head, & already shaking off the rubbish which lay so heavy on it. We have seen since His Majesties return, many Dramatick Poems which yield not to those of any forreign Nation, and which deserve all Lawrels but the English. I will set aside Flattery and Envy: it cannot be deny'd but we have had some little blemish either in the Plot or writing of all those Playes which have been made within these seven years: (and perhaps there is no Nation in the world so quick to discern them, or so difficult to pardon them, as ours:) yet if we can perswade our selves to use the candour of that Poet, who (though the most severe of Criticks) has left us this caution by which to moderate our censures;

Vbi plura nitent in carmine non ego paucis offendar maculis.

If in consideration of their many and great beauties, we can wink at some slight, and little imperfections; if we, I say, can be thus equal to our selves, I ask no favour from the French. And if I do not venture upon any particular judgment of our late Playes, 'tis out of the consideration which an Ancient Writer gives me; *Vivorum, ut magna admiratio ita censura difficilis*: betwixt the extreams of admiration and malice, 'tis hard to judge uprightly of the living. Onely I think it may be permitted me to say, that as it is no less'ning to us to yield to some Playes, and those not many of our own Nation in the last Age, so can it be no addition to pronounce of our present Poets that they have far surpass'd all the Ancients, and the Modern Writers of other Countreys.

This, my Lord, was the substance of what was then spoke on that occasion; and *Lisideius*, I think was going to reply, when he was prevented thus by *Crites*: I am confident, said he, the most material things that can be said, have been already urg'd on either side; if they have not, I must beg of *Lisideius* that he will defer his answer till another time: for I confess I have a joynt quarrel to you both, because you have concluded, without any reason given for it, that Rhyme is proper for the Stage. I will not dispute how ancient it hath been among us to write this way; perhaps our Ancestours knew no better till

Shakespeare's time. I will grant it was not altogether left by him, and that *Fletcher* and *Ben. Johnson* us'd it frequently in their Pastorals, and sometimes in other Playes. Farther, I will not argue whether we receiv'd it originally from our own Countrymen, or from the French; for that is an inquiry of as little benefit, as theirs who in the midst of the great Plague were not so sollicitous to provide against it, as to know whether we had it from the malignity of our own air, or by transportation from *Holland*. I have therefore onely to affirm, that it is not allowable in serious Playes; for Comedies I find you already concluding with me.

To prove this, I might satisfie my self to tell you, how much in vain it is for you to strive against the stream of the peoples inclination; the greatest part of which are prepossess'd so much with those excellent Playes of *Shakespeare, Fletcher*, and *Ben. Johnson*, (which have been written out of Rhyme) that except you could bring them such as were written better in it, and those too by persons of equal reputation with them, it will be impossible for you to gain your cause with them, who will still be judges. This it is to which in fine all your reasons must submit. The unanimous consent of an Audience is so powerful, That even *Julius Cæsar* (as *Macrobius* reports of him) when he was perpetual Dictator, was not able to ballance it on the other side. But when *Laberius*, a *Roman* Knight, at his request contended in the *Mime* with another Poet, he was forc'd to cry out, *Etiam favente me victus es Liberi*. But I will not on this occasion, take the advantage of the greater number, but onely urge such reasons against Rhyme, as I find in the Writings of those who have argu'd for the other way.

First then I am of opinion, that Rhyme is unnatural in a Play, because Dialogue there is presented as the effect of sudden thought. For a Play is the imitation of Nature; and since no man, without premeditation speaks in Rhyme, neither ought he to do it on the Stage; this hinders not but the Fancy may be there elevated to a higher pitch of thought then it is in ordinary discourse: for there is a probability that men of excellent and quick parts may speak noble things *ex tempore*: but those thoughts are never fetter'd with the numbers or sound of Verse without study, and therefore it cannot be but unnatural to present the most free way of speaking, in that which is the most constrain'd. For this Reason, sayes *Aristotle*, 'Tis best to write Tragedy in that kind of Verse which is the least such, or which is nearest Prose: and this amongst the Ancients was the Iambique, and with us is blank verse, or the measure of verse, kept exactly without rhyme. These numbers therefore are fittest for a Play; the others for a paper of Verses, or a Poem.

Blank verse being as much below them as rhyme is improper for the *Drama*. And if it be objected that neither are blank verses made *ex tempore*, yet as nearest Nature, they are still to be preferr'd. But there are two particular exceptions which many besides my self have had to verse; by which it will appear yet more plainly, how improper it is in Playes. And the first of them is grounded upon that very reason for which some have commended Rhyme: they say the quickness of repartees in argumentative Scenes receives an ornament from verse. Now what is more unreasonable then to imagine that a man should not onely light upon the Wit, but the Rhyme too upon the sudden? This nicking of him who spoke before both in sound and measure, is so great an happiness, that you must at least suppose the persons of your Play to be born Poets, *Arcades omnes & cantare pares & respondere parati*: they must have arriv'd to the degree of *quicquid conabar dicere*: to make Verses almost whether they will or no: if they are any thing below this, it will look rather like the design of two then the answer of one: it will appear that your Actors hold intelligence together, that they perform their tricks like Fortune-tellers, by confederacy. The hand of Art will be too visible in it against that maxime of all Professions; *Ars est celare artem.*

That it is the greatest perfection of Art to keep it self undiscover'd. Nor will it serve you to object, that however you manage it, 'tis still known to be a Play; and consequently the Dialogue of two persons understood to be the labour of one Poet. For a Play is still an imitation of Nature; we know we are to be deceiv'd, and we desire to be so; but no man ever was deceiv'd but with a probability of truth, for who will suffer a grose lie to be fasten'd on him? Thus we sufficiently understand that the Scenes which represent Cities and Countries to us, are not really such, but onely painted on boards and Canvass: But shall that excuse the ill Painture or designment of them; Nay rather ought they not to be labour'd with so much the more diligence and exactness to help the imagination? since the mind of man does naturally tend to, and seek after Truth; and therefore the nearer any thing comes to the imitation of it, the more it pleases.

Thus, you see, your Rhyme is uncapable of expressing the greatest thoughts naturally, and the lowest it cannot with any grace: for what is more unbefitting the Majesty of Verse, then to call a Servant, or bid a door be shut in Rhime? And yet this miserable necessity you are forc'd upon. But Verse, you say, circumscribes a quick and luxuriant fancy, which would extend it self too far on every subject, did not the labour which is requir'd to well turn'd and polish'd Rhyme, set bounds to it. Yet this Argument, if granted, would onely prove that we may write better in Verse, but not more naturally. Neither is it able to evince that; for he who wants judgment to confine his fancy in blank Verse, may want it as much in Rhyme; and he who has it will avoid errours in both kinds. Latine verse was as great a confinement to the imagination of those Poets, as Rhime to ours: and yet you find *Ovid* saying too much on every subject. *Nescivit* (sayes *Seneca*) *quod bene cessit relinquere*: of which he gives you one famous instance in his Discription of the Deluge.

Omnia pontus erat, deerant quoque Litora Ponto: Now all was Sea, Nor had that Sea a shore. Thus *Ovid's* fancy was not limited by verse, and *Virgil* needed not verse to have bounded his.

In our own language we see *Ben. Johnson* confining himself to what ought to be said, even in the liberty of blank Verse; and yet *Corneille*, the most judicious of the *French* Poets, is still varying the same sence an hundred wayes, and dwelling eternally upon the same subject, though confin'd by Rhyme. Some other exceptions I have to Verse, but being these I have nam'd are for the most part already publick; I conceive it reasonable they should first be answer'd. It concerns me less then any, said *Neander*, (seeing he had ended) to reply to this Discourse; because when I should have prov'd that Verse may be natural in Playes, yet I should alwayes be ready to confess, that those which I have written in this kind come short of that perfection which is requir'd. Yet since you are pleas'd I should undertake this Province, I will do it, though with all imaginable respect and deference both to that person from whom you have borrow'd your strongesst Arguments, and to whose judgment when I have said all, I finally submit.

But before I proceed to answer your objections, I must first remember you, that I exclude all Comedy from my defence; and next that I deny not but blank verse may be also us'd, and content my self onely to assert, that in serious Playes where the subject and characters are great, and the Plot unmix'd with mirth, which might allay or divert these concernments which are produc'd, Rhyme is there as natural, and more effectual then blank Verse. And now having laid down this as a foundation, to begin with *Crites*, I must crave leave to tell him, that some of his Arguments against rhyme reach no farther then from the faults or defects of ill rhime, to conclude against the use of it in general. May not I conclude against blank verse by the same reason? If the words of some Poets who write in it, are either ill chosen, or ill placed (which makes not onely rhime, but all kind of verse in any language unnatural;) Shall I, for their vitious affection condemn those excellent lines of *Fletcher*, which are written in that kind?

Is there any thing in rhyme more constrain'd than this line in blank verse? I Heav'n invoke, and strong resistance make, where you see both the clauses are plac'd unnaturally; that is, contrary to the common way of speaking, and that without the excuse of a rhyme to cause it: yet you would think me very ridiculous, if I should accuse the stubbornness of blank Verse for this, and not rather the stifness of the Poet. Therefore, *Crites*, you must either prove that words, though well chosen, and duly plac'd, yet render not Rhyme natural in it self; or, that however natural and easie the rhyme may be, yet it is not proper for a Play. If you insist upon the former part, I would ask you what other conditions are requir'd to make Rhyme natural in it self, besides an election of apt words, and a right disposing of them? For the due choice of your words expresses your sence naturally, and the due placing them adapts the rhyme to it. If you object that one verse may be made for the sake of another, though both the words and rhyme be apt; I answer it cannot possibly so fall out; for either there is a dependance of sence betwixt the first line and the second, or there is none: if there be that connection, then in the natural position of the words, the latter line must of necessity flow from the former: if there be no dependance, yet still the due ordering of words makes the last line as natural in itself as the other: so that the necessity of a rhime never forces any but bad or lazy Writers to say what they would not otherwise.

'Tis true, there is both care and Art requir'd to write in Verse; A good Poet never concludes upon the first line, till he has sought out such a rhime as may fit the sense, already prepar'd to heighten the second: many times the close of the sense falls into the middle of the next verse, or farther of, and he may often prevail himself of the same advantages in English which *Virgil* had in Latine. He may break off in the *Hemystich*, and begin another line: indeed, the not observing these two last things, makes Playes which are writ in verse so tedious: for though, most commonly, the sence is to be confin'd to the Couplet, yet nothing that does *perpetuo tenore fluere*, run in the same channel, can please alwayes. 'Tis like the murmuring of a stream, which not varying in the fall, causes at first attention, at last drowsiness. Variety of cadences is the best rule, the greatest help to the Actors, and refreshment to the Audience.

If then Verse may be made natural in it self, how becomes it improper to a Play? You say the Stage is the representation of Nature, and no man in ordinary conversation speaks in rhime. But you foresaw when you said this, that it might be answer'd; neither does any man speak in blank verse, or in measure without rhime. Therefore you concluded, that which is nearest Nature is still to be preferr'd. But you took no notice that rhime might be made as natural as blank verse, by the well placing of the words, *&c.* all the difference between them when they are both correct, is the sound in one, which the other wants; and if so, the sweetness of it, and all the advantage resulting from it, which are handled in the Preface to the *Rival Ladies,* will yet stand good. As for that place of *Aristotle,* where he sayes Playes should be writ in that kind of Verse which is nearest Prose; it makes little for you, blank verse being properly but measur'd Prose. Now measure alone in any modern Language, does not constitute verse; those of the Ancients in Greek and Latine, consisted in quantity of words, and a determinate number of feet.

But when, by the inundation of the *Goths* and *Vandals* into *Italy* new Languages were brought in, and barbarously mingled with the Latine (of which the *Italian, Spanish, French,* and ours, (made out of them and the *Teutonick*) are Dialects:) a new way of Poesie was practis'd; new, I say in those Countries, for in all probability it was that of the Conquerours in their own Nations. This new way consisted in measure or number of feet and rhyme. The sweetness of Rhyme, and observation of Accent, supplying the place of quantity in words, which could neither exactly be observ'd by those *Barbarians* who knew not the Rules of it, neither was it suitable to their tongues as it had been to the Greek and Latine. No man is tied in modern Poesie to observe any farther rule in the feet of his verse, but that they be dissylables; whether *Spondee, Trochee,* or *Iambique,* it matters not; onely he is obliged to rhyme: Neither do the *Spanish, French, Italian* or *Germans* acknowledge at all, or very rarely any such kind of Poesie as blank verse amongst them.

Therefore at most 'tis but a Poetick Prose, *a Sermo pedestris,* and as such most fit for Comedies, where I acknowledge Rhyme to be improper. Farther, as to that quotation of *Aristotle,* our Couplet Verses may be rendred as near Prose as blank verse it self, by using those advantages I lately nam'd, as breaks in a Hemistick, or running the sence into another line, thereby making Art and Order appear as loose and free as Nature: or not tying our selves to Couplets strictly, we may use the benefit of the Pindarique way, practis'd in the Siege of *Rhodes;* where the numbers vary and the rhyme is dispos'd carelesly, and far from often chymeing. Neither is that other advantage of the Ancients to be despis'd, of changing the kind of verse when they please with the change of the Scene, or some new entrance: for they confine not themselves alwayes to Iambiques, but extend their liberty to all Lyrique numbers, and sometimes, even to Hexameter. But I need not go so far to prove that Rhyme, as it succeeds to all other offices of Greek and Latine Verse, so especially to this of Playes, since the custome of all Nations at this day confirms it: All the *French*, *Italian* and *Spanish* Tragedies are generally writ in it, and sure the Universal consent of the most civiliz'd parts of the world, ought in this, as it doth in other customs, include the rest.

But perhaps you may tell me I have propos'd such a way to make rhyme natural, and consequently proper to Playes, as is unpracticable, and that I shall scarce find six or eight lines together in any Play, where the words are so plac'd and chosen as is requir'd to make it natural. I answer, no Poet need constrain himself at all times to it. It is enough he makes it his general Rule; for I deny not but sometimes there may be a greatness in placing the words otherwise; and sometimes they may sound better, sometimes also the variety it self is excuse enough. But if, for the most part, the words be plac'd as they are in the negligence of Prose, it is sufficient to denominate the way practicable; for we esteem that to be such, which in the Tryal oftner succeeds then misses. And thus far you may find the practice made good in many Playes; where you do not, remember still, that if you cannot find six natural Rhymes together, it will be as hard for you to produce as many lines in blank Verse, even among the greatest of our Poets, against which I cannot make some reasonable exception.

And this, Sir, calls to my remembrance the beginning of your discourse, where you told us we should never find the Audience favourable to this kind of writing, till we could produce as good Playes in Rhyme, as *Ben. Johnson*, *Fletcher*, and *Shakespeare*, had writ out of it. But it is to raise envy to the living, to compare them with the dead. They are honour'd, and almost ador'd by us, as they deserve; neither do I know any so presumptuous of themselves as to contend with them.

Yet give me leave to say thus much without injury to their Ashes, that not onely we shall never equal them, but they could never equal themselves, were they to rise and write again. We acknowledge them our Fathers in wit, but they have ruin'd their Estates themselves before they came to their childrens hands. There is scarce an Humour, a Character, or any kind of Plot, which they have not blown upon: all comes sullied or wasted to us: and were they to entertain this Age, they could not make so plenteous treatments out of such decay'd Fortunes. This therefore will be a good Argument to us either not to write at all, or to attempt some other way. There is no bayes to be expected in their Walks; *Tentanda via est quà me quoque possum tollere humo.*

This way of writing in Verse, they have onely left free to us; our age is arriv'd to a perfection in it, which they never knew; and which (if we may guess by what of theirs we have seen in Verse (as in the *Faithful Shepherdess*, and *Sad Shepherd*:) 'tis probable they never could have reach'd. For the Genius of every Age is different; and though ours excel in this, I deny not but that to imitate Nature in that perfection which they did in Prose, is a greater commendation then to write in verse exactly. As for what you have added, that the people are not generally inclin'd to like this way; if it were true, it would be no wonder, that betwixt the shaking off an old habit, and the introducing of a new, there should be difficulty.

Do we not see them stick to *Hopkins* and *Sternholds* Psalmes, and forsake those of *David*, I mean *Sandys* his Translation of them? If by the people you understand the multitude, the *hoi polloi*. 'Tis no matter what they think; they are sometimes in the right, sometimes in the wrong; their judgment is a meer Lottery. *Est ubi plebs rectè putat, est ubi peccat. Horace* sayes it of the vulgar, judging Poesie. But if you mean the mix'd audience of the populace, and the Noblesse, I dare confidently affirm that a great part of the latter sort are already favourable to verse; and that no serious Playes written since the Kings return have been more kindly receiv'd by them, then the Seige of *Rhodes*, the *Mustapha*, the *Indian* Queen, and *Indian* Emperour.

But I come now to the inference of your first Argument. You said the Dialogue of Playes is presented as the effect of sudden thought, but no man speaks suddenly, or *ex tempore* in Rhyme: And you inferr'd from thence, that Rhyme, which you acknowledge to be proper to Epique Poesie cannot equally be proper to Dramatick, unless we could suppose all men born so much more then Poets, that verses should be made in them, not by them. It has been formerly urg'd by you, and confess'd by me, that since no man spoke any kind of verse *ex tempore*, that which was nearest Nature was to be preferr'd. I answer you therefore, by distinguishing betwixt what is nearest to the nature of Comedy, which is the imitation of common persons and ordinary speaking, and what is nearest the nature of a serious Play: this last is indeed the representation of Nature, but 'tis Nature wrought up to an higher pitch. The Plot, the Characters, the Wit, the Passions, the Descriptions, are all exalted above the level of common converse, as high as the imagination of the Poet can carry them, with proportion to verisimility. Tragedy we know is wont to image to us the minds and fortunes of noble persons, and to portray these exactly, Heroick Rhime is nearest Nature, as being the noblest kind of modern verse.

Indignatur enim privatis, & prope socco.
Dignis carminibus narrari coena Thyestæ. (Sayes Horace.)
And in another place,
Essutire leveis indigna tragoedia versus.

Blank Verse is acknowledg'd to be too low for a Poem, nay more, for a paper of verses; but if too low for an ordinary Sonnet, how much more for Tragedy, which is by *Aristotle* in the dispute betwixt the Epique Poesie and the Dramatick; for many reasons he there alledges ranck'd above it.

But setting this defence aside, your Argument is almost as strong against the use of Rhyme in Poems as in Playes; for the Epique way is every where interlac'd with Dialogue, or discoursive Scenes; and therefore you must either grant Rhyme to be improper there, which is contrary to your assertion, or admit it into Playes by the same title which you have given it to Poems. For though Tragedy be justly preferr'd above the other, yet there is a great affinity between them as may easily be discover'd in that definition of a Play which *Lisideius* gave us. The Genus of them is the same, a just and lively Image of human nature, in its Actions, Passions, and traverses of Fortune: so is the end, namely for the delight and benefit of Mankind. The Characters and Persons are still the same, *viz.* the greatest of both sorts, onely the manner of acquainting us with those Actions, Passions and Fortunes is different.

Tragedy performs it *viva voce*, or by action, in Dialogue, wherein it excels the Epique Poem which does it chiefly by narration, and therefore is not so lively an Image of Humane Nature. However, the agreement betwixt them is such, that if Rhyme be proper for one, it must be for the other. Verse 'tis true is not the effect of sudden thought; but this hinders not that sudden thought may be represented in verse, since those thoughts are such as must be higher then Nature can raise them without premeditation, especially to a continuance of them even out of verse, and consequently you cannot imagine them to have been sudden either in the Poet, or the Actors. A Play, as I had said to be like Nature, is to be set above it; as Statues which are plac'd on high are made greater then the life, that they may descend to the sight in their just proportion.

Perhaps I have insisted too long upon this objection; but the clearing of it will make my stay shorter on the rest. You tell us *Crites*, that rhyme appears most unnatural in repartees, or short replyes: when he who answers, (it being presum'd he knew not what the other would say, yet) makes up that part of the verse which was left incompleat, and supplies both the sound and measure of it. This you say looks rather like the confederacy of two, then the answer of one. This, I confess, is an objection which is in every ones mouth who loves not rhyme: but suppose, I beseech you, the repartee were made onely in blank verse, might not part of the same argument be turn'd against you? for the measure is as often supply'd there as it is in Rhyme. The latter half of the Hemystich as commonly made up, or a second line subjoyn'd as a reply to the former; which any one leaf in *Johnson's* Playes will sufficiently clear to you. You will often find in the Greek Tragedians, and in *Seneca*, that when a Scene grows up in the warmth of repartees (which is the close sighting of it) the latter part of the Trimeter is supply'd by him who answers; and yet it was never observ'd as a fault in them by any of the Ancient or Modern Criticks. The case is the same in our verse as it was in theirs; Rhyme to us being in lieu of quantity to them. But if no latitude is to be allow'd a Poet, you take from him not onely his license of *quidlibet audendi*, but you tie him up in a straighter compass then you would a Philosopher.

This is indeed *Musas colere severiores*: You would have him follow Nature, but he must follow her on foot: you have dismounted him from his *Pegasus*. But you tell us this supplying the last half of a verse, or adjoyning a whole second to the former, looks more like the design of two then the answer of one. Suppose we acknowledge it: how comes this confederacy to be more displeasing to you then in a Dance which is well contriv'd? You see there the united design of many persons to make up one Figure: after they have seperated themselves in many petty divisions, they rejoyn one by one into a gross: the confederacy is plain amongst them; for chance could never produce any thing so beautiful, and yet there is nothing in it that shocks your sight. I acknowledg the hand of Art appears in repartee, as of necessity it must in all kind of verse. But there is also the quick and poynant brevity of it (which is an high imitation of Nature in those sudden gusts of passion) to mingle with it: and this joyn'd with the cadency and sweetness of the Rhyme, leaves nothing in the soul of the hearer to desire.

'Tis an Art which appears; but it appears onely like the shadowings of Painture, which being to cause the rounding of it, cannot be absent; but while that is consider'd they are lost: so while we attend to the other beauties of the matter, the care and labour of the Rhyme is carry'd from us, or at least drown'd in its own sweetness, as Bees are sometimes bury'd in their Honey. When a Poet has found the repartee, the last perfection he can add to it, is to put it into verse. However good the thought may be; however apt the words in which 'tis couch'd, yet he finds himself at a little unrest while Rhyme is wanting: he cannot leave it till that comes naturally, and then is at ease, and sits down contented. From Replies, which are the most elevated thoughts of Verse, you pass to the most mean ones; those which are common with the lowest of houshold conversation. In these, you say, the Majesty of Verse suffers. You instance in the calling of a servant, or commanding a door to be shut in rhyme. This, *Crites,* is a good observation of yours, but no argument: for it proves no more but that such thoughts should be wav'd, as often as may be, by the address of the Poet. But suppose they are necessary in the places where he uses them, yet there is no need to put them into rhime. He may place them in the beginning of a Verse, and break it off, as unfit, when so debas'd for any other use: or granting the worst, that they require more room then the Hemystich will allow; yet still there is a choice to be made of the best words, and least vulgar (provided they be apt) to express such thoughts. Many have blam'd Rhyme in general, for this fault, when the Poet, with a little care, might have redress'd it. But they do it with no more justice, then if English Poesie should be made ridiculous for the sake of the Water Poet's Rhymes. Our language is noble, full and significant; and I know not why he who is Master of it may not cloath ordinary things in it as decently as the Latine; if he use the same diligence in his choice of words.

Delectus verborum Origo est Eloquentiæ: It was the saying of *Julius Cæsar,* one so curious in his, that none of them can be chang'd but for a worse. One would think unlock the door was a thing as vulgar as could be spoken; and yet *Seneca* could make it sound high and lofty in his Latine.

Reserate clusos Regii postes Laris: But I turn from this exception, both because it happens not above twice or thrice in any Play that those vulgar thoughts are us'd; and then too (were there no other Apology to be made, yet) the necessity of them (which is alike in all kind of writing) may excuse them. Besides that the great eagerness and præcipitation with which they are spoken makes us rather mind the substance then the dress; that for which they are spoken, rather then what is spoke. For they are alwayes the effect of some hasty concernment, and something of consequence depends upon them. Thus, *Crites,* I have endeavour'd to answer your objections; it remains onely that I should vindicate an Argument for Verse, which you have gone about to overthrow. It had formerly been said, that the easiness of blank verse, renders the Poet too luxuriant; but that the labour of Rhyme bounds and circumscribes an over-fruitful fancy, The sence there being commonly confin'd to the couplet, and the words so order'd that the Rhyme naturally follows them, not they the Rhyme.

To this you answer'd, that it was no Argument to the question in hand, for the dispute was not which way a man may write best: but which is most proper for the subject on which he writes. First, give me leave, Sir, to remember you that the Argument against which you rais'd this objection, was onely secondary: it was built upon this *Hypothesis*, that to write in verse was proper for serious Playes.

Which supposition being granted (as it was briefly made out in that discourse, by showing how verse might be made natural) it asserted, that this way of writing was an help to the Poets judgment, by putting bounds to a wilde overflowing Fancy. I think therefore it will not be hard for me to make good what it was to prove: But you add, that were this let pass, yet he who wants judgment in the liberty of his fancy, may as well show the defect of it when he is confin'd to verse: for he who has judgment will avoid errours, and he who has it not, will commit them in all kinds of writing.

This Argument, as you have taken it from a most acute person, so I confess it carries much weight in it. But by using the word Judgment here indefinitely, you seem to have put a fallacy upon us: I grant he who has Judgment, that is, so profound, so strong, so infallible a judgment, that he needs no helps to keep it alwayes pois'd and upright, will commit no faults either in rhyme or out of it. And on the other extream, he who has a judgment so weak and craz'd that no helps can correct or amend it, shall write scurvily out of Rhyme, and worse in it.

But the first of these judgments is no where to be found, and the latter is not fit to write at all. To speak therefore of judgment as it is in the best Poets; they who have the greatest proportion of it, want other helps than from it within. As for example, you would be loth to say, that he who was indued with a sound judgment had no need of History, Geography, or Moral Philosophy, to write correctly. Judgment is indeed the Master-workman in a Play: but he requires many subordinate hands, many tools to his assistance.

And Verse I affirm to be one of these: 'Tis a Rule and line by which he keeps his building compact and even, which otherwise lawless imagination would raise either irregularly or loosly. At least if the Poet commits errours with this help, he would make greater and more without it: 'tis a slow and painfull, but the surest kind of working. *Ovid* whom you accuse for luxuriancy in Verse, had perhaps been farther guilty of it had he writ in Prose. And for your instance of *Ben. Johnson*, who you say, writ exactly without the help of Rhyme; you are to remember 'tis onely an aid to a luxuriant Fancy, which his was not: As he did not want imagination, so none ever said he had much to spare. Neither was verse then refin'd so much to be an help to that Age as it is to ours.

Thus then the second thoughts being usually the best, as receiving the maturest digestion from judgment, and the last and most mature product of those thoughts being artful and labour'd verse, it may well be inferr'd, that verse is a great help to a luxuriant Fancy, and this is what that Argument which you oppos'd was to evince. *Neander* was pursuing this Discourse so eagerly, that *Eugenius* had call'd to him twice or thrice ere he took notice that the Barge stood still, and that they were at the foot of *Somerset*-Stairs, where they had appointed it to land. The company were all sorry to separate so soon, though a great part of the evening was already spent; and stood a while looking back upon the water, which the Moon-beams play'd upon, and made it appear like floating quick-silver: at last they went up through a crowd of French people who were merrily dancing in the open air, and nothing concern'd for the noise of Guns which had allarm'd the Town that afternoon. Walking thence together to th *Piazze* they parted there; *Eugenius* and *Lysideius* to some pleasant appointment they had made, and *Crites* and *Neander* to their several Lodgings.FINIS.

Chapter 6

Summary

An Essay of Dramatic Poesy (sometimes also referred to as *Of Dramatic Poesy: An Essay,* which more closely matches the form of the original Latin title) is a critical examination of English literature presented in dialogue form. There are four characters who participate in the dialogue (which takes place on a barge that the characters are taking down the Thames in order to observe the battle raging between the English Navy and Dutch Navy, purportedly the most revered sea powers of the time): Crites, who prefers classical literature, Eugenius, a modern who prefers recent English literature, Lisideius, who prefers modern French drama and Neander, a lover of Elizabethan writers such as Ben Jonson and Shakespeare.

The discussion begins when the characters comment on the terrible poems that the scenic battle will no doubt inspire; Crites says that they will never be able to duplicate (much less surpass) the achievements of the ancients, while Eugenius disagrees. This part of the discussion very much resembles standard debates between the ancients and moderns: Crites's main argument is that all of the conventions of modern literature come from the ancients; Egenius's main argument is that just as the ancient built upon the foundation of poets who came before them, modern poets have built upon the foundation laid by the ancients.

Eventually, the combatants decide to restrict their discussion to one form of literature: drama. Lisideius then enters the argument in order to defend the strict formalism of the modern French dramatists, while Neander cites the richer emotional content and wit of the Elizabethans, particularly

Shakespeare. From there, the discussion evolves into a discussion on whether or not rhymed verse is the most appropriate for the stage. Each of the characters has a tenable position here, with the main point of contention being whether the requirement for verisimilitude is better filled with plain prose, blank verse or elegantly-composed rhyming verse.

Comments: Throughout the first part of the *Essay*, the debate that takes place primarily between Crites and Eugenius contains very strong echoes of the larger debate between the ancients and moderns. The two characters' arguments (as briefly characterized above) fall in line almost perfectly with the debates as presented in other words such as Swift's *Battle of the Books*.

Also on a very macro level, the *Essay* deals very directly with the relationship between form, rules and the artist's genius. Lisideius's preference for the French's strict observance of the rules of drama (particularly those presented in Aristotle's *Poetics*) is hardly presented in satirical fashion, and the astute reader certainly must come up with a way to justify this apparent shortcoming in classical and (particularly) English drama. Ultimately, this argument is Neander's strongest support for his preference for Shakespeare, who had so much natural genius that he actually created archetypes of his own rather than simply relying on those formulated in classical times.

For those who prefer nuts-and-bolts style literary criticism, the debate over how to achieve verisimilitude in drama is extremely interesting. An assumption running through most of the characters' arguments is that the closer an author can come to representing real time on the stage, the easier it will be for the audience to digest, which is why the action of a play should never take place over the course of more than one day (the characters even debate whether "one day" should be interpreted as 12 or 24 hours). All of the characters have (to modern readers, at least) very little faith in the audience's mind to "imagine" aspects of the play that are not explicitly represented, so jarring changes in setting must be avoided as much as possible.

Finally, any discussion of the *Essay* must pay attention to its use of the conventions of dialogue. By presenting four characters with very different but equally tenable views (even if critics have suspected that Neander is something of a stand-in for Dryden himself), Dryden highlights the complexities facing the dramatist, and argues that there are no easy answers for any of these questions.

Chapter 7

Comments on: "An Essay of Dramatic Poesy"

Purpose of Thinking

Primarily focusing on drama, the poetry of plays, Dryden ultimately wants to make a case for the achievements of the British in that respect. In somewhat "Platonic" method, he creates a dialogue between poet/critics of the day who have different viewpoints about the strengths and weaknesses of, and influences on, British poesy. The benefit of this is to mount an argument which takes a variety of positions into consideration. Rather than attempting to create a new set of "rules" for drama, comedy, or verse, he chooses instead to review the existing, generally accepted conventions and decide in what respects they are being followed, or whether they should be followed by English writers. Further, through the use of the four-way dialogue, he is able to provide some insight on the prevailing notions of the day.

It may be worth noting that the "characters" in this dialogue are associated for the purpose of argument with specific points of view: Crites praises the Greeks and Romans suggesting that they cannot be surpassed; Eugenius recognizes their worth but suggests that they have indeed been exceeded and in many instances are not consistent in their adherence to Aristotle's conventions; Lisideius suggests that the French are superior to the English; and Neander (ostensibly Dryden) counters that, based on their agreed definition of what "a play ought to be," the English are superior.

Question at Issue (Problem)

What are the merits and demerits of English writing of the time? What are the influences for English writing? Can the English writing during that time be compared favorably or not to the writers of antiquity? Are French drama and verse superior to English? What is the value of the three unities? Are they consistently applied by the ancients? By the French? By the English? If not, why not? Should these conventions be an over-riding consideration? What is, or is not, the value of rhyme in verse and drama? What is its place if any? What about the place of verse in drama?

Information/Interpretations/Concepts/Crucial Assumptions

The dialogue begins with Crites complaining about two types of "bad" English poets: the first are the poets who "perpetually pay us with clenches upon words and a certain clownish kind of raillery;" (bad metaphysicals?) and the second is he who " affects plainness to cover his want of imagination" (bad Puritans?) He goes on to suggest that no one writing can surpass the ancients or even the previous generation of English writers, to which Eugenius responds that he might be rejecting everything recent just because it is recent. The debate begins in earnest when the four decide that they will "limit their dispute" to a discussion of dramatic poesy and whether the "ancients were superior to the moderns." Additionally, they must decide on a definition of what a play should be. Lisideius offers the agreed upon terms: just and lively image of human nature, representing its passions and humors, and the changes of fortune to which it is subject, for the delight and instruction of mankind.

Crites develops the main points in defending the ancients and the objections to modern plays. The moderns are still imitating the ancients and using their forms and subjects, relying on Aristotle and Horace, adding nothing new and yet not following their good advice closely enough, especially with respect to the unities of time, place and action. While the unity of time suggests that all the action should be portrayed within a single day, English plays attempt to use long periods of time, sometimes years. In terms of place, the setting should be the same from beginning to end with the scenes marked by the entrances and exits of the persons having business within each. The English, on the other hand, try to have all kinds of places, even far off countries, shown within a single play.

The third unity, that of action, requires that the play "aim at one great and complete action", but the English have all kinds of sub-plots which destroy the unity of the action. In anticipating the objection that the ancients' language is not as vital as the moderns, Crites say that we have to remember that we are probably missing a lot of subtleties because the languages are dead and the customs far removed from this time. Crites uses Ben Jonson (Father Ben) as the example of the best in English drama, saying that he followed the ancients "in all things" and offered nothing really new in terms of "serious thoughts".

Eugenius responds that though "the moderns have profited by the rules of the ancients" they have "excelled them." He points first to some discrepancies in the applications of the unities, mentioning that there seem to be four parts in Aristotle's method: the entrance, the intensifying of the plot, the counter-turn, and the catastrophe. But he points out that somewhere along the line, and by way of Horace, plays developed five acts (the Spanish only 3). As far as the action. Eugenius contends that they are transparent, everybody already knows what will happen; that the Romans borrowed from the Greeks; and that the deus ex machina convention is a weak escape. As far as the unity of place, he suggests that the ancients weren't the ones to insist on it so much as the French, and that that insistence has caused some artificial entrances and exits of characters.

The unity of time is often ignored in both. As to the liveliness of language, Eugenius counters Crites by suggesting that even if we don't know all the contexts, good writing is always good, wit is always discernible, if done well. He goes on to say also that while the ancients portrayed many emotions and action, they neglected love, "which is the most frequent of all passions" and known to everyone. He mentions Shakespeare and Fletcher as offering "excellent scenes of passion." Lisideius' discussion of the French follows. He declares them the best of all Europe because of their adherence to the unities, and the most important point here is that they maintain the unity of action by not adding confusing sub-plots. Here he begins the discussion of the English tragi-comedy, which he calls "absurd". He commends the French as well for basing their tragedies on "some known history," that in this way fiction is combined with reality so that some truth can be revealed. He compares Shakespeare's history plays, saying that "they are rather so many chronicles of kings," years of history packed into a 2 1/2 hour play so that the point is lost.

He reports that the French do several things much better than the English. First, they keep the plot to one action which they then develop fully where the English add all kinds of actions that don't always follow from the main one. The French also focus on one main character and all the characters have some connection with him and have a purpose that advances the plot. Additionally, the French use narration (reporting by the characters) to describe things that happen, like battles and deaths, that Lisideius says are ridiculous when shown on stage. "The representation" of incidents that cannot be portrayed as realistic, possible, or believable anyway, are better omitted.

This goes, I think, to the issue of decorumsince he says "some parts of the action are more fit to be represented, some to be related." Further, he says the French never end their plays with "conversions" or "changes of will" without setting up the proper justification for it. The English, by contrast, show their characters having changes of heart that are over-reactions to circumstances and therefore not believable. Also, in the French plays, the characters never come in or leave a scene without the proper justifications being supplied. Finally, he compliments the "beauty of their rhyme" suggesting that it would help English poetry, though he doesn't think there's anyone capable of doing it properly.

Neander has the last word, suggesting that based on the definition of a play, the English are best at "the lively imitation of nature" (human nature), conceding that while French poesy is beautiful, it is beautiful like a "statue". He even says that the newer French writers are imitating the English. One fault he finds in their plots is that the regularity, which has been complimented as uncluttered, also make the plays too much alike. He defends the English invention of tragi-comedy by suggesting that the use of mirth with tragedy provides "contraries" that "set each other off" and give the audience relief from the heaviness of straight tragedy. He suggest that the use of sub-plots, if they are well-ordered, make the plays interesting and help the main action. Further, he suggests that English plays are more entertaining and instructive because they offer an element of surprise that the ancients and the French do not. As far as decorum, things the French choose not to portray on-stage, he brings up the idea of the suspension of disbelief. The audience knows that none of it is real, why should they think scenes of death or battles any less "real" than the rest? I think here he credits the English audience with a certain robustness in suggesting that they want their battles and "other objects of horror." Ultimately, in discussing the English habit of breaking the rules, he suggests that it maybe there are simply too many rules and often that following them creates more absurdities than they prevent.

In the last of the essay, a discussion of the proper use of rhyme and verse ensues, mostly between Crites, who wants to eliminate the use of rhyme, which he sees as sounding artificial, and Neander, who says if you want to eliminate rhyme on that basis, why not verse on the same grounds. Neander suggests that comedy should not be rhymed but that the heroic tragedy should be. To Crites' charge that it is too much invention, Neander says that if a writer must choose every word, that is artificial. If properly done, the additional artifices of verse and rhyme are no less contrived, but can add to the effect of the play.

Implications/Consequences/Points of View

That Dryden concerns himself with the influence of the French is no surprise. Charles II, installed as King after the fall of the commonwealth under Cromwell, returned from exile in France, and court society during his reign adopted much of French fashion and taste. Corneille, especially in his heroic tragedies, was a favourite, and in this genre, Dryden would never surpass him. His concerns expressed in the essay about the Roman and Greek influences naturally follow because of Corneille's adherence, and that of the French writers in general, to the conventions of unity and considerations of decorum. Dryden's strength in writing for the stage would be in the comedies which reflected the changing social milieu.

As far as discussion of the influences in English plays, he focuses on Shakespeare and Ben Jonson, the Homer and Virgil of English play-writing, respectively. Shakespeare he admits can be inconsistent, sometimes flat and bombastic, yet Dryden says he had "the largest and most comprehensive soul." Jonson, on the other hand, he calls the "most learned and judicious writer which any theatre ever had." Jonson could use all the conventions as well as the ancients of the French. Dryden, commenting on the two together notes that he "admires" Jonson but he "loves" Shakespeare.

But for the British loyal to the king, and Dryden was, the restoration was also time of renewed nationalism, and Dryden seems, at least in this essay, to be interested in defending British sensibilities. Dryden was also very concerned in his art with the events of the day. Even this piece of criticism begins at the moment of the second British victory over the Dutch. Some of Dryden's best works are his later ones, particularly Absolom and Achitophel prompted by the Popish plot, and are inspired by specific political and social issues of the day.

In that respect, as well as stylistically in the use of heroic couplet, they contrast works of broader scope such as Paradise Lost published in 1666 by John Milton, who Dryden would compare to Homer and Virgil in his 1688 "Epigram on Milton." (By contrast to Dryden, Milton seems clearly from a different era). Dryden's real strengths were translations, the later satires, and the solidifying of a base for continuing British criticism.

Although he was Poet Laureate during the reigns of Charles II and James, he was relieved of the honour with the ascension of William and Mary, remained loyal to James, and converted to Catholicism. His "Secular Masque," written for the turn of the century, registers a disenchantment with the entire age. It is interesting, in light of what he says in "An Essay..." to look at a play like Congrieve's "The Way of the World" which is marked by the shift from verse to prose, the more natural reflection of conversation that Dryden seems to suggest as a possibility for comedy.

Chapter 8

Discourses on Satire and Epic Poetry

Introduction.

Dryden's discourses upon Satire and Epic Poetry belong to the latter years of his life, and represent maturer thought than is to be found in his "Essay of Dramatic Poesie." That essay, published in 1667, draws its chief interest from the time when it was written. A Dutch fleet was at the mouth of the Thames. Dryden represents himself taking a boat down the river with three friends, one of them his brother-in-law Sir Robert Howard, another Sir Charles Sedley, and another Charles Sackville Lord Buckhurst to whom, as Earl of Dorset, the "Discourse of Satire" is inscribed. They go down the river to hear the guns at sea, and judge by the sound whether the Dutch fleet be advancing or retreating.

On the way they talk of the plague of Odes that will follow an English victory; their talk of verse proceeds to plays, with particular attention to a question that had been specially argued before the public between Dryden and his brother-in-law Sir Robert Howard. The question touched the use of blank verse in the drama. Dryden had decided against it as a worthless measure, and the chief feature of the Essay, which was written in dialogue, was its support of Dryden's argument. But in that year "Paradise Lost" was published, and Milton's blank verse was the death of Dryden's theories. After a few years Dryden recanted his error. The "Essay of Dramatic Poesie" is interesting as a setting forth in 1667 of mistaken critical opinions which were at that time in the ascendant, but had not very long to live. Dryden always wrote good masculine prose, and all his critical essays are good reading as pieces of English. His "Essay of Dramatic Poesie" is good reading as illustrative of the weakness of our literature in the days of the influence of France after the Restoration. The essays on Satire and on Epic Poetry represent also the influence of the French critical school, but represent it in a larger way, with indications of its strength as well as of its weakness. They represent also Dryden himself with a riper mind covering a larger field of thought, and showing abundantly the strength and independence of his own critical judgment, while he cites familiarly and frequently the critics, little remembered and less cared for now, who then passed for the arbiters of taste.

If English literature were really taught in schools, and the eldest boys had received training that brought them in their last school-year to a knowledge of the changes of intellectual fashion that set their outward mark upon successive periods, there is no prose writing of Dryden that could be used by a teacher more instructively than these Discourses on Satire and on Epic Poetry. They illustrate abundantly both Dryden and his time, and give continuous occasion for discussion of first principles, whether in disagreement or agreement with the text. Dryden was on his own ground as a critic of satire; and the ideal of an epic that the times, and perhaps also the different bent of his own genius, would not allow him to work out, at least finds such expression as might be expected from a man who had high aspirations, and whose place, in times unfavourable to his highest aims, was still among the master-poets of the world.

The Discourse on Satire was prefixed to a translation of the satires of Juvenal and Persius, and is dated the 18th of August, 1692, when the poet's age was sixty-one. In translating Juvenal, Dryden was helped by his sons Charles and John. William Congreve translated one satire; other translations were by Nahum Tate and George Stepney. Time modern reader of the introductory discourse has first to pass through the unmeasured compliments to the Earl of Dorset, which represent a real esteem and gratitude in the extravagant terms then proper to the art of dedication. We get to the free sea over a slimy shore. We must remember that Charles the Second upon his death was praised by Charles Montague, who knew his faults, as "the best good man that ever filled a throne," and compared to God Himself at the end of the first paragraph of Montague's poem. But when we are clear of the conventional unmeasured flatteries, and Dryden lingers among epic poets on his way to the satirists, there is equal interest in the mistaken criticisms, in the aspirations that are blended with them, and in the occasional touches of the poet's personality in quiet references to his critics. The comparisons between Horace and Juvenal in this discourse, and much of the criticism on Virgil in the discourse on epic poetry, are the utterances of a poet upon poets, and full of right suggestions from an artist's mind. The second discourse was prefixed in 1697—three years before Dryden's death—to his translation of the AEneid.

H. M.

A discourse on the original and progress of satire:
Addressed to the right honourable
Charles, earl of dorset and middlesex,
Lord chamberlain of his majesty's household, knight of the most
Noble order of the garter, etc.

My Lord,

The wishes and desires of all good men, which have attended your lordship from your first appearance in the world, are at length accomplished, from your obtaining those honours and dignities which you have so long deserved. There are no factions, though irreconcilable to one another, that are not united in their affection to you, and the respect they pay you. They are equally pleased in your prosperity, and would be equally concerned in your afflictions. Titus Vespasian was not more the delight of human kind. The universal empire made him only more known and more powerful, but could not make him more beloved. He had greater ability of doing good, but your inclination to it is not less: and though you could not extend your beneficence to so many persons, yet you have lost as few days as that excellent emperor; and never had his complaint to make when you went to bed, that the sun had shone upon you in vain, when you had the opportunity of relieving some unhappy man. This, my lord, has justly acquired you as many friends as there are persons who have the honour to be known to you.

Mere acquaintance you have none; you have drawn them all into a nearer line; and they who have conversed with you are for ever after inviolably yours. This is a truth so generally acknowledged that it needs no proof: it is of the nature of a first principle, which is received as soon as it is proposed; and needs not the reformation which Descartes used to his; for we doubt not, neither can we properly say, we think we admire and love you above all other men: there is a certainty in the proposition, and we know it. With the same assurance I can say, you neither have enemies, nor can scarce have any; for they who have never heard of you can neither love or hate you; and they who have, can have no other notion of you than that which they receive from the public, that you are the best of men. After this, my testimony can be of no farther use, than to declare it to be daylight at high noon: and all who have the benefit of sight can look up as well and see the sun.

It is true, I have one privilege which is almost particular to myself, that I saw you in the east at your first arising above the hemisphere: I was as soon sensible as any man of that light when it was but just shooting out and beginning to travel upwards to the meridian. I made my early addresses to your lordship in my "Essay of Dramatic Poetry," and therein bespoke you to the world; wherein I have the right of a first discoverer. When I was myself in the rudiments of my poetry, without name or reputation in the world, having rather the ambition of a writer than the skill; when I was drawing the outlines of an art, without any living master to instruct me in it—an art which had been better praised than studied here in England; wherein Shakespeare, who created the stage among us, had rather written happily than knowingly and justly; and Jonson, who, by studying Horace, had been acquainted with the rules, yet seemed to envy to posterity that knowledge, and, like an inventor of some useful art, to make a monopoly of his learning— when thus, as I may say, before the use of the loadstone or knowledge of the compass, I was sailing in a vast ocean without other help than the pole-star of the ancients and the rules of the French stage amongst the moderns (which are extremely different from ours, by reason of their opposite taste), yet even then I had the presumption to dedicate to your lordship—a very unfinished piece, I must confess, and which only can be excused by the little experience of the author and the modesty of the title—"An Essay." Yet I was stronger in prophecy than I was in criticism: I was inspired to foretell you to mankind as the restorer of poetry, the greatest genius, the truest judge, and the best patron.

Good sense and good nature are never separated, though the ignorant world has thought otherwise. Good nature, by which I mean beneficence and candour, is the product of right reason; which of necessity will give allowance to the failings of others by considering that there is nothing perfect in mankind; and by distinguishing that which comes nearest to excellency, though not absolutely free from faults, will certainly produce a candour in the judge.

It is incident to an elevated understanding like your lordship's to find out the errors of other men; but it is your prerogative to pardon them; to look with pleasure on those things which are somewhat congenial and of a remote kindred to your own conceptions; and to forgive the many failings of those who, with their wretched art, cannot arrive to those heights that you possess from a happy, abundant, and native genius which are as inborn to you as they were to Shakespeare, and, for aught I know, to Homer; in either of whom we find all arts and sciences, all moral and natural philosophy, without knowing that they ever studied them. There is not an English writer this day living who is not perfectly convinced that your lordship excels all others in all the several parts of poetry which you have undertaken to adorn. The most vain and the most ambitions of our age have not dared to assume so much as the competitors of Themistocles: they have yielded the first place without dispute; and have been arrogantly content to be esteemed as second to your lordship, and even that also with a longo, sed proximi intervallo. If there have been, or are, any who go farther in their self-conceit, they must be very singular in their opinion; they must be like the officer in a play who was called captain, lieutenant, and company. The world will easily conclude whether such unattended generals can ever be capable of making a revolution in Parnassus.

I will not attempt in this place to say anything particular of your lyric poems, though they are the delight and wonder of the age, and will be the envy of the next. The subject of this book confines me to satire; and in that an author of your own quality, whose ashes I will not disturb, has given you all the commendation which his self-sufficiency could afford to any man—"The best good man, with the worst-natured muse." In that character, methinks, I am reading Jonson's verses to the memory of Shakespeare; an insolent, sparing, and invidious panegyric: where good nature—the most godlike commendation of a man—is only attributed to your person, and denied to your writings; for they are everywhere so full of candour, that, like Horace, you only expose the follies of men without arraigning their vices; and in this excel him, that you add that pointedness of thought which is visibly wanting in our great Roman. There is more of salt in all your verses than I have seen in any of the moderns, or even of the ancients: but you have been sparing of the gall; by which means you have pleased all readers and offended none.

Donne alone, of all our countrymen, had your talent, but was not happy enough to arrive at your versification; and were he translated into numbers and English, he would yet be wanting in the dignity of expression. That which is the prime virtue and chief ornament of Virgil, which distinguishes him from the rest of writers, is so conspicuous in your verses that it casts a shadow on all your contemporaries; we cannot be seen, or but obscurely, while you are present. You equal Donne in the variety, multiplicity, and choice of thoughts; you excel him in the manner and the words. I read you both with the same admiration, but not with the same delight. He affects the metaphysics, not only in his satires, but in his amorous verses, where Nature only should reign; and perplexes the minds of the fair sex with nice speculations of philosophy, when he should engage their hearts and entertain them with the softnesses of love. In this (if I may be pardoned for so bold a truth) Mr. Cowley has copied him to a fault: so great a one, in my opinion, that it throws his "Mistress" infinitely below his "Pindarics" and his later compositions, which are undoubtedly the best of his poems and the most correct. For my own part I must avow it freely to the world that I never attempted anything in satire wherein I have not studied your writings as the most perfect model.

I have continually laid them before me; and the greatest commendation which my own partiality can give to my productions is that they are copies, and no farther to be allowed than as they have something more or less of the original. Some few touches of your lordship, some secret graces which I have endeavoured to express after your manner, have made whole poems of mine to pass with approbation: but take your verses all together, and they are inimitable. If, therefore, I have not written better, it is because you have not written more. You have not set me sufficient copy to transcribe; and I cannot add one letter of my own invention of which I have not the example there.

It is a general complaint against your lordship, and I must have leave to upbraid you with it, that, because you need not write, you will not. Mankind that wishes you so well in all things that relate to your prosperity, have their intervals of wishing for themselves, and are within a little of grudging you the fulness of your fortune: they would be more malicious if you used it not so well and with so much generosity.

Fame is in itself a real good, if we may believe Cicero, who was perhaps too fond of it; but even fame, as Virgil tells us, acquires strength by going forward. Let Epicurus give indolency as an attribute to his gods, and place in it the happiness of the blest: the Divinity which we worship has given us not only a precept against it, but His own example to the contrary. The world, my lord, would be content to allow you a seventh day for rest; or, if you thought that hard upon you, we would not refuse you half your time: if you came out, like some great monarch, to take a town but once a year, as it were for your diversion, though you had no need to extend your territories. In short, if you were a bad, or, which is worse, an indifferent poet, we would thank you for our own quiet, and not expose you to the want of yours.

But when you are so great, and so successful, and when we have that necessity of your writing that we cannot subsist entirely without it, any more (I may almost say) than the world without the daily course of ordinary Providence, methinks this argument might prevail with you, my lord, to forego a little of your repose for the public benefit. It is not that you are under any force of working daily miracles to prove your being, but now and then somewhat of extraordinary—that is, anything of your production—is requisite to refresh your character.

This, I think, my lord, is a sufficient reproach to you, and should I carry it as far as mankind would authorise me, would be little less than satire. And indeed a provocation is almost necessary, in behalf of the world, that you might be induced sometimes to write; and in relation to a multitude of scribblers, who daily pester the world with their insufferable stuff, that they might be discouraged from writing any more. I complain not of their lampoons and libels, though I have been the public mark for many years. I am vindictive enough to have repelled force by force if I could imagine that any of them had ever reached me: but they either shot at rovers, and therefore missed; or their powder was so weak that I might safely stand them at the nearest distance.

I answered not the "Rehearsal" because I knew the author sat to himself when he drew the picture, and was the very Bayes of his own farce; because also I knew that my betters were more concerned than I was in that satire; and, lastly, because Mr. Smith and Mr. Johnson, the main pillars of it, were two such languishing gentlemen in their conversation that I could liken them to nothing but to their own relations, those noble characters of men of wit and pleasure about the town. The like considerations have hindered me from dealing with the lamentable companions of their prose and doggerel. I am so far from defending my poetry against them that I will not so much as expose theirs. And for my morals, if they are not proof against their attacks, let me be thought by posterity what those authors would be thought if any memory of them or of their writings could endure so long as to another age. But these dull makers of lampoons, as harmless as they have been to me, are yet of dangerous example to the public. Some witty men may perhaps succeed to their designs, and, mixing sense with malice, blast the reputation of the most innocent amongst men, and the most virtuous amongst women.

Heaven be praised, our common libellers are as free from the imputation of wit as of morality, and therefore whatever mischief they have designed they have performed but little of it. Yet these ill writers, in all justice, ought themselves to be exposed, as Persius has given us a fair example in his first Satire, which is levelled particularly at them; and none is so fit to correct their faults as he who is not only clear from any in his own writings, but is also so just that he will never defame the good, and is armed with the power of verse to punish and make examples of the bad. But of this I shall have occasion to speak further when I come to give the definition and character of true satires.

In the meantime, as a counsellor bred up in the knowledge of the municipal and statute laws may honestly inform a just prince how far his prerogative extends, so I may be allowed to tell your lordship, who by an undisputed title are the king of poets, what an extent of power you have, and how lawfully you may exercise it over the petulant scribblers of this age. As Lord Chamberlain, I know, you are absolute by your office in all that belongs to the decency and good manners of the stage. You can banish from thence scurrility and profaneness, and restrain the licentious insolence of poets and their actors in all things that shock the public quiet, or the reputation of private persons, under the notion of humour. But I mean not the authority which is annexed to your office, I speak of that only which is inborn and inherent to your person; what is produced in you by an excellent wit, a masterly and commanding genius over all writers: whereby you are empowered, when you please, to give the final decision of wit, to put your stamp on all that ought to pass for current and set a brand of reprobation on clipped poetry and false coin. A shilling dipped in the bath may go for gold amongst the ignorant, but the sceptres on the guineas show the difference. That your lordship is formed by nature for this supremacy I could easily prove (were it not already granted by the world) from the distinguishing character of your writing, which is so visible to me that I never could be imposed on to receive for yours what was written by any others, or to mistake your genuine poetry for their spurious productions. I can farther add with truth, though not without some vanity in saying it, that in the same paper written by divers hands, whereof your lordship's was only part, I could separate your gold from their copper; and though I could not give back to every author his own brass (for there is not the same rule for distinguishing betwixt bad and bad as betwixt ill and excellently good), yet I never failed of knowing what was yours and what was not, and was absolutely certain that this or the other part was positively yours, and could not possibly be written by any other.

True it is that some bad poems, though not all, carry their owners' marks about them. There is some peculiar awkwardness, false grammar, imperfect sense, or, at the least, obscurity; some brand or other on this buttock or that ear that it is notorious who are the owners of the cattle, though they should not sign it with their names. But your lordship, on the contrary, is distinguished not only by the excellency of your thoughts, but by your style and manner of expressing them. A painter judging of some admirable piece may affirm with certainty that it was of Holbein or Vandyck; but vulgar designs and common draughts are easily mistaken and misapplied. Thus, by my long study of your lordship, I am arrived at the knowledge of your particular manner. In the good poems of other men, like those artists, I can only say, "This is like the draught of such a one, or like the colouring of another;" in short, I can only be sure that it is the hand of a good master: but in your performances it is scarcely possible for me to be deceived. If you write in your strength, you stand revealed at the first view, and should you write under it, you cannot avoid some peculiar graces which only cost me a second consideration to discover you: for I may say it with all the severity of truth, that every line of yours is precious. Your lordship's only fault is that you have not written more, unless I could add another, and that yet greater, but I fear for the public the accusation would not be true—that you have written, and out of a vicious modesty will not publish. Virgil has confined his works within the compass of eighteen thousand lines, and has not treated many subjects, yet he ever had, and ever will have, the reputation of the best poet. Martial says of him that he could have excelled Varius in tragedy and Horace in lyric poetry, but out of deference to his friends he attempted neither.

The same prevalence of genius is in your lordship, but the world cannot pardon your concealing it on the same consideration, because we have neither a living Varius nor a Horace, in whose excellences both of poems, odes, and satires, you had equalled them, if our language had not yielded to the Roman majesty, and length of time had not added a reverence to the works of Horace. For good sense is the same in all or most ages, and course of time rather improves nature than impairs her. What has been, may be again; another Homer and another Virgil may possible arise from those very causes which produced the first, though it would be impudence to affirm that any such have yet appeared.

It is manifest that some particular ages have been more happy than others in the production of great men in all sorts of arts and sciences, as that of Euripides, Sophocles, Aristophanes, and the rest, for stage-poetry amongst the Greeks; that of Augustus for heroic, lyric, dramatic, elegiac, and indeed all sorts of poetry in the persons of Virgil, Horace, Varius, Ovid, and many others, especially if we take into that century the latter end of the commonwealth, wherein we find Varro, Lucretius, and Catullus; and at the same time lived Cicero and Sallust and Caesar. A famous age in modern times for learning in every kind was that of Lorenzo de Medici and his son Leo the Tenth, wherein painting was revived, and poetry flourished, and the Greek language was restored. Examples in all these are obvious, but what I would infer is this— that in such an age it is possible some great genius may arise to equal any of the ancients, abating only for the language; for great contemporaries whet and cultivate each other, and mutual borrowing and commerce makes the common riches of learning, as it does of the civil government. But suppose that Homer and Virgil were the only of their species, and that nature was so much worn out in producing them that she is never able to hear the like again, yet the example only holds in heroic poetry; in tragedy and satire I offer myself to maintain, against some of our modern critics, that this age and the last, particularly in England, have excelled the ancients in both those kinds, and I would instance in Shakespeare of the former, of your lordship in the latter sort.

Thus I might safely confine myself to my native country. But if I would only cross the seas, I might find in France a living Horace and a Juvenal in the person of the admirable Boileau, whose numbers are excellent, whose expressions are noble, whose thoughts are just, whose language is pure, whose satire is pointed and whose sense is close. What he borrows from the ancients, he repays with usury of his own in coin as good and almost as universally valuable: for, setting prejudice and partiality apart, though he is our enemy, the stamp of a Louis, the patron of all arts, is not much inferior to the medal of an Augustus Caesar. Let this be said without entering into the interests of factions and parties, and relating only to the bounty of that king to men of learning and merit—a praise so just that even we, who are his enemies, cannot refuse it to him.

Now if it may be permitted me to go back again to the consideration of epic poetry, I have confessed that no man hitherto has reached or so much as approached to the excellences of Homer or of Virgil; I must farther add that Statius, the best versificator next to Virgil, knew not how to design after him, though he had the model in his eye; that Lucan is wanting both in design and subject, and is besides too full of heat and affectation; that amongst the moderns, Ariosto neither designed justly nor observed any unity of action, or compass of time, or moderation in the vastness of his draught: his style is luxurious without majesty or decency, and his adventures without the compass of nature and possibility. Tasso, whose design was regular, and who observed the roles of unity in time and place more closely than Virgil, yet was not so happy in his action: he confesses himself to have been too lyrical—that is, to have written beneath the dignity of heroic verse—in his episodes of Sophronia, Erminia, and Armida. His story is not so pleasing as Ariosto's; he is too flatulent sometimes, and sometimes too dry; many times unequal, and almost always forced; and, besides, is full of conceits, points of epigram, and witticisms; all which are not only below the dignity of heroic verse, but contrary to its nature: Virgil and Homer have not one of them.

And those who are guilty of so boyish an ambition in so grave a subject are so far from being considered as heroic poets that they ought to be turned down from Homer to the "Anthologia," from Virgil to Martial and Owen's Epigrams, and from Spenser to Flecknoe—that is, from the top to the bottom of all poetry. But to return to Tasso: he borrows from the invention of Boiardo, and in his alteration of his poem, which is infinitely for the worse, imitates Homer so very servilely that he gives the King of Jerusalem fifty sons, only because Homer had bestowed the like number on King Priam; he kills the youngest in the same manner; and has provided his hero with a Patroclus, under another name, only to bring him back to the wars when his friend was killed.

The French have performed nothing in this kind which is not far below those two Italians, and subject to a thousand more reflections, without examining their "St. Louis," their "Pucelle," or their "Alaric." The English have only to boast of Spenser and Milton, who neither of them wanted either genius or learning to have been perfect poets; and yet both of them are liable to many censures. For there is no uniformity in the design of Spenser; he aims at the accomplishment of no one action; he raises up a hero for every one of his adventures, and endows each of them with some particular moral virtue, which renders them all equal, without subordination or preference: every one is most valiant in his own legend: only we must do him that justice to observe that magnanimity, which is the character of Prince Arthur, shines throughout the whole poem, and succours the rest when they are in distress. The original of every knight was then living in the court of Queen Elizabeth, and he attributed to each of them that virtue which he thought was most conspicuous in them—an ingenious piece of flattery, though it turned not much to his account. Had he lived to finish his poem in the six remaining legends, it had certainly been more of a piece; but could not have been perfect, because the model was not true.

But Prince Arthur, or his chief patron Sir Philip Sidney, whom he intended to make happy by the marriage of his Gloriana, dying before him, deprived the poet both of means and spirit to accomplish his design. For the rest, his obsolete language and the ill choice of his stanza are faults but of the second magnitude; for, notwithstanding the first, he is still intelligible—at least, after a little practice; and for the last, he is the more to be admired that, labouring under such a difficulty, his verses are so numerous, so various and so harmonious, that only Virgil, whom he professedly imitated, has surpassed him among the Romans, and only Mr. Waller among the English.

As for Mr. Milton, whom we all admire with so much justice, his subject is not that of an heroic poem, properly so called. His design is the losing of our happiness; his event is not prosperous, like that of all other epic works; his heavenly machines are many, and his human persons are but two. But I will not take Mr. Rymer's work out of his hands: he has promised the world a critique on that author wherein, though he will not allow his poem for heroic, I hope he will grant us that his thoughts are elevated, his words sounding, and that no man has so happily copied the manner of Homer, or so copiously translated his Grecisms and the Latin elegances of Virgil. It is true, he runs into a flat of thought, sometimes for a hundred lines together, but it is when he has got into a track of Scripture. His antiquated words were his choice, not his necessity; for therein he imitated Spenser, as Spencer did

Chaucer. And though, perhaps, the love of their masters may have transported both too far in the frequent use of them, yet in my opinion obsolete words may then be laudably revived when either they are more sounding or more significant than those in practice, and when their obscurity is taken away by joining other words to them which clear the sense— according to the rule of Horace for the admission of new words. But in both cases a moderation is to be observed in the use of them; for unnecessary coinage, as well as unnecessary revival, runs into affectation—a fault to be avoided on either hand. Neither will I justify Milton for his blank verse, though I may excuse him by the example of Hannibal Caro and other Italians who have used it; for, whatever causes he alleges for the abolishing of rhyme (which I have not now the leisure to examine), his own particular reason is plainly this—that rhyme was not his talent; he had neither the ease of doing it, nor the graces of it: which is manifest in his "Juvenilia" or verses written in his youth, where his rhyme is always constrained and forced, and comes hardly from him, at an age when the soul is most pliant, and the passion of love makes almost every man a rhymer, though not a poet.

By this time, my lord, I doubt not but that you wonder why I have run off from my bias so long together, and made so tedious a digression from satire to heroic poetry; but if you will not excuse it by the tattling quality of age (which, as Sir William Davenant says, is always narrative), yet I hope the usefulness of what I have to say on this subject will qualify the remoteness of it; and this is the last time I will commit the crime of prefaces, or trouble the world with my notions of anything that relates to verse. I have then, as you see, observed the failings of many great wits amongst the moderns who have attempted to write an epic poem. Besides these, or the like animadversions of them by other men, there is yet a farther reason given why they cannot possibly succeed so well as the ancients, even though we could allow them not to be inferior either in genius or learning, or the tongue in which they write, or all those other wonderful qualifications which are necessary to the forming of a true accomplished heroic poet. The fault is laid on our religion; they say that Christianity is not capable of those embellishments which are afforded in the belief of those ancient heathens.

And it is true that in the severe notions of our faith the fortitude of a Christian consists in patience, and suffering for the love of God whatever hardships can befall in the world—not in any great attempt, or in performance of those enterprises which the poets call heroic, and which are commonly the effects of interest, ostentation, pride, and worldly honour; that humility and resignation are our prime virtues; and that these include no action but that of the soul, whereas, on the contrary, an heroic poem requires to its necessary design, and as its last perfection, some great action of war, the accomplishment of some extraordinary undertaking, which requires the strength and vigour of the body, the duty of a soldier, the capacity and prudence of a general, and, in short, as much or more of the active virtue than the suffering. But to this the answer is very obvious. God has placed us in our several stations; the virtues of a private Christian are patience, obedience, submission, and the like; but those of a magistrate or a general or a king are prudence, counsel, active fortitude, coercive power, awful command, and the exercise of magnanimity as well as justice. So that this objection hinders not but that an epic poem, or the heroic action of some great commander, enterprised for the common good and honour of the Christian cause, and executed happily, may be as well written now as it was of old by the heathens, provided the poet be endued with the same talents; and the language, though not of equal dignity, yet as near approaching to it as our modern barbarism will allow—which is all that can be expected from our own or any other now extant, though more refined; and therefore we are to rest contented with that only inferiority, which is not possibly to be remedied.

I wish I could as easily remove that other difficulty which yet remains. It is objected by a great French critic as well as an admirable poet, yet living, and whom I have mentioned with that honour which his merit exacts from me (I mean, Boileau), that the machines of our Christian religion in heroic poetry are much more feeble to support that weight than those of heathenism. Their doctrine, grounded as it was on ridiculous fables, was yet the belief of the two victorious monarchies, the Grecian and Roman.

Their gods did not only interest themselves in the event of wars (which is the effect of a superior Providence), but also espoused the several parties in a visible corporeal descent, managed their intrigues and fought their battles, sometimes in opposition to each other; though Virgil (more discreet than Homer in that last particular) has contented himself with the partiality of his deities, their favours, their counsels or commands, to those whose cause they had espoused, without bringing them to the outrageousness of blows. Now our religion, says he, is deprived of the greatest part of those machines—at least, the most shining in epic poetry. Though St. Michael in Ariosto seeks out Discord to send her amongst the Pagans, and finds her in a convent of friars, where peace should reign (which indeed is fine satire); and Satan in Tasso excites Soliman to an attempt by night on the Christian camp, and brings a host of devils to his assistance; yet the Archangel in the former example, when Discord was restive and would not be drawn from her beloved monastery with fair words, has the whip-hand of her, drags her out with many stripes, sets her on God's name about her business, and makes her know the difference of strength betwixt a nuncio of heaven and a minister of hell.

The same angel in the latter instance from Tasso (as if God had never another messenger belonging to the court, but was confined, like Jupiter to Mercury, and Juno to Iris), when he sees his time—that is, when half of the Christians are already killed, and all the rest are in a fair way to be routed—stickles betwixt the remainders of God's host and the race of fiends, pulls the devils backward by the tails, and drives them from their quarry; or otherwise the whole business had miscarried, and Jerusalem remained untaken. This, says Boileau, is a very unequal match for the poor devils, who are sure to come by the worst of it in the combat; for nothing is more easy than for an Almighty Power to bring His old rebels to reason when

He pleases. Consequently what pleasure, what entertainment, can be raised from so pitiful a machine, where we see the success of the battle from the very beginning of it? unless that as we are Christians, we are glad that we have gotten God on our side to maul our enemies when we cannot do the work ourselves. For if the poet had given the faithful more courage, which had cost him nothing, or at least have made them exceed the Turks in number, he might have gained the victory for us Christians without interesting Heaven in the quarrel, and that with as much ease and as little credit to the conqueror as when a party of a hundred soldiers defeats another which consists only of fifty.

This, my lord, I confess is such an argument against our modern poetry as cannot be answered by those mediums which have been used. We cannot hitherto boast that our religion has furnished us with any such machines as have made the strength and beauty of the ancient buildings.

But what if I venture to advance an invention of my own to supply the manifest defect of our new writers? I am sufficiently sensible of my weakness, and it is not very probable that I should succeed in such a project, whereof I have not had the least hint from any of my predecessors the poets, or any of their seconds or coadjutors the critics. Yet we see the art of war is improved in sieges, and new instruments of death are invented daily. Something new in philosophy and the mechanics is discovered almost every year, and the science of former ages is improved by the succeeding. I will not detain you with a long preamble to that which better judges will, perhaps, conclude to be little worth.

It is this, in short—that Christian poets have not hitherto been acquainted with their own strength. If they had searched the Old Testament as they ought, they might there have found the machines which are proper for their work, and those more certain in their effect than it may be the New Testament is in the rules sufficient for salvation. The perusing of one chapter in the prophecy of Daniel, and accommodating what there they find with the principles of Platonic philosophy as it is now Christianised, would have made the ministry of angels as strong an engine for the working up heroic poetry in our religion as that of the ancients has been to raise theirs by all the fables of their gods, which were only received for truths by the most ignorant and weakest of the people.

It is a doctrine almost universally received by Christians, as well Protestants as Catholics, that there are guardian angels appointed by God Almighty as His vicegerents for the protection and government of cities, provinces, kingdoms, and monarchies; and those as well of heathens as of true believers. All this is so plainly proved from those texts of Daniel that it admits of no farther controversy. The prince of the Persians, and that other of the Grecians, are granted to be the guardians and protecting ministers of those empires. It cannot be denied that they were opposite and resisted one another. St. Michael is mentioned by his name as the patron of the Jews, and is now taken by the Christians as the protector-general of our religion. These tutelar genii, who presided over the several people and regions committed to their charge, were watchful over them for good, as far as their commissions could possibly extend. The general purpose and design of all was certainly the service of their great Creator.

But it is an undoubted truth that, for ends best known to the Almighty Majesty of Heaven, His providential designs for the benefit of His creatures, for the debasing and punishing of some nations, and the exaltation and temporal reward of others, were not wholly known to these His ministers; else why those factious quarrels, controversies, and battles amongst themselves, when they were all united in the same design, the service and honour of their common master? But being instructed only in the general, and zealous of the main design, and as finite beings not admitted into the secrets of government, the last resorts of Providence, or capable of discovering the final purposes of God (who can work good out of evil as He pleases, and irresistibly sways all manner of events on earth, directing them finally for the best to His creation in general, and to the ultimate end of His own glory in particular), they must of necessity be sometimes ignorant of the means conducing to those ends, in which alone they can jar and oppose each other— one angel, as we may suppose (the Prince of Persia, as he is called), judging that it would be more for God's honour and the benefit of His people that the Median and Persian monarchy, which delivered them from the Babylonish captivity, should still be uppermost; and the patron of the Grecians, to whom the will of God might be more particularly revealed, contending on the other side for the rise of Alexander and his successors, who were appointed to punish the backsliding Jews, and thereby to put them in mind of their offences, that they might repent and become more virtuous and more observant of the law revealed.

But how far these controversies and appearing enmities of those glorious creatures may be carried; how these oppositions may be best managed, and by what means conducted, is not my business to show or determine: these things must be left to the invention and judgment of the poet, if any of so happy a genius be now living, or any future age can produce a man who, being conversant in the philosophy of Plato as it is now accommodated to Christian use (for, as Virgil gives us to understand by his example, that is the only proper, of all others, for an epic poem), who to his natural endowments of a large invention, a ripe judgment, and a strong memory, has joined the knowledge of the liberal arts and sciences (and particularly moral philosophy, the mathematics, geography, and history), and with all these qualifications is born a poet, knows, and can practise the variety of numbers, and is master of the language in which he writes—if such a man, I say, be now arisen, or shall arise, I am vain enough to think that I have proposed a model to him by which he may build a nobler, a more beautiful, and more perfect poem than any yet extant since the ancients.

There is another part of these machines yet wanting; but by what I have said, it would have been easily supplied by a judicious writer. He could not have failed to add the opposition of ill spirits to the good; they have also their design, ever opposite to that of Heaven; and this alone has hitherto been the practice of the moderns: but this imperfect system, if I may call it such, which I have given, will infinitely advance and carry farther that hypothesis of the evil spirits contending with the good. For being so much weaker since their fall than those blessed beings, they are yet supposed to have a permitted power from God of acting ill, as from their own depraved nature they have always the will of designing it—a great testimony of which we find in Holy Writ, when God Almighty suffered Satan to appear in the holy synod of the angels (a thing not hitherto drawn into example by any of the poets), and also gave him power over all things belonging to his servant Job, excepting only life.

Now what these wicked spirits cannot compass by the vast disproportion of their forces to those of the superior beings, they may by their fraud and cunning carry farther in a seeming league, confederacy, or subserviency to the designs of some good angel, as far as consists with his purity to suffer such an aid, the end of which may possibly be disguised and concealed from his finite knowledge. This is indeed to suppose a great error in such a being; yet since a devil can appear like an angel of light, since craft and malice may sometimes blind for a while a more perfect understanding; and lastly, since Milton has given us an example of the like nature, when Satan, appearing like a cherub to Uriel, the intelligence of the sun, circumvented him even in his own province, and passed only for a curious traveller through those new-created regions, that he might observe therein the workmanship of God and praise Him in His works—I know not why, upon the same supposition, or some other, a fiend may not deceive a creature of more excellency than himself, but yet a creature; at least, by the connivance or tacit permission of the Omniscient Being.

Thus, my lord, I have, as briefly as I could, given your lordship, and by you the world, a rude draught of what I have been long labouring in my imagination, and what I had intended to have put in practice (though far unable for the attempt of such a poem), and to have left the stage, to which my genius never much inclined me, for a work which would have taken up my life in the performance of it. This, too, I had intended chiefly for the honour of my native country, to which a poet is particularly obliged. Of two subjects, both relating to it, I was doubtful—whether I should choose that of King Arthur conquering the Saxons (which, being farther distant in time, gives the greater scope to my invention), or that of Edward the Black Prince in subduing Spain and restoring it to the lawful prince, though a great tyrant, Don Pedro the Cruel—which for the compass of time, including only the expedition of one year; for the greatness of the action, and its answerable event; for the magnanimity of the English hero, opposed to the ingratitude of the person whom he restored; and for the many beautiful episodes which I had interwoven with the principal design, together with the characters of the chiefest English persons (wherein, after Virgil and Spenser, I would have taken occasion to represent my living friends and patrons of the noblest families, and also shadowed the events of future ages in the succession of our imperial line)—with these helps, and those of the machines which I have mentioned, I might perhaps have done as well as some of my predecessors, or at least chalked out a way for others to amend my errors in a like design; but being encouraged only with fair words by King Charles the Second, my little salary ill paid, and no prospect of a future subsistence.

I was then discouraged in the beginning of my attempt; and now age has overtaken me, and want (a more insufferable evil) through the change of the times has wholly disenabled me; though I must ever acknowledge, to the honour of your lordship, and the eternal memory of your charity, that since this Revolution, wherein I have patiently suffered the ruin of my small fortune, and the loss of that poor subsistence which I had from two kings, whom I had served more faithfully than profitably to myself—then your lordship was pleased, out of no other motive but your own nobleness, without any desert of mine, or the least solicitation from me, to make me a most bountiful present, which at that time, when I was most in want of it, came most seasonably and unexpectedly to my relief. That favour, my lord, is of itself sufficient to bind any grateful man to a perpetual acknowledgment, and to all the future service which one of my mean condition can be ever able to perform. May the Almighty God return it for me, both in blessing you here and rewarding you hereafter! I must not presume to defend the cause for which I now suffer, because your lordship is engaged against it; but the more you are so, the greater is my obligation to you for your laying aside all the considerations of factions and parties to do an action of pure disinterested charity.

This is one amongst many of your shining qualities which distinguish you from others of your rank. But let me add a farther truth—that without these ties of gratitude, and abstracting from them all, I have a most particular inclination to honour you, and, if it were not too bold an expression, to say I love you. It is no shame to be a poet, though it is to be a bad one. Augustus Caesar of old, and Cardinal Richelieu of late, would willingly have been such; and David and Solomon were such. You who, without flattery, are the best of the present age in England, and would have been so had you been born in any other country, will receive more honour in future ages by that one excellency than by all those honours to which your birth has entitled you, or your merits have acquired you.

"Ne forte pudori
Sit tibi Musa lyrae solers, et cantor Apollo."

I have formerly said in this epistle that I could distinguish your writings from those of any others; it is now time to clear myself from any imputation of self-conceit on that subject. I assume not to myself any particular lights in this discovery; they are such only as are obvious to every man of sense and judgment who loves poetry and understands it. Your thoughts are always so remote from the common way of thinking that they are, as I may say, of another species than the conceptions of other poets; yet you go not out of nature for any of them. Gold is never bred upon the surface of the ground, but lies so hidden and so deep that the mines of it are seldom found; but the force of waters casts it out from the bowels of mountains, and exposes it amongst the sands of rivers, giving us of her bounty what we could not hope for by our search.

This success attends your lordship's thoughts, which would look like chance if it were not perpetual and always of the same tenor. If I grant that there is care in it, it is such a care as would be ineffectual and fruitless in other men; it is the curiosa felicitas which Petronius ascribes to Horace in his odes. We have not wherewithal to imagine so strongly, so justly, and so pleasantly: in short, if we have the same knowledge, we cannot draw out of it the same quintessence; we cannot give it such a turn, such a propriety, and such a beauty. Something is deficient in the manner or the words, but more in the nobleness of our conception. Yet when you have finished all, and it appears in its full lustre; when the diamond is not only found, but the roughness smoothed; when it is cut into a form and set in gold, then we cannot but acknowledge that it is the perfect work of art and nature; and every one will be so vain to think he himself could have performed the like until he attempts it. It is just the description that Horace makes of such a finished piece; it appears so easy,

"Ut sibi quivis
Speret idem, sudet multum, frustraque laboret,
Ausus idem."

And besides all this, it is your lordship's particular talent to lay your thoughts so chose together that, were they closer, they would be crowded, and even a due connection would be wanting. We are not kept in expectation of two good lines which are to come after a long parenthesis of twenty bad; which is the April poetry of other writers, a mixture of rain and sunshine by fits: you are always bright, even almost to a fault, by reason of the excess. There is continual abundance, a magazine of thought, and yet a perpetual variety of entertainment; which creates such an appetite in your reader that he is not cloyed with anything, but satisfied with all.

It is that which the Romans call caena dubia; where there is such plenty, yet withal so much diversity, and so good order, that the choice is difficult betwixt one excellency and another; and yet the conclusion, by a due climax, is evermore the best—that is, as a conclusion ought to be, ever the most proper for its place. See, my lord, whether I have not studied your lordship with some application: and since you are so modest that you will not be judge and party, I appeal to the whole world if I have not drawn your picture to a great degree of likeness, though it is but in miniature, and that some of the best features are yet wanting. Yet what I have done is enough to distinguish you from any other, which is the proposition that I took upon me to demonstrate.

And now, my lord, to apply what I have said to my present business: the satires of Juvenal and Persius, appearing in this new English dress, cannot so properly be inscribed to any man as to your lordship, who are the first of the age in that way of writing. Your lordship, amongst many other favours, has given me your permission for this address; and you have particularly encouraged me by your perusal and approbation of the sixth and tenth satires of Juvenal as I have translated them. My fellow-labourers have likewise commissioned me to perform in their behalf this office of a dedication to you, and will acknowledge, with all possible respect and gratitude, your acceptance of their work.

Some of them have the honour to be known to your lordship already; and they who have not yet that happiness, desire it now. Be pleased to receive our common endeavours with your wonted candour, without entitling you to the protection of our common failings in so difficult an undertaking. And allow me your patience, if it be not already tired with this long epistle, to give you from the best authors the origin, the antiquity, the growth, the change, and the completement of satire among the Romans; to describe, if not define, the nature of that poem, with its several qualifications and virtues, together with the several sorts of it; to compare the excellencies of Horace, Persius, and Juvenal, and show the particular manners of their satires; and, lastly, to give an account of this new way of version which is attempted in our performance: all which, according to the weakness of my ability, and the best lights which I can get from others, shall be the subject of my following discourse.

The most perfect work of poetry, says our master Aristotle, is tragedy. His reason is because it is the most united; being more severely confined within the rules of action, time, and place. The action is entire of a piece, and one without episodes; the time limited to a natural day; and the place circumscribed at least within the compass of one town or city. Being exactly proportioned thus, and uniform in all its parts, the mind is more capable of comprehending the whole beauty of it without distraction. But after all these advantages an heroic poem is certainly the greatest work of human nature. The beauties and perfections of the other are but mechanical; those of the epic are more noble.

Though Homer has limited his place to Troy and the fields about it; his actions to forty-eight natural days, whereof twelve are holidays, or cessation from business during the funeral of Patroclus. To proceed: the action of the epic is greater; the extension of time enlarges the pleasure of the reader, and the episodes give it more ornament and more variety. The instruction is equal; but the first is only instructive, the latter forms a hero and a prince. If it signifies anything which of them is of the more ancient family, the best and most absolute heroic poem was written by Homer long before tragedy was invented. But if we consider the natural endowments and acquired parts which are necessary to make an accomplished writer in either kind, tragedy requires a less and more confined knowledge; moderate learning and observation of the rules is sufficient if a genius be not wanting.

But in an epic poet, one who is worthy of that name, besides an universal genius is required universal learning, together with all those qualities and acquisitions which I have named above, and as many more as I have through haste or negligence omitted. And, after all, he must have exactly studied Homer and Virgil as his patterns, Aristotle and Horace as his guides, and Vida and Bossu as their commentators, with many others (both Italian and French critics) which I want leisure here to recommend.

In a word, what I have to say in relation to this subject, which does not particularly concern satire, is that the greatness of an heroic poem beyond that of a tragedy may easily be discovered by observing how few have attempted that work, in comparison to those who have written dramas; and of those few, how small a number have succeeded. But leaving the critics on either side to contend about the preference due to this or that sort of poetry, I will hasten to my present business, which is the antiquity and origin of satire, according to those informations which I have received from the learned Casaubon, Heinsius, Rigaltius, Dacier, and the Dauphin's Juvenal, to which I shall add some observations of my own.

There has been a long dispute among the modern critics whether the Romans derived their satire from the Grecians or first invented it themselves. Julius Scaliger and Heinsius are of the first opinion; Casaubon, Rigaltius, Dacier, and the publisher of Dauphin's Juvenal maintain the latter. If we take satire in the general signification of the word, as it is used in all modern languages, for an invective, it is certain that it is almost as old as verse; and though hymns, which are praises of God, may be allowed to have been before it, yet the defamation of others was not long after it. After God had cursed Adam and Eve in Paradise, the husband and wife excused themselves by laying the blame on one another, and gave a beginning to those conjugal dialogues in prose which the poets have perfected in verse. The third chapter of Job is one of the first instances of this poem in Holy Scripture, unless we will take it higher, from the latter end of the second, where his wife advises him to curse his Maker.

This original, I confess, is not much to the honour of satire; but here it was nature, and that depraved: when it became an art, it bore better fruit. Only we have learnt thus much already—that scoffs and revilings are of the growth of all nations; and consequently that neither the Greek poets borrowed from other people their art of railing, neither needed the Romans to take it from them. But considering satire as a species of poetry, here the war begins amongst the critics. Scaliger, the father, will have it descend from Greece to Rome; and derives the word "satire" from Satyrus, that mixed kind of animal (or, as the ancients thought him, rural god) made up betwixt a man and a goat, with a human head, hooked nose, pouting lips, a bunch or struma under the chin, pricked ears, and upright horns; the body shagged with hair, especially from the waist, and ending in a goat, with the legs and feet of that creature. But Casaubon and his followers, with reason, condemn this derivation, and prove that from Satyrus the word satira, as it signifies a poem, cannot possibly descend. For satira is not properly a substantive, but an adjective; to which the word lanx (in English a "charger" or "large platter") is understood: so that the Greek poem made according to the manners of a Satyr, and expressing his qualities, must properly be called satirical, and not satire. And thus far it is allowed that the Grecians had such poems, but that they were wholly different in species from that to which the Romans gave the name of satire.

Aristotle divides all poetry, in relation to the progress of it, into nature without art, art begun, and art completed. Mankind, even the most barbarous, have the seeds of poetry implanted in them. The first specimen of it was certainly shown in the praises of the Deity and prayers to Him; and as they are of natural obligation, so they are likewise of divine institution: which Milton observing, introduces Adam and Eve every morning adoring God in hymns and prayers. The first poetry was thus begun in the wild notes of natural poetry before the invention of feet and measures. The Grecians and Romans had no other original of their poetry.

Festivals and holidays soon succeeded to private worship, and we need not doubt but they were enjoined by the true God to His own people, as they were afterwards imitated by the heathens; who by the light of reason knew they were to invoke some superior being in their necessities, and to thank him for his benefits. Thus the Grecian holidays were celebrated with offerings to Bacchus and Ceres and other deities, to whose bounty they supposed they were owing for their corn and wine and other helps of life. And the ancient Romans, as Horace tells us, paid their thanks to Mother Earth or Vesta, to Silvanus, and their Genius in the same manner.

But as all festivals have a double reason of their institution—the first of religion, the other of recreation for the unbending of our minds—so both the Grecians and Romans agreed (after their sacrifices were performed) to spend the remainder of the day in sports and merriments; amongst which songs and dances, and that which they called wit (for want of knowing better), were the chiefest entertainments. The Grecians had a notion of Satyrs, whom I have already described; and taking them and the Sileni—that is, the young Satyrs and the old—for the tutors, attendants, and humble companions of their Bacchus, habited themselves like those rural deities, and imitated them in their rustic dances, to which they joined songs with some sort of rude harmony, but without certain numbers; and to these they added a kind of chorus.

The Romans also, as nature is the same in all places, though they knew nothing of those Grecian demi-gods, nor had any communication with Greece, yet had certain young men who at their festivals danced and sang after their uncouth manner to a certain kind of verse which they called Saturnian. What it was we have no certain light from antiquity to discover; but we may conclude that, like the Grecian, it was void of art, or, at least, with very feeble beginnings of it. Those ancient Romans at these holy days, which were a mixture of devotion and debauchery, had a custom of reproaching each other with their faults in a sort of extempore poetry, or rather of tunable hobbling verse, and they answered in the same kind of gross raillery—their wit and their music being of a piece. The Grecians, says Casaubon, had formerly done the same in the persons of their petulant Satyrs; but I am afraid he mistakes the matter, and confounds the singing and dancing of the Satyrs with the rustical entertainments of the first Romans.

The reason of my opinion is this: that Casaubon finding little light from antiquity of these beginnings of poetry amongst the Grecians, but only these representations of Satyrs who carried canisters and cornucopias full of several fruits in their hands, and danced with them at their public feasts, and afterwards reading Horace, who makes mention of his homely Romans jesting at one another in the same kind of solemnities, might suppose those wanton Satyrs did the same; and especially because Horace possibly might seem to him to have shown the original of all poetry in general (including the Grecians as well as Romans), though it is plainly otherwise that he only described the beginning and first rudiments of poetry in his own country. The verses are these, which he cites from the First Epistle of the Second Book, which was written to Augustus:-

"Agricolae prisci, fortes, parvoque beati,
Condita post frumenta, levantes tempore festo
Corpus, et ipsum animum spe finis dura ferentem,
Cum sociis operum, et pueris, et conjuge fida,
Tellurem porco, Silvanum lacte piabant;
Floribus et vino Genium memorem brevis aevi.
Fescennina per hunc inventa licentia morem
Versibus alternis opprobria rustica fudit."
"Our brawny clowns of old, who turned the soil,
Content with little, and inured to toil,
At harvest-home, with mirth and country cheer,
Restored their bodies for another year,
Refreshed their spirits, and renewed their hope
Of such a future feast and future crop.
Then with their fellow-joggers of the ploughs,
Their little children, and their faithful spouse,
A sow they slew to Vesta's deity,
And kindly milk, Silvanus, poured to thee.
With flowers and wine their Genius they adored;
A short life and a merry was the word.
From flowing cups defaming rhymes ensue,
And at each other homely taunts they threw."

Yet since it is a hard conjecture that so great a man as Casaubon should misapply what Horace writ concerning ancient Rome to the ceremonies and manners of ancient Greece, I will not insist on this opinion, but rather judge in general that since all poetry had its original from religion, that of the Grecians and Rome had the same beginning. Both were invented at festivals of thanksgiving, and both were prosecuted with mirth and raillery and rudiments of verses; amongst the Greeks by those who represented Satyrs, and amongst the Romans by real clowns.

For, indeed, when I am reading Casaubon on these two subjects methinks I hear the same story told twice over with very little alteration. Of which Dacier, taking notice in his interpretation of the Latin verses which I have translated, says plainly that the beginning of poetry was the same, with a small variety, in both countries, and that the mother of it in all nations was devotion. But what is yet more wonderful, that most learned critic takes notice also, in his illustrations on the First Epistle of the Second Book, that as the poetry of the Romans and that of the Grecians had the same beginning at feasts and thanksgiving (as it has been observed), and the old comedy of the Greeks (which was invective) and the satire of the Romans (which was of the same nature) were begun on the very same occasion, so the fortune of both in process of time was just the same—the old comedy of the Grecians was forbidden for its too much licence in exposing of particular persons, and the rude satire of the Romans was also punished by a law of the Decemviri, as Horace tells us in these words:-

"Libertasque recurrentes accepta per annos
Lusit amabiliter; donec jam saevus apertam
In rabiem verti caepit jocus, et per honestas
Ire domos impune minax: doluere cruento
Dente lacessiti; fuit intactis quoque cura
Conditione super communi: quinetiam lex,
Paenaque lata, malo quae nollet carmine quenquam
Describi: vertere modum, formidine fustis
Ad benedicendum delectandumque redacti."

The law of the Decemviri was this: Siquis occentassit malum carmen, sive condidissit, quod infamiam faxit, flagitiumve alteri, capital esto. A strange likeness, and barely possible; but the critics being all of the same opinion, it becomes me to be silent and to submit to better judgments than my own. But to return to the Grecians, from whose satiric dramas the elder Scaliger and Heinsius will have the Roman satire to proceed; I am to take a view of them first, and see if there be any such descent from them as those authors have pretended.

Thespis, or whoever he were that invented tragedy (for authors differ), mingled with them a chorus and dances of Satyrs which had before been used in the celebration of their festivals, and there they were ever afterwards retained. The character of them was also kept, which was mirth and wantonness; and this was given, I suppose, to the folly of the common audience, who soon grow weary of good sense, and, as we daily see in our own age and country, are apt to forsake poetry, and still ready to return to buffoonery and farce. From hence it came that in the Olympic Games, where the poets contended for four prizes, the satiric tragedy was the last of them, for in the rest the Satyrs were excluded from the chorus. Amongst the plays of Euripides which are yet remaining, there is one of these satirics, which is called The Cyclops, in which we may see the nature of those poems, and from thence conclude what likeness they have to the Roman satire.

The story of this Cyclops, whose name was Polyphemus (so famous in the Grecian fables), was that Ulysses, who with his company was driven on the coast of Sicily, where those Cyclops inhabited, coming to ask relief from Silenus and the Satyrs, who were herdsmen to that one-eyed giant, was kindly received by them, and entertained till, being perceived by Polyphemus, they were made prisoners against the rites of hospitality (for which Ulysses eloquently pleaded), were afterwards put down into the den, and some of them devoured; after which Ulysses (having made him drunk when he was asleep) thrust a great fire-brand into his eye, and so revenging his dead followers escaped with the remaining party of the living, and Silenus and the Satyrs were freed from their servitude under Polyphemus and remitted to their first liberty of attending and accompanying their patron Bacchus.

This was the subject of the tragedy, which, being one of those that end with a happy event, is therefore by Aristotle judged below the other sort, whose success is unfortunate; notwithstanding which, the Satyrs (who were part of the dramatis personae, as well as the whole chorus) were properly introduced into the nature of the poem, which is mixed of farce and tragedy. The adventure of Ulysses was to entertain the judging part of the audience, and the uncouth persons of Silenus and the Satyrs to divert the common people with their gross railleries.

Your lordship has perceived by this time that this satiric tragedy and the Roman satire have little resemblance in any of their features. The very kinds are different; for what has a pastoral tragedy to do with a paper of verses satirically written? The character and raillery of the Satyrs is the only thing that could pretend to a likeness, were Scaliger and Heinsius alive to maintain their opinion. And the first farces of the Romans, which were the rudiments of their poetry, were written before they had any communication with the Greeks, or indeed any knowledge of that people.

And here it will be proper to give the definition of the Greek satiric poem from Casaubon before I leave this subject. "The 'satiric,'" says he, "is a dramatic poem annexed to a tragedy having a chorus which consists of Satyrs. The persons represented in it are illustrious men, the action of it is great, the style is partly serious and partly jocular, and the event of the action most commonly is happy."

The Grecians, besides these satiric tragedies, had another kind of poem, which they called "silli," which were more of kin to the Roman satire. Those "silli" were indeed invective poems, but of a different species from the Roman poems of Ennius, Pacuvius, Lucilius, Horace, and the rest of their successors. "They were so called," says Casaubon in one place, "from Silenus, the foster-father of Bacchus;" but in another place, bethinking himself better, he derives their name [Greek text which cannot be reproduced] from their scoffing and petulancy. From some fragments of the "silli" written by Timon we may find that they were satiric poems, full of parodies; that is, of verses patched up from great poets, and turned into another sense than their author intended them. Such amongst the Romans is the famous Cento of Ausonius, where the words are Virgil's, but by applying them to another sense they are made a relation of a wedding-night, and the act of consummation fulsomely described in the very words of the most modest amongst all poets.

Of the same manner are our songs which are turned into burlesque, and the serious words of the author perverted into a ridiculous meaning. Thus in Timon's "silli" the words are generally those of Homer and the tragic poets, but he applies them satirically to some customs and kinds of philosophy which he arraigns. But the Romans not using any of these parodies in their satires—sometimes indeed repeating verses of other men, as Persius cites some of Nero's, but not turning them into another meaning—the "silli" cannot be supposed to be the original of Roman satire. To these "silli," consisting of parodies, we may properly add the satires which were written against particular persons, such as were the iambics of Archilochus against Lycambes, which Horace undoubtedly imitated in some of his odes and epodes, whose titles bear sufficient witness of it: I might also name the invective of Ovid against Ibis, and many others. But these are the underwood of satire rather than the timber-trees; they are not of general extension, as reaching only to some individual person. And Horace seems to have purged himself from those splenetic reflections in those odes and epodes before he undertook the noble work of satires, which were properly so called.

Thus, my lord, I have at length disengaged myself from those antiquities of Greece, and have proved, I hope, from the best critics, that the Roman satire was not borrowed from thence, but of their own manufacture. I am now almost gotten into my depth; at least, by the help of Dacier, I am swimming towards it. Not that I will promise always to follow him, any more than he follows Casaubon; but to keep him in my eye as my best and truest guide; and where I think he may possibly mislead me, there to have recourse to my own lights, as I expect that others should do by me.

Quintilian says in plain words, Satira quidem tota nostra est; and Horace had said the same thing before him, speaking of his predecessor in that sort of poetry, et Graecis intacti carminis auctor. Nothing can be clearer than the opinion of the poet and the orator (both the best critics of the two best ages of the Roman empire), that satire was wholly of Latin growth, and not transplanted to Rome from Athens. Yet, as I have said, Scaliger the father, according to his custom (that is, insolently enough), contradicts them both, and gives no better reason than the derivation of satyrus from [Greek text which cannot be reproduced] salacitas; and so, from the lechery of those fauns, thinks he has sufficiently proved that satire is derived from them: as if wantonness and lubricity were essential to that sort of poem, which ought to be avoided in it. His other allegation, which I have already mentioned, is as pitiful—that the Satyrs carried platters and canisters full of fruit in their hands. If they had entered empty-handed, had they been ever the less Satyrs? Or were the fruits and flowers which they offered anything of kin to satire? or any argument that this poem was originally Grecian? Casaubon judged better, and his opinion is grounded on sure authority: that satire was derived from satura, a Roman word which signifies full and abundant, and full also of variety, in which nothing is wanting to its due perfection.

It is thus, says Denier, that we say a full colour, when the wool has taken the whole tincture and drunk in as much of the dye as it can receive. According to this derivation, from setur comes satura or satira, according to the new spelling, as optumus and maxumus are now spelled optimus and maximus. Satura, as I have formerly noted, is an adjective, and relates to the word lanx, which is understood; and this lanx (in English a "charger" or "large platter") was yearly filled with all sorts of fruits, which were offered to the gods at their festivals as the premices or first gatherings. These offerings of several sorts thus mingled, it is true, were not unknown to the Grecians, who called them Greek text which cannot be reproduced] a sacrifice of all sorts of fruits; and Greek text which cannot be reproduced, when they offered all kinds of grain. Virgil has mentioned these sacrifices in his "Georgics":-

"Lancibus et pandis fumantia reddimus exta;"and in another place, lancesque et liba feremus—that is, "We offer the smoking entrails in great platters; and we will offer the chargers and the cakes." This word satura has been afterward applied to many other sorts of mixtures; as Festus calls it, a kind of olla or hotch-potch made of several sorts of meats. Laws were also called leges saturae when they were of several heads and titles, like our tacked Bills of Parliament; and per saturam legem ferre in the Roman senate was to carry a law without telling the senators, or counting voices, when they were in haste. Sallust uses the word, per saturam sententias exquirere, when the majority was visibly on one side. From hence it might probably be conjectured that the Discourses or Satires of Ennius, Lucilius, and Horace, as we now call them, took their name, because they are full of various matters, and are also written on various subjects—as Porphyrius says. But Dacier affirms that it is not immediately from thence that these satires are so called, for that name had been used formerly for other things which bore a nearer resemblance to those discourses of Horace; in explaining of which, continues Dacier, a method is to be pursued of which Casaubon himself has never thought, and which will put all things into so clear a light that no further room will be left for the least dispute.

During the space of almost four hundred years since the building of their city the Romans had never known any entertainments of the stage. Chance and jollity first found out those verses which they called Saturnian and Fescennine; or rather human nature, which is inclined to poetry, first produced them rude and barbarous and unpolished, as all other operations of the soul are in their beginnings before they are cultivated with art and study. However, in occasions of merriment, they were first practised; and this rough-cast, unhewn poetry was instead of stage-plays for the space of a hundred and twenty years together.

They were made extempore, and were, as the French call them, impromptus; for which the Tarsians of old were much renowned, and we see the daily examples of them in the Italian farces of Harlequin and Scaramucha. Such was the poetry of that savage people before it was tuned into numbers and the harmony of verse. Little of the Saturnian verses is now remaining; we only know from authors that they were nearer prose than poetry, without feet or measure. They were [Greek text which cannot be reproduced] but not [Greek text which cannot be reproduced]. Perhaps they might be used in the solemn part of their ceremonies; and the Fescennine, which were invented after them, in their afternoons' debauchery, because they were scoffing and obscene.

The Fescennine and Saturnian were the same; for as they were called Saturnian from their ancientness, when Saturn reigned in Italy, they were also called Fescennine, from Fescennia, a town in the same country where they were first practised. The actors, with a gross and rustic kind of raillery, reproached each other with their failings, and at the same time were nothing sparing of it to their audience. Somewhat of this custom was afterwards retained in their Saturnalia, or Feasts of Saturn, celebrated in December; at least, all kind of freedom in speech was then allowed to slaves, even against their masters; and we are not without some imitation of it in our Christmas gambols.

Soldiers also used those Fescennine verses, after measure and numbers had been added to them, at the triumph of their generals; of which we have an example in the triumph of Julius Caesar over Gaul in these expressions: Caesar Gallias subegit, Nicomedes Caesarem. Ecce Caesar nunc triumphat, qui subegit Gallias; Nicomedes non triumphat, qui subegit Caesarem. The vapours of wine made those first satirical poets amongst the Romans, which, says Dacier, we cannot better represent than by imagining a company of clowns on a holiday dancing lubberly and upbraiding one another in extempore doggerel with their defects and vices, and the stories that were told of them in bake-houses and barbers' shops.

When they began to be somewhat better bred, and were entering, as I may say, into the first rudiments of civil conversation, they left these hedge-notes for another sort of poem, somewhat polished, which was also full of pleasant raillery, but without any mixture of obscenity. This sort of poetry appeared under the name of "satire" because of its variety; and this satire was adorned with compositions of music, and with dances; but lascivious postures were banished from it. In the Tuscan language, says Livy, the word hister signifies a player; and therefore those actors which were first brought from Etruria to Rome on occasion of a pestilence, when the Romans were admonished to avert the anger of the gods by plays (in the year ab urbe condita CCCXC.)—those actors, I say, were therefore called histriones: and that name has since remained, not only to actors Roman born, but to all others of every nation. They played, not the former extempore stuff of Fescennine verses or clownish jests, but what they acted was a kind of civil cleanly farce, with music and dances, and motions that were proper to the subject.

In this condition Livius Andronicus found the stage when he attempted first, instead of farces, to supply it with a nobler entertainment of tragedies and comedies. This man was a Grecian born, and being made a slave by Livius Salinator, and brought to Rome, had the education of his patron's children committed to him, which trust he discharged so much to the satisfaction of his master that he gave him his liberty.

Andronicus, thus become a freeman of Rome, added to his own name that of Livius, his master; and, as I observed, was the first author of a regular play in that commonwealth. Being already instructed in his native country in the manners and decencies of the Athenian theatre, and conversant in the archaea comaedia or old comedy of Aristophanes and the rest of the Grecian poets, he took from that model his own designing of plays for the Roman stage, the first of which was represented in the year CCCCCXIV. since the building of Rome, as Tully, from the Commentaries of Atticus, has assured us; it was after the end of the first Punic War, the year before Atticus was born. Dacier has not carried the matter altogether thus far; he only says that one Livius Andronicus was the first stage-poet at Rome.

But I will adventure on this hint to advance another proposition, which I hope the learned will approve; and though we have not anything of Andronicus remaining to justify my conjecture, yet it is exceeding probable that, having read the works of those Grecian wits, his countrymen, he imitated not only the groundwork, but also the manner of their writing; and how grave soever his tragedies might be, yet in his comedies he expressed the way of Aristophanes, Eupolis, and the rest, which was to call some persons by their own names, and to expose their defects to the laughter of the people (the examples of which we have in the fore-mentioned Aristophanes, who turned the wise Socrates into ridicule, and is also very free with the management of Cleon, Alcibiades, and other ministers of the Athenian government). Now if this be granted, we may easily suppose that the first hint of satirical plays on the Roman stage was given by the Greeks—not from the satirica, for that has been reasonably exploded in the former part of this discourse— but from their old comedy, which was imitated first by Livius Andronicus. And then Quintilian and Horace must be cautiously interpreted, where they affirm that satire is wholly Roman, and a sort of verse which was not touched on by the Grecians.

The reconcilement of my opinion to the standard of their judgment is not, however, very difficult, since they spoke of satire, not as in its first elements, but as it was formed into a separate work—begun by Ennius, pursued by Lucilius, and completed afterwards by Horace. The proof depends only on this postalatum—that the comedies of Andronicus, which were imitations of the Greek, were also imitations of their railleries and reflections on particular persons. For if this be granted me, which is a most probable supposition, it is easy to infer that the first light which was given to the Roman theatrical satire was from the plays of Livius Andronicus, which will be more manifestly discovered when I come to speak of Ennius. In the meantime I will return to Dacier.

The people, says he, ran in crowds to these new entertainments of Andronicus, as to pieces which were more noble in their kind, and more perfect than their former satires, which for some time they neglected and abandoned; but not long after they took them up again, and then they joined them to their comedies, playing them at the end of every drama, as the French continue at this day to act their farces, in the nature of a separate entertainment from their tragedies. But more particularly they were joined to the "Atellane" fables, says Casaubon; which were plays invented by the Osci. Those fables, says Valerius Maximus, out of Livy, were tempered with the Italian severity, and free from any note of infamy or obsceneness; and, as an old commentator on Juvenal affirms, the Exodiarii, which were singers and dancers, entered to entertain the people with light songs and mimical gestures, that they might not go away oppressed with melancholy from those serious pieces of the theatre. So that the ancient satire of the Romans was in extempore reproaches; the next was farce, which was brought from Tuscany; to that succeeded the plays of Andronicus, from the old comedy of the Grecians; and out of all these sprang two several branches of new Roman satire, like different scions from the same root, which I shall prove with as much brevity as the subject will allow.

A year after Andronicus had opened the Roman stage with his new dramas, Ennius was born; who, when he was grown to man's estate, having seriously considered the genius of the people, and how eagerly they followed the first satires, thought it would be worth his pains to refine upon the project, and to write satires, not to be acted on the theatre, but read. He preserved the groundwork of their pleasantry, their venom, and their raillery on particular persons and general vices; and by this means, avoiding the danger of any ill success in a public representation, he hoped to be as well received in the cabinet as Andronicus had been upon the stage. The event was answerable to his expectation. He made discourses in several sorts of verse, varied often in the same paper, retaining still in the title their original name of satire.

Both in relation to the subjects, and the variety of matters contained in them, the satires of Horace are entirely like them; only Ennius, as I said, confines not himself to one sort of verse, as Horace does, but taking example from the Greeks, and even from Homer himself in his "Margites" (which is a kind of satire, as Scaliger observes), gives himself the licence, when one sort of numbers comes not easily, to run into another, as his fancy dictates; for he makes no difficulty to mingle hexameters with iambic trimeters or with trochaic tetrameters, as appears by those fragments which are yet remaining of him. Horace has thought him worthy to be copied, inserting many things of his into his own satires, as Virgil has done into his "AEneids."

Here we have Dacier making out that Ennius was the first satirist in that way of writing, which was of his invention—that is, satire abstracted from the stage and new modelled into papers of verses on several subjects. But he will have Ennius take the groundwork of satire from the first farces of the

Romans rather than from the formed plays of Livius Andronicus, which were copied from the Grecian comedies. It may possibly be so; but Dacier knows no more of it than I do. And it seems to me the more probable opinion that he rather imitated the fine railleries of the Greeks, which he saw in the pieces of Andronicus, than the coarseness of his own countrymen in their clownish extemporary way of jeering. But besides this, it is universally granted that Ennius, though an Italian, was excellently learned in the Greek language.

His verses were stuffed with fragments of it, even to a fault; and he himself believed, according to the Pythagorean opinion, that the soul of Homer was transfused into him, which Persius observes in his sixth satire—postquam destertuit esse Maeonides. But this being only the private opinion of so inconsiderable a man as I am, I leave it to the further disquisition of the critics, if they think it worth their notice. Most evident it is that, whether he imitated the Roman farce or the Greek comedies, he is to be acknowledged for the first author of Roman satire, as it is properly so called, and distinguished from any sort of stage-play.

Of Pacuvius, who succeeded him, there is little to be said, because there is so little remaining of him; only that he is taken to be the nephew of Ennius, his sister's son; that in probability he was instructed by his uncle in his way of satire, which we are told he has copied; but what advances he made, we know not. Lucilius came into the world when Pacuvius flourished most. He also made satires after the manner of Ennius; but he gave them a more graceful turn, and endeavoured to imitate more closely the vetus comaedia of the Greeks, of the which the old original Roman satire had no idea till the time of Livius Andronicus. And though Horace seems to have made Lucilius the first author of satire in verse amongst the Romans in these words-"Quid? cum est Lucilius auses Primus in hunc operis componere carmina morem"-

He is only thus to be understood—that Lucilius had given a more graceful turn to the satire of Ennius and Pacuvius, not that he invented a new satire of his own; and Quintilian seems to explain this passage of Horace in these words: Satira quidem tota nostra est; in qua primus insignem laudem adeptus est Luciluis. Thus both Horace and Quintilian give a kind of primacy of honour to Lucilius amongst the Latin satirists; for as the Roman language grew more refined, so much more capable it was of receiving the Grecian beauties, in his time. Horace and Quintilian could mean no more than that Lucilius writ better than Ennius and Pacuvius, and on the same account we prefer Horace to Lucilius.

Both of them imitated the old Greek comedy; and so did Ennius and Pacuvius before them. The polishing of the Latin tongue, in the succession of times, made the only difference; and Horace himself in two of his satires, written purposely on this subject, thinks the Romans of his age were too partial in their commendations of Lucilius, who writ not only loosely and muddily, with little art and much less care, but also in a time when the Latin tongue was not yet sufficiently purged from the dregs of barbarism; and many significant and sounding words which the Romans wanted were not admitted even in the times of Lucretius and Cicero, of which both complain. But to proceed: Dacier justly taxes Casaubon for saying that the satires of Lucilius were wholly different in species from those of Ennius and Pacuvius, Casaubon was led into that mistake by Diomedes the grammarian, who in effect says this:-"Satire amongst the Romans but not amongst the Greeks, was a biting invective poem, made after the model of the ancient comedy, for the reprehension of vices; such as were the poems of Lucilius, of Horace, and of Persius.

But in former times the name of satire was given to poems which were composed of several sorts of verses, such as were made by Ennius and Pacuvius"—more fully expressing the etymology of the word satire from satura, which we have observed. Here it is manifest that Diomedes makes a specifical distinction betwixt the satires of Ennius and those of Lucilius. But this, as we say in English, is only a distinction without a difference; for the reason of it is ridiculous and absolutely false. This was that which cozened honest Casaubon, who, relying on Diomedes, had not sufficiently examined the origin and nature of those two satires, which were entirely the same both in the matter and the form; for all that Lucilius performed beyond his predecessors, Ennius and Pacuvius, was only the adding of more politeness and more salt, without any change in the substance of the poem.

And though Lucilius put not together in the same satire several sorts of verses, as Ennius did, yet he composed several satires of several sorts of verses, and mingled them with Greek verses: one poem consisted only of hexameters, and another was entirely of iambics; a third of trochaics; as is visible by the fragments yet remaining of his works. In short, if the satires of Lucilius are therefore said to be wholly different from those of Ennius because he added much more of beauty and polishing to his own poems than are to be found in those before him, it will follow from hence that the satires of Horace are wholly different from those of Lucilius, because Horace has not less surpassed Lucilius in the elegancy of his writing than Lucilius surpassed Ennius in the turn and ornament of his. This passage of Diomedes has also drawn Dousa the son into the same error of Casaubon, which I say, not to expose the little failings of those judicious men, but only to make it appear with how much diffidence and caution we are to read their works when they treat a subject of so much obscurity and so very ancient as is this of satire.

Having thus brought down the history of satire from its original to the times of Horace, and shown the several changes of it, I should here discover some of those graces which Horace added to it, but that I think it will be more proper to defer that undertaking till I make the comparison betwixt him and Juvenal. In the meanwhile, following the order of time, it will be necessary to say somewhat of another kind of satire which also was descended from the ancient; it is that which we call the Varronian satire (but which Varro himself calls the Menippean) because Varro, the most learned of the Romans, was the first author of it, who imitated in his works the manners of Menippus the Gadarenian, who professed the philosophy of the Cynics.

This sort of satire was not only composed of several sorts of verse, like those of Ennius, but was also mixed with prose, and Greek was sprinkled amongst the Latin. Quintilian, after he had spoken of the satire of Lucilius, adds what follows:-"There is another and former kind of satire, composed by Terentius Varro, the most learned of the Romans, in which he was not satisfied alone with mingling in it several sorts of verse." The only difficulty of this passage is that Quintilian tells us that this satire of Varro was of a former kind; for how can we possibly imagine this to be, since Varro, who was contemporary to Cicero, must consequently be after Lucilius? But Quintilian meant not that the satire of Varro was in order of time before Lucilius; he would only give us to understand that the Varronian satire, with mixture of several sorts of verses, was more after the manner of Ennius and Pacuvius than that of Lucilius, who was more severe and more correct, and gave himself less liberty in the mixture of his verses in the same poem.

We have nothing remaining of those Varronian satires excepting some inconsiderable fragments, and those for the most part much corrupted. The tithes of many of them are indeed preserved, and they are generally double; from whence, at least, we may understand how many various subjects were treated by that author. Tully in his "Academics" introduces Varro himself giving us some light concerning the scope and design of those works; wherein, after he had shown his reasons why he did not ex professo write of philosophy, he adds what follows:-"Notwithstanding," says he, "that those pieces of mine wherein I have imitated Menippus, though I have not translated him, are sprinkled with a kind of mirth and gaiety, yet many things are there inserted which are drawn from the very entrails of philosophy, and many things severely argued which I have mingled with pleasantries on purpose that they may more easily go down with the common sort of unlearned readers." The rest of the sentence is so lame that we can only make thus much out of it—that in the composition of his satires he so tempered philology with philosophy that his work was a mixture of them both. And Tully himself confirms us in this opinion when a little after he addresses himself to Varro in these words:-"And you yourself have composed a most elegant and complete poem; you have begun philosophy in many places; sufficient to incite us, though too little to instruct us." Thus it appears that Varro was one of those writers whom they called [Greek text which cannot be reproduced] (studious of laughter); and that, as learned as he was, his business was more to divert his reader than to teach him.

And he entitled his own satires Menippean; not that Menippus had written any satires (for his were either dialogues or epistles), but that Varro imitated his style, his manner, and his facetiousness. All that we know further of Menippus and his writings, which are wholly lost, is that by some he is esteemed, as, amongst the rest, by Varro; by others he is noted of cynical impudence and obscenity; that he was much given to those parodies which I have already mentioned (that is, he often quoted the verses of Homer and the tragic poets, and turned their serious meaning into something that was ridiculous); whereas Varro's satires are by Tully called absolute, and most elegant and various poems. Lucian, who was emulous of this Menippus, seems to have imitated both his manners and his style in many of his dialogues, where Menippus himself is often introduced as a speaker in them and as a perpetual buffoon; particularly his character is expressed in the beginning of that dialogue which is called [Greek text which cannot be reproduced]. But Varro in imitating him avoids his impudence and filthiness, and only expresses his witty pleasantry.

This we may believe for certain—that as his subjects were various, so most of them were tales or stories of his own invention; which is also manifest from antiquity by those authors who are acknowledged to have written Varronian satires in imitation of his—of whom the chief is Petronius Arbiter, whose satire, they say, is now printing in Holland, wholly recovered, and made complete; when it is made public, it will easily be seen by any one sentence whether it be supposititious or genuine. Many of Lucian's dialogues may also properly be called Varronian satires, particularly his true history; and consequently the "Golden Ass" of Apuleius, which is taken from him. Of the same stamp is the mock deification of Claudius by Seneca, and the Symposium or "Caesars" of Julian the Emperor. Amongst the moderns we may reckon the "Encomium Moriae" of Erasmus, Barclay's "Euphormio," and a volume of German authors which my ingenious friend Mr. Charles Killigrew once lent me. In the English I remember none which are mixed with prose as Varro's were; but of the same kind is "Mother Hubbard's Tale" in Spenser, and (if it be not too vain to mention anything of my own) the poems of "Absalom" and "MacFlecnoe."

This is what I have to say in general of satire: only, as Dacier has observed before me, we may take notice that the word satire is of a more general signification in Latin than in French or English; for amongst the Romans it was not only used for those discourses which decried vice or exposed folly, but for others also, where virtue was recommended. But in our modern languages we apply it only to invective poems, where the very name of satire is formidable to those persons who would appear to the world what they are not in themselves; for in English, to say satire is to mean reflection, as we use that word in the worst sense; or as the French call it, more properly, medisance. In the criticism of spelling, it ought to be with i, and not with y, to distinguish its true derivation from satura, not from Satyrus; and if this be so, then it is false spelled throughout this book, for here it is written "satyr," which having not considered at the first, I thought it not worth correcting afterwards. But the French are more nice, and never spell it any otherwise than "satire."

I am now arrived at the most difficult part of my undertaking, which is to compare Horace with Juvenal and Persius. It is observed by Rigaltius in his preface before Juvenal, written to Thuanus, that these three poets have all their particular partisans and favourers. Every commentator, as he has taken pains with any of them, thinks himself obliged to prefer his author to the other two; to find out their failings, and decry them, that he may make room for his own darling. Such is the partiality of mankind, to set up that interest which they have once espoused, though it be to the prejudice of truth, morality, and common justice, and especially in the productions of the brain. As authors generally think themselves the best poets, because they cannot go out of themselves to judge sincerely of their betters, so it is with critics, who, having first taken a liking to one of these poets, proceed to comment on him and to illustrate him; after which they fall in love with their own labours to that degree of blind fondness that at length they defend and exalt their author, not so much for his sake as for their own.

It is a folly of the same nature with that of the Romans themselves in their games of the circus. The spectators were divided in their factions betwixt the Veneti and the Prasini; some were for the charioteer in blue, and some for him in green. The colours themselves were but a fancy; but when once a man had taken pains to set out those of his party, and had been at the trouble of procuring voices for them, the case was altered: he was concerned for his own labour, and that so earnestly that disputes and quarrels, animosities, commotions, and bloodshed often happened; and in the declension of the Grecian empire, the very sovereigns themselves engaged in it, even when the barbarians were at their doors, and stickled for the preference of colours when the safety of their people was in question.

I am now myself on the brink of the same precipice; I have spent some time on the translation of Juvenal and Persius, and it behoves me to be wary, lest for that reason I should be partial to them, or take a prejudice against Horace. Yet on the other side I would not be like some of our judges, who would give the cause for a poor man right or wrong; for though that be an error on the better hand, yet it is still a partiality, and a rich man unheard cannot be concluded an oppressor. I remember a saying of King Charles II. on Sir Matthew Hale (who was doubtless an uncorrupt and upright man), that his servants were sure to be cast on any trial which was heard before him; not that he thought the judge was possibly to be bribed, but that his integrity might be too scrupulous, and that the causes of the Crown were always suspicious when the privileges of subjects were concerned.

It had been much fairer if the modern critics who have

embarked in the quarrels of their favourite authors had rather given to each his proper due without taking from another's heap to raise their own. There is praise enough for each of them in particular, without encroaching on his fellows, and detracting from them or enriching themselves with the spoils of others. But to come to particulars: Heinsius and Dacier are the most principal of those who raise Horace above Juvenal and Persius. Scaliger the father, Rigaltius, and many others debase Horace that they may set up Juvenal; and Casaubon, who is almost single, throws dirt on Juvenal and Horace that he may exalt Persius, whom he understood particularly well, and better than any of his former commentators, even Stelluti, who succeeded him. I will begin with him who, in my opinion, defends the weakest cause, which is that of Persius; and labouring, as Tacitus professes of his own writing, to divest myself of partiality or prejudice, consider Persius, not as a poet whom I have wholly translated, and who has cost me more labour and time than Juvenal, but according to what I judge to be his own merit, which I think not equal in the main to that of Juvenal or Horace, and yet in some things to be preferred to both of them.

First, then, for the verse; neither Casaubon himself, nor any for him, can defend either his numbers or the purity of his Latin. Casaubon gives this point for lost, and pretends not to justify either the measures or the words of Persius; he is evidently beneath Horace and Juvenal in both. Then, as his verse is scabrous and hobbling, and his words not everywhere well chosen (the purity of Latin being more corrupted than in the time of Juvenal, and consequently of Horace, who wrote when the language was in the height of its perfection), so his diction is hard, his figures are generally too bold and daring, and his tropes, particularly his metaphors, insufferably strained. In the third place, notwithstanding all the diligence of Casaubon, Stelluti, and a Scotch gentleman whom I have heard extremely commended for his illustrations of him, yet he is still obscure; whether he affected not to be understood but with difficulty; or whether the fear of his safety under Nero compelled him to this darkness in some places, or that it was occasioned by his close way of thinking, and the brevity of his style and crowding of his figures; or lastly, whether after so long a time many of his words have been corrupted, and many customs and stories relating to them lost to us; whether some of these reasons, or all, concurred to render him so cloudy, we may be bold to affirm that the best of commentators can but guess at his meaning in many passages, and none can be certain that he has divined rightly.

After all he was a young man, like his friend and contemporary Lucan—both of them men of extraordinary parts and great acquired knowledge, considering their youth; but neither of them had arrived to that maturity of judgment which is necessary to the accomplishing of a formed poet. And this consideration, as on the one hand it lays some imperfections to their charge, so on the other side it is a candid excuse for those failings which are incident to youth and inexperience; and we have more reason to wonder how they, who died before the thirtieth year of their age, could write so well and think so strongly, than to accuse them of those faults from which human nature (and more especially in youth) can never possibly be exempted. To consider Persius yet more closely: he rather insulted over vice and folly than exposed them like Juvenal and Horace; and as chaste and modest as he is esteemed, it cannot be denied but that in some places he is broad and fulsome, as the latter verses of the fourth satire and of the sixth sufficiently witness.

And it is to be believed that he who commits the same crime often and without necessity cannot but do it with some kind of pleasure. To come to a conclusion: he is manifestly below Horace because he borrows most of his greatest beauties from him; and Casaubon is so far from denying this that he has written a treatise purposely concerning it, wherein he shows a multitude of his translations from Horace, and his imitations of him, for the credit of his author, which he calls "Imitatio Horatiana."

To these defects (which I casually observed while I was translating this author) Scaliger has added others; he calls him in plain terms a silly writer and a trifler, full of ostentation of his learning, and, after all, unworthy to come into competition with Juvenal and Horace.

After such terrible accusations, it is time to hear what his patron Casaubon can allege in his defence. Instead of answering, he excuses for the most part; and when he cannot, accuses others of the same crimes. He deals with Scaliger as a modest scholar with a master. He compliments him with so much reverence that one would swear he feared him as much at least as he respected him. Scaliger will not allow Persius to have any wit; Casaubon interprets this in the mildest sense, and confesses his author was not good at turning things into a pleasant ridicule, or, in other words, that he was not a laughable writer. That he was ineptus, indeed, but that was non aptissimus ad jocandum; but that he was ostentatious of his learning, that by Scaliger's good favour he denies. Persius showed his learning, but was no boaster of it; he did ostendere, but not ostentare; and so, he says, did Scaliger (where, methinks, Casaubon turns it handsomely upon that supercilious critic, and silently insinuates that he himself was sufficiently vain-glorious and a boaster of his own knowledge). All the writings of this venerable censor, continues Casaubon, which are [Greek text which cannot be reproduced] (more golden than gold itself), are everywhere smelling of that thyme which, like a bee, he has gathered from ancient authors; but far be ostentation and vain-glory from a gentleman so well born and so nobly educated as Scaliger.

But, says Scaliger, he is so obscure that he has got himself the name of Scotinus—a dark writer. "Now," says Casaubon, "it is a wonder to me that anything could be obscure to the divine wit of Scaliger, from which nothing could be hidden." This is, indeed, a strong compliment, but no defence; and Casaubon, who could not but be sensible of his author's blind side, thinks it time to abandon a post that was untenable. He acknowledges that Persius is obscure in some places; but so is Plato, so is Thucydides; so are Pindar, Theocritus, and Aristophanes amongst the Greek poets; and even Horace and Juvenal, he might have added, amongst the Romans. The truth is, Persius is not sometimes, but generally obscure; and therefore Casaubon at last is forced to excuse him by alleging that it was se defendendo, for fear of Nero, and that he was commanded to write so cloudily by Cornutus, in virtue of holy obedience to his master. I cannot help my own opinion; I think Cornutus needed not to have read many lectures to him on that subject. Persius was an apt scholar, and when he was bidden to be obscure in some places where his life and safety were in question, took the same counsel for all his book, and never afterwards wrote ten lines together clearly. Casaubon, being upon this chapter, has not failed, we may be sure, of making a compliment to his own dear comment. "If Persius," says he, "be in himself obscure, yet my interpretation has made him intelligible." There is no question but he deserves that praise which he has given to himself; but the nature of the thing, as Lucretius says, will not admit of a perfect explanation. Besides many examples which I could urge, the very last verse of his last satire (upon which he particularly values himself in his preface) is not yet sufficiently explicated.

It is true, Holyday has endeavoured to justify his construction; but Stelluti is against it: and, for my part, I can have but a very dark notion of it. As for the chastity of his thoughts, Casaubon denies not but that one particular passage in the fourth satire is not only the most obscure, but the most obscene, of all his works. I understood it, but for that reason turned it over.

In defence of his boisterous metaphors he quotes Longinus, who accounts them as instruments of the sublime, fit to move and stir up the affections, particularly in narration; to which it may be replied that where the trope is far-fetched and hard, it is fit for nothing but to puzzle the understanding, and may be reckoned amongst those things of Demosthenes which AEschines called [Greek text which cannot be reproduced] not [Greek text which cannot be reproduced]—that is, prodigies, not words.

It must be granted to Casaubon that the knowledge of many things is lost in our modern ages which were of familiar notice to the ancients, and that satire is a poem of a difficult nature in itself, and is not written to vulgar readers; and (through the relation which it has to comedy) the frequent change of persons makes the sense perplexed, when we can but divine who it is that speaks—whether Persius himself, or his friend and monitor, or, in some places, a third person. But Casaubon comes back always to himself, and concludes that if Persius had not been obscure, there had been no need of him for an interpreter. Yet when he had once enjoined himself so hard a task, he then considered the Greek proverb, that he must Greek text which cannot be reproduced (either eat the whole snail or let it quite alone); and so he went through with his laborious task, as I have done with my difficult translation.

Thus far, my lord, you see it has gone very hard with Persius. I think he cannot be allowed to stand in competition either with Juvenal or Horace. Yet, for once, I will venture to be so vain as to affirm that none of his hard metaphors or forced expressions are in my translation. But more of this in its proper place, where I shall say somewhat in particular of our general performance in making these two authors English. In the meantime I think myself obliged to give Persius his undoubted due, and to acquaint the world, with Casaubon, in what he has equalled and in what excelled his two competitors.

A man who is resolved to praise an author with any appearance of justice must be sure to take him on the strongest side, and where he is least liable to exceptions; he is therefore obliged to choose his mediums accordingly. Casaubon (who saw that Persius could not laugh with a becoming grace, that he was not made for jesting, and that a merry conceit was not his talent) turned his feather, like an Indian, to another light, that he might give it the better gloss. "Moral doctrine," says he, "and urbanity or well-mannered wit are the two things which constitute the Roman satire; but of the two, that which is most essential to this poem, and is, as it were, the very soul which animates it, is the scourging of vice and exhortation to virtue." Thus wit, for a good reason, is already almost out of doors, and allowed only for an instrument—a kind of tool or a weapon, as he calls it—of which the satirist makes use in the compassing of his design. The end and aim of our three rivals is consequently the same; but by what methods they have prosecuted their intention is further to be considered. Satire is of the nature of moral philosophy, as being instructive; he therefore who instructs most usefully will carry the palm from his two antagonists.

The philosophy in which Persius was educated, and which he professes through his whole book, is the Stoic—the most noble, most generous, most beneficial to humankind amongst all the sects who have given us the rules of ethics, thereby to form a severe virtue in the soul, to raise in us an undaunted courage against the assaults of fortune, to esteem as nothing the things that are without us, because they are not in our power; not to value riches, beauty, honours, fame, or health any farther than as conveniences and so many helps to living as we ought, and doing good in our generation. In short, to be always happy while we possess our minds with a good conscience, are free from the slavery of vices, and conform our actions and conversation to the rules of right reason. See here, my lord, an epitome of Epictetus, the doctrine of Zeno, and the education of our Persius; and this he expressed, not only in all his satires, but in the manner of his life. I will not lessen this commendation of the Stoic philosophy by giving you an account of some absurdities in their doctrine, and some perhaps impieties (if we consider them by the standard of Christian faith).

Persius has fallen into none of them, and therefore is free from those imputations. What he teaches might be taught from pulpits with more profit to the audience than all the nice speculations of divinity and controversies concerning faith, which are more for the profit of the shepherd than for the edification of the flock. Passion, interest, ambition, and all their bloody consequences of discord and of war are banished from this doctrine. Here is nothing proposed but the quiet and tranquillity of the mind; virtue lodged at home, and afterwards diffused in her general effects to the improvement and good of humankind. And therefore I wonder not that the present Bishop of Salisbury has recommended this our author and the tenth satire of Juvenal (in his pastoral letter) to the serious perusal and practice of the divines in his diocese as the best commonplaces for their sermons, as the storehouses and magazines of moral virtues, from whence they may draw out, as they have occasion, all manner of assistance for the accomplishment of a virtuous life, which the Stoics have assigned for the great end and perfection of mankind. Herein, then, it is that Persius has excelled both Juvenal and Horace. He sticks to his own philosophy; he shifts not sides, like Horace (who is sometimes an Epicurean, sometimes a Stoic, sometimes an Eclectic, as his present humour leads him), nor declaims, like Juvenal, against vices more like an orator than a philosopher.

Persius is everywhere the same—true to the dogmas of his master. What he has learnt, he teaches vehemently; and what he teaches, that he practises himself. There is a spirit of sincerity in all he says; you may easily discern that he is in earnest, and is persuaded of that truth which he inculcates. In this I am of opinion that he excels Horace, who is commonly in jest, and laughs while he instructs; and is equal to Juvenal, who was as honest and serious as Persius, and more he could not be. Hitherto I have followed Casaubon, and enlarged upon him, because I am satisfied that he says no more than truth; the rest is almost all frivolous. For he says that Horace, being the son of a tax-gatherer (or a collector, as we call it) smells everywhere of the meanness of his birth and education; his conceits are vulgar, like the subjects of his satires; that he does plebeium sepere, and writes not with that elevation which becomes a satirist; that Persius, being nobly born and of an opulent family, had likewise the advantage of a better master (Cornutus being the most learned of his time, a man of a most holy life, the chief of the Stoic sect at Rome, and not only a great philosopher, but a poet himself, and in probability a coadjutor of Persius: that as for Juvenal, he was long a declaimer, came late to poetry, and had not been much conversant in philosophy.

It is granted that the father of Horace was libertinus—that is, one degree removed from his grandfather, who had been once a slave. But Horace, speaking of him, gives him the best character of a father which I ever read in history; and I wish a witty friend of mine, now living, had such another. He bred him in the best school, and with the best company of young noblemen; and Horace, by his gratitude to his memory, gives a certain testimony that his education was ingenuous. After this he formed himself abroad by the conversation of great men. Brutus found him at Athens, and was so pleased with him that he took him thence into the army, and made him Tribunus Militum (a colonel in a legion), which was the preferment of an old soldier.

All this was before his acquaintance with Maecenas, and his introduction into the court of Augustus, and the familiarity of that great emperor; which, had he not been well bred before, had been enough to civilise his conversation, and render him accomplished and knowing in all the arts of complacency and good behaviour; and, in short, an agreeable companion for the retired hours and privacies of a favourite who was first minister. So that upon the whole matter Persius may be acknowledged to be equal with him in those respects, though better born, and Juvenal inferior to both. If the advantage be anywhere, it is on the side of Horace, as much as the court of Augustus Caesar was superior to that of Nero. As for the subjects which they treated, it will appear hereafter that Horace wrote not vulgarly on vulgar subjects, nor always chose them. His style is constantly accommodated to his subject, either high or low. If his fault be too much lowness, that of Persius is the fault of the hardness of his metaphors and obscurity; and so they are equal in the failings of their style, where Juvenal manifestly triumphs over both of them.

The comparison betwixt Horace and Juvenal is more difficult, because their forces were more equal. A dispute has always been, and ever will continue, betwixt the favourers of the two poets. Non nostrum est tantas componere lites. I shall only venture to give my own opinion, and leave it for better judges to determine. If it be only argued in general which of them was the better poet, the victory is already gained on the side of Horace. Virgil himself must yield to him in the delicacy of his turns, his choice of words, and perhaps the purity of his Latin. He who says that Pindar is inimitable, is himself inimitable in his odes; but the contention betwixt these two great masters is for the prize of satire, in which controversy all the odes and epodes of Horace are to stand excluded. I say this because Horace has written many of them satirically against his private enemies; yet these, if justly considered, are somewhat of the nature of the Greek silli, which were invectives against particular sects and persons.

But Horace had purged himself of this choler before he entered on those discourses which are more properly called the Roman satire. He has not now to do with a Lyce, a Canidia, a Cassius Severus, or a Menas; but is to correct the vices and the follies of his time, and to give the rules of a happy and virtuous life. In a word, that former sort of satire which is known in England by the name of lampoon is a dangerous sort of weapon, and for the most part unlawful. We have no moral right on the reputation of other men; it is taking from them what we cannot restore to them. There are only two reasons for which we may be permitted to write lampoons, and I will not promise that they can always justify us. The first is revenge, when we have been affronted in the same nature, or have been anywise notoriously abused, and can make ourselves no other reparation. And yet we know that in Christian charity all offences are to be forgiven, as we expect the like pardon for those which we daily commit against Almighty God.

And this consideration has often made me tremble when I was saying our Saviour's prayer, for the plain condition of the forgiveness which we beg is the pardoning of others the offences which they have done to us; for which reason I have many times avoided the commission of that fault, even when I have been notoriously provoked. Let not this, my lord, pass for vanity in me; for it is truth. More libels have been written against me than almost any man now living; and I had reason on my side to have defended my own innocence. I speak not of my poetry, which I have wholly given up to the critics—let them use it as they please— posterity, perhaps, may be more favourable to me; for interest and passion will lie buried in another age, and partiality and prejudice be forgotten. I speak of my morals, which have been sufficiently aspersed—that only sort of reputation ought to be dear to every honest man, and is to me. But let the world witness for me that I have been often wanting to myself in that particular; I have seldom answered any scurrilous lampoon when it was in my power to have exposed my enemies; and, being naturally vindicative, have suffered in silence, and possessed my soul in quiet.

Anything, though never so little, which a man speaks of himself, in my opinion, is still too much; and therefore I will waive this subject, and proceed to give the second reason which may justify a poet when he writes against a particular person, and that is when he is become a public nuisance. All those whom Horace in his satires, and Persius and Juvenal have mentioned in theirs with a brand of infamy, are wholly such. It is an action of virtue to make examples of vicious men. They may and ought to be upbraided with their crimes and follies, both for their own amendment (if they are not yet incorrigible), and for the terror of others, to hinder them from falling into those enormities, which they see are so severely punished in the persons of others. The first reason was only an excuse for revenge; but this second is absolutely of a poet's office to perform. But how few lampooners are there now living who are capable of this duty!

When they come in my way, it is impossible sometimes to avoid reading them. But, good God! how remote they are in common justice from the choice of such persons as are the proper subject of satire, and how little wit they bring for the support of their injustice! The weaker sex is their most ordinary theme; and the best and fairest are sure to be the most severely handled. Amongst men, those who are prosperously unjust are entitled to a panegyric, but afflicted virtue is insolently stabbed with all manner of reproaches; no decency is considered, no fulsomeness omitted; no venom is wanting, as far as dulness can supply it, for there is a perpetual dearth of wit, a barrenness of good sense and entertainment. The neglect of the readers will soon put an end to this sort of scribbling. There can be no pleasantry where there is no wit, no impression can be made where there is no truth for the foundation. To conclude: they are like the fruits of the earth in this unnatural season; the corn which held up its head is spoiled with rankness, but the greater part of the harvest is laid along, and little of good income and wholesome nourishment is received into the barns. This is almost a digression, I confess to your lordship; but a just indignation forced it from me. Now I have removed this rubbish I will return to the comparison of Juvenal and Horace.

I would willingly divide the palm betwixt them upon the two heads of profit and delight, which are the two ends of poetry in general. It must be granted by the favourers of Juvenal that Horace is the more copious and more profitable in his instructions of human life; but in my particular opinion, which I set not up for a standard to better judgments, Juvenal is the more delightful author. I am profited by both, I am pleased with both; but I owe more to Horace for my instruction, and more to Juvenal for my pleasure. This, as I said, is my particular taste of these two authors. They who will have either of them to excel the other in both qualities, can scarce give better reasons for their opinion than I for mine. But all unbiassed readers will conclude that my moderation is not to be condemned; to such impartial men I must appeal, for they who have already formed their judgment may justly stand suspected of prejudice; and though all who are my readers will set up to be my judges, I enter my caveat against them, that they ought not so much as to be of my jury; or; if they be admitted, it is but reason that they should first hear what I have to urge in the defence of my opinion.

That Horace is somewhat the better instructor of the two is proved from hence—that his instructions are more general, Juvenal's more limited. So that, granting that the counsels which they give are equally good for moral use, Horace, who gives the most various advice, and most applicable to all occasions which can occur to us in the course of our lives—as including in his discourses not only all the rules of morality, but also of civil conversation—is undoubtedly to be preferred to him, who is more circumscribed in his instructions, makes them to fewer people, and on fewer occasions, than the other. I may be pardoned for using an old saying, since it is true and to the purpose: Bonum quo communius, eo melius. Juvenal, excepting only his first satire, is in all the rest confined to the exposing of some particular vice; that he lashes, and there he sticks. His sentences are truly shining and instructive; but they are sprinkled here and there.

Horace is teaching us in every line, and is perpetually moral; he had found out the skill of Virgil to hide his sentences, to give you the virtue of them without showing them in their full extent, which is the ostentation of a poet, and not his art. And this Petronius charges on the authors of his time as a vice of writing, which was then growing on the age: ne sententiae extra corpus orationis emineant; he would have them weaved into the body of the work, and not appear embossed upon it, and striking directly on the reader's view. Folly was the proper quarry of Horace, and not vice; and as there are but few notoriously wicked men in comparison with a shoal of fools and fops, so it is a harder thing to make a man wise than to make him honest; for the will is only to be reclaimed in the one, but the understanding is to be informed in the other. There are blind sides and follies even in the professors of moral philosophy, and there is not any one sect of them that Horace has not exposed; which, as it was not the design of Juvenal, who was wholly employed in lashing vices (some of them the most enormous that can be imagined), so perhaps it was not so much his talent.

"Omne vafer vitium ridenti Flaccus amico
Tangit, et admissus circum praecordia ludit."

This was the commendation which Persius gave him; where by vitium he means those little vices which we call follies, the defects of human understanding, or at most the peccadilloes of life, rather than the tragical vices to which men are hurried by their unruly passions and exorbitant desires. But in the word omne, which is universal, he concludes with me that the divine wit of Horace left nothing untouched; that he entered into the inmost recesses of nature; found out the imperfections even of the most wise and grave, as well as of the common people; discovering even in the great Trebatius (to whom he addresses the first satire) his hunting after business and following the court, as well as in the prosecutor Crispinus, his impertinence and importunity. It is true, he exposes Crispinus openly as a common nuisance; but he rallies the other, as a friend, more finely. The exhortations of Persius are confined to noblemen, and the Stoic philosophy is that alone which he recommends to them; Juvenal exhorts to particular virtues, as they are opposed to those vices against which he declaims; but Horace laughs to shame all follies, and insinuates virtue rather by familiar examples than by the severity of precepts.

This last consideration seems to incline the balance on the side of Horace, and to give him the preference to Juvenal, not only in profit, but in pleasure. But, after all, I must confess that the delight which Horace gives me is but languishing (be pleased still to understand that I speak of my own taste only); he may ravish other men, but I am too stupid and insensible to be tickled. Where he barely grins himself, and, as Scaliger says, only shows his white teeth, he cannot provoke me to any laughter. His urbanity—that is, his good manners—are to be commended; but his wit is faint, and his salt (if I may dare to say so) almost insipid. Juvenal is of a more vigorous and masculine wit; he gives me as much pleasure as I can bear; he fully satisfies my expectation; he treats his subject home; his spleen is raised, and he raises mine. I have the pleasure of concernment in all he says; he drives his reader along with him, and when he is at the end of his way, I willingly stop with him. If he went another stage, it would be too far; it would make a journey of a progress, and turn delight into fatigue.

When he gives over, it is a sign the subject is exhausted, and the wit of man can carry it no farther. If a fault can be justly found in him, it is that he is sometimes too luxuriant, too redundant; says more than he needs, like my friend "the Plain Dealer," but never more than pleases. Add to this that his thoughts are as just as those of Horace, and much more elevated; his expressions are sonorous and more noble; his verse more numerous; and his words are suitable to his thoughts, sublime and lofty. All these contribute to the pleasure of the reader; and the greater the soul of him who reads, his transports are the greater. Horace is always on the amble, Juvenal on the gallop, but his way is perpetually on carpet-ground. He goes with more impetuosity than Horace, but as securely; and the swiftness adds a more lively agitation to the spirits. The low style of Horace is according to his subject—that is, generally grovelling. I question not but he could have raised it, for the first epistle of the second book, which he writes to Augustus (a most instructive satire concerning poetry), is of so much dignity in the words, and of so much elegancy in the numbers, that the author plainly shows the sermo pedestris in his other satires was rather his choice than his necessity.

He was a rival to Lucilius, his predecessor, and was resolved to surpass him in his own manner. Lucilius, as we see by his remaining fragments, minded neither his style, nor his numbers, nor his purity of words, nor his run of verse. Horace therefore copes with him in that humble way of satire, writes under his own force, and carries a dead weight, that he may match his competitor in the race. This, I imagine, was the chief reason why he minded only the clearness of his satire, and the cleanness of expression, without ascending to those heights to which his own vigour might have carried him. But limiting his desires only to the conquest of Lucilius, he had his ends of his rival, who lived before him, but made way for a new conquest over himself by Juvenal his successor. He could not give an equal pleasure to his reader, because he used not equal instruments.

The fault was in the tools, and not in the workman. But versification and numbers are the greatest pleasures of poetry. Virgil knew it, and practised both so happily that, for aught I know, his greatest excellency is in his diction. In all other parts of poetry he is faultless, but in this he placed his chief perfection. And give me leave, my lord, since I have here an apt occasion, to say that Virgil could have written sharper satires than either Horace or Juvenal if he would have employed his talent that way. I will produce a verse and half of his, in one of his Eclogues, to justify my opinion, and with commas after every word, to show that he has given almost as many lashes as he has written syllables. It is against a bad poet, whose ill verses he describes

"Non tu, in triviis indocte, solebas
Stridenti, miserum, stipula, disperdere carmen?"

But to return to my purpose. When there is anything deficient in numbers and sound, the reader is uneasy and unsatisfied; he wants something of his complement, desires somewhat which he finds not: and this being the manifest defect of Horace, it is no wonder that, finding it supplied in Juvenal, we are more delighted with him. And besides this, the sauce of Juvenal is more poignant, to create in us an appetite of reading him. The meat of Horace is more nourishing, but the cookery of Juvenal more exquisite; so that, granting Horace to be the more general philosopher, we cannot deny that Juvenal was the greater poet—I mean, in satire. His thoughts are sharper, his indignation against vice is more vehement, his spirit has more of the commonwealth genius; he treats tyranny, and all the vices attending it, as they deserve, with the utmost rigour; and consequently a noble soul is better pleased with a zealous vindicator of Roman liberty than with a temporising poet, a well-mannered court slave, and a man who is often afraid of laughing in the right place—who is ever decent, because he is naturally servile.

After all, Horace had the disadvantage of the times in which he lived; they were better for the man, but worse for the satirist. It is generally said that those enormous vices which were practised under the reign of Domitian were unknown in the time of Augustus Caesar; that therefore Juvenal had a larger field than Horace. Little follies were out of doors when oppression was to be scourged instead of avarice; it was no longer time to turn into ridicule the false opinions of philosophers when the Roman liberty was to be asserted. There was more need of a Brutus in Domitian's days to redeem or mend, than of a Horace, if he had then been living, to laugh at a fly-catcher. This reflection at the same time excuses Horace, but exalts Juvenal. I have ended, before I was aware, the comparison of Horace and Juvenal upon the topics of instruction and delight; and indeed I may safely here conclude that commonplace: for if we make Horace our minister of state in satire, and Juvenal of our private pleasures, I think the latter has no ill bargain of it. Let profit have the pre-eminence of honour in the end of poetry; pleasure, though but the second in degree, is the first in favour. And who would not choose to be loved better rather than to be more esteemed! But I am entered already upon another topic, which concerns the particular merits of these two satirists. However, I will pursue my business where I left it, and carry it farther than that common observation of the several ages in which these authors flourished.

When Horace writ his satires, the monarchy of his Caesar was in its newness, and the government but just made easy to the conquered people. They could not possibly have forgotten the usurpation of that prince upon their freedom, nor the violent methods which he had used in the compassing of that vast design; they yet remembered his proscriptions, and the slaughter of so many noble Romans their defenders—amongst the rest, that horrible action of his when he forced Livia from the arms of her husband (who was constrained to see her married, as Dion relates the story), and, big with child as she was, conveyed to the bed of his insulting rival. The same Dion Cassius gives us another instance of the crime before mentioned— that Cornelius Sisenna, being reproached in full senate with the licentious conduct of his wife, returned this answer: that he had married her by the counsel of Augustus (intimating, says my author, that Augustus had obliged him to that marriage, that he might under that covert have the more free access to her).

His adulteries were still before their eyes, but they must be patient where they had not power. In other things that emperor was moderate enough; propriety was generally secured, and the people entertained with public shows and donatives, to make them more easily digest their lost liberty. But Augustus, who was conscious to himself of so many crimes which he had committed, thought in the first place to provide for his own reputation by making an edict against lampoons and satires, and the authors of those defamatory writings, which my author Tacitus, from the law-term, calls famosos libellos.

In the first book of his Annals he gives the following account of it in these words:-Primus Augustus cognitionem de famosis libellis, specie legis ejus, tractavit; commotus Cassii Severi libidine, qua viros faeminasque illustres procacibus scriptis diffamaverat. Thus in English:-"Augustus was the first who, under the colour of that law, took cognisance of lampoons, being provoked to it by the petulancy of Cassius Severus, who had defamed many illustrious persons of both sexes in his writings." The law to which Tacitus refers was Lex laesae majestatis; commonly called, for the sake of brevity, majestas; or, as we say, high-treason. He means not that this law had not been enacted formerly (for it had been made by the Decemviri, and was inscribed amongst the rest in the Twelve Tables, to prevent the aspersion of the Roman majesty, either of the people themselves, or their religion, or their magistrates; and the infringement of it was capital—that is, the offender was whipped to death with the fasces which were borne before their chief officers of Rome), but Augustus was the first who restored that intermitted law.

By the words "under colour of that law" he insinuates that Augustus caused it to be executed on pretence of those libels which were written by Cassius Severus against the nobility, but in truth to save himself from such defamatory verses. Suetonius likewise makes mention of it thus:-Sparsos de se in curia famosos libellos, nec exparit, et magna cura redarguit. Ac ne requisitis quidem auctoribus, id modo censuit, cognoscendum posthac de iis qui libellos aut carmina ad infamiam cujuspiam sub alieno nomine edant. "Augustus was not afraid of libels," says that author, "yet he took all care imaginable to have them answered, and then decreed that for the time to come the authors of them should be punished." But Aurelius makes it yet more clear, according to my sense, that this emperor for his own sake durst not permit them:-Fecit id Augustus in speciem, et quasi gratificaretur populo

Romano, et primoribus urbis; sed revera ut sibi consuleret: nam habuit in animo comprimere nimiam quorundam procacitatem in loquendo, a qua nec ipse exemptus fuit. Nam suo nomine compescere erat invidiosum, sub alieno facile et utile. Ergo specie legis tractavit, quasi populi Romani majestas infamaretur. This, I think, is a sufficient comment on that passage of Tacitus. I will add only by the way that the whole family of the Caesars and all their relations were included in the law, because the majesty of the Romans in the time of the Empire was wholly in that house: Omnia Caesar erat; they were all accounted sacred who belonged to him. As for Cassius Severus, he was contemporary with Horace, and was the same poet against whom he writes in his epodes under this title, In Cassium Severum, maledicum poctam—perhaps intending to kill two crows, according to our proverb, with one stone, and revenge both himself and his emperor together.

From hence I may reasonably conclude that Augustus, who was not altogether so good as he was wise, had some by-respect in the enacting of this law; for to do anything for nothing was not his maxim. Horace, as he was a courtier, complied with the interest of his master; and, avoiding the lashing of greater crimes, confined himself to the ridiculing of petty vices and common follies, excepting only some reserved cases in his odes and epodes of his own particular quarrels (which either with permission of the magistrate or without it, every man will revenge, though I say not that he should; for prior laesit is a good excuse in the civil law if Christianity had not taught us to forgive).

However, he was not the proper man to arraign great vices; at least, if the stories which we hear of him are true—that he practised some which I will not here mention, out of honour to him. It was not for a Clodius to accuse adulterers, especially when Augustus was of that number. So that, though his age was not exempted from the worst of villainies, there was no freedom left to reprehend them by reason of the edict; and our poet was not fit to represent them in an odious character, because himself was dipped in the same actions. Upon this account, without further insisting on the different tempers of Juvenal and Horace, I conclude that the subjects which Horace chose for satire are of a lower nature than those of which Juvenal has written.

Thus I have treated, in a new method, the comparison betwixt Horace, Juvenal, and Persius. Somewhat of their particular manner, belonging to all of them, is yet remaining to be considered. Persius was grave, and particularly opposed his gravity to lewdness, which was the predominant vice in Nero's court at the time when he published his satires, which was before that emperor fell into the excess of cruelty. Horace was a mild admonisher, a court satirist, fit for the gentle times of Augustus, and more fit for the reasons which I have already given. Juvenal was as proper for his times as they for theirs; his was an age that deserved a more severe chastisement; vices were more gross and open, more flagitious, more encouraged by the example of a tyrant, and more protected by his authority. Therefore, wheresoever Juvenal mentions Nero, he means Domitian, whom he dares not attack in his own person, but scourges him by proxy. Heinsius urges in praise of Horace that, according to the ancient art and law of satire, it should be nearer to comedy than to tragedy; not declaiming against vice, but only laughing at it. Neither Persius nor Juvenal was ignorant of this, for they had both studied Horace. And the thing itself is plainly true. But as they had read Horace, they had likewise read Lucilius, of whom Persius says, Secuit urbem;... et genuinum fregit in illis; meaning Mutius and Lupus; and Juvenal also mentions him in these words

"Ense velut stricto, quoties Lucilius ardens
Infremuit, rubet auditor, cui frigida mens est
Criminibus, tacita sulant praecordia culpa."

So that they thought the imitation of Lucilius was more proper to their purpose than that of Horace. "They changed satire," says Holyday, "but they changed it for the better; for the business being to reform great vices, chastisement goes farther than admonition; whereas a perpetual grin, like that of Horace, does rather anger than amend a man."

Thus far that learned critic Barten Holyday, whose interpretation and illustrations of Juvenal are as excellent as the verse of his translation and his English are lame and pitiful; for it is not enough to give us the meaning of a poet (which I acknowledge him to have performed most faithfully) but he must also imitate his genius and his numbers as far as the English will come up to the elegance of the original. In few words, it is only for a poet to translate a poet. Holyday and Stapleton had not enough considered this when they attempted Juvenal; but I forbear reflections: only I beg leave to take notice of this sentence, where Holyday says, "a perpetual grin, like that of Horace, rather angers than amends a man." I cannot give him up the manner of Horace in low satire so easily.

Let the chastisements of Juvenal be never so necessary for his new kind of satire, let him declaim as wittily and sharply as he pleases, yet still the nicest and most delicate touches of satire consist in fine raillery. This, my lord, is your particular talent, to which even Juvenal could not arrive. It is not reading, it is not imitation of, an author which can produce this fineness; it must be inborn; it must proceed from a genius, and particular way of thinking, which is not to be taught, and therefore not to be imitated by him who has it not from nature. How easy it is to call rogue and villain, and that wittily! but how hard to make a man appear a fool, a blockhead, or a knave, without using any of those opprobrious terms! To spare the grossness of the names, and to do the thing yet more severely, is to draw a full face and to make the nose and cheeks stand out, and yet not to employ any depth of shadowing.

This is the mystery of that noble trade, which yet no master can teach to his apprentice; he may give the rules, but the scholar is never the nearer in his practice. Neither is it true that this fineness of raillery is offensive; a witty man is tickled, while he is hurt in this manner; and a fool feels it not. The occasion of an offence may possibly be given, but he cannot take it. If it be granted that in effect this way does more mischief; that a man is secretly wounded, and though he be not sensible himself, yet the malicious world will find it for him; yet there is still a vast difference betwixt the slovenly butchering of a man, and the fineness of a stroke that separates the head from the body and leaves it standing in its place. A man may be capable, as Jack Ketch's wife said of his servant, of a plain piece of work, a bare hanging; but to make a malefactor die sweetly was only belonging to her husband. I wish I could apply it to myself, if the reader would be kind enough to think it belongs to me.

The character of Zimri, in my "Absalom" is, in my opinion, worth the whole poem; it is not bloody, but it is ridiculous enough; and he for whom it was intended was too witty to resent it as an injury. If I had railed, I might have suffered for it justly; but I managed my own work more happily, perhaps more dexterously. I avoided the mention of great crimes, and applied myself to the representing of blind-sides and little extravagances; to which the wittier a man is, he is generally the more obnoxious. It succeeded as I wished; the jest went round, and he was laughed at in his turn who began the frolic. And thus, my lord, you see I have preferred the manner of Horace and of your lordship in this kind of satire to that of Juvenal, and, I think, reasonably. Holyday ought not to have arraigned so great an author for that which was his excellency and his merit; or, if he did, on such a palpable mistake he might expect that some one might possibly arise (either in his own time, or after him) to rectify his error, and restore to Horace that commendation of which he has so unjustly robbed him. And let the manes of Juvenal forgive me if I say that this way of Horace was the best for amending manners, as it is the most difficult.

His was an ense rescindendum; but that of Horace was a pleasant cure, with all the limbs preserved entire, and, as our mountebanks tell us in their bills, without keeping the patient within doors for a day. What they promise only, Horace has effectually performed. Yet I contradict not the proposition which I formerly advanced. Juvenal's times required a more painful kind of operation; but if he had lived in the age of Horace, I must needs affirm that he had it not about him. He took the method which was prescribed him by his own genius, which was sharp and eager; he could not railly, but he could declaim: and as his provocations were great, he has revenged them tragically. This, notwithstanding I am to say another word which, as true as it is, will yet displease the partial admirers of our Horace; I have hinted it before, but it is time for me now to speak more plainly.

This manner of Horace is indeed the best; but Horace has not executed it altogether so happily—at least, not often. The manner of Juvenal is confessed to be inferior to the former; but Juvenal has excelled him in his performance. Juvenal has railed more wittily than Horace has rallied. Horace means to make his reader laugh, but he is not sure of his experiment. Juvenal always intends to move your indignation, and he always brings about his purpose. Horace, for aught I know, might have tickled the people of his age, but amongst the moderns he is not so successful. They who say he entertains so pleasantly, may perhaps value themselves on the quickness of their own understandings, that they can see a jest farther off than other men; they may find occasion of laughter in the wit-battle of the two buffoons Sarmentus and Cicerrus, and hold their sides for fear of bursting when Rupilius and Persius are scolding. For my own part, I can only like the characters of all four, which are judiciously given; but for my heart I cannot so much as smile at their insipid raillery.

I see not why Persius should call upon Brutus to revenge him on his adversary; and that because he had killed Julius Caesar for endeavouring to be a king, therefore he should be desired to murder Rupilius, only because his name was Mr. King. A miserable clench, in my opinion, for Horace to record; I have heard honest Mr. Swan make many a better, and yet have had the grace to hold my countenance. But it may be puns were then in fashion, as they were wit in the sermons of the last age, and in the court of King Charles the Second. I am sorry to say it, for the sake of Horace; but certain it is, he has no fine palate who can feed so heartily on garbage. But I have already wearied myself, and doubt not but I have tired your lordship's patience, with this long, rambling, and, I fear, trivial discourse. Upon the one-half of the merits, that is, pleasure, I cannot but conclude that Juvenal was the better satirist. They who will descend into his particular praises may find them at large in the dissertation of the learned Rigaltius to Thuanus. As for Persius, I have given the reasons why I think him inferior to both of them; yet I have one thing to add on that subject.

Barten Holyday, who translated both Juvenal and Persius, has made this distinction betwixt them, which is no less true than witty— that in Persius, the difficulty is to find a meaning; in Juvenal, to choose a meaning; so crabbed is Persius, and so copious is Juvenal; so much the understanding is employed in one, and so much the judgment in the other; so difficult is it to find any sense in the former, and the best sense of the latter. If, on the other side, any one suppose I have commended Horace below his merit, when I have allowed him but the second place, I desire him to consider if Juvenal (a man of excellent natural endowments, besides the advantages of diligence and study, and coming after him and building upon his foundations) might not probably, with all these helps, surpass him; and whether it be any dishonour to Horace to be thus surpassed, since no art or science is at once begun and perfected but that it must pass first through many hands and even through several ages.

If Lucilius could add to Ennius and Horace to Lucilius, why, without any diminution to the fame of Horace, might not Juvenal give the last perfection to that work? Or rather, what disreputation is it to Horace that Juvenal excels in the tragical satire, as Horace does in the comical? I have read over attentively both Heinsius and Dacier in their commendations of Horace, but I can find no more in either of them for the preference of him to Juvenal than the instructive part (the part of wisdom, and not that of pleasure), which therefore is here allowed him, notwithstanding what Scaliger and Rigaltius have pleaded to the contrary for Juvenal. And to show I am impartial I will here translate what Dacier has said on that subject:-"I cannot give a more just idea of the two books of satires made by Horace than by comparing them to the statues of the Sileni, to which Alcibiades compares Socrates in the Symposium. They were figures which had nothing of agreeable, nothing of beauty on their outside; but when any one took the pains to open them and search into them, he there found the figures of all the deities. So in the shape that Horace presents himself to us in his satires we see nothing at the first view which deserves our attention; it seems that he is rather an amusement for children than for the serious consideration of men. But when we take away his crust, and that which hides him from our sight, when we discover him to the bottom, then we find all the divinities in a full assembly—that is to say, all the virtues which ought to be the continual exercise of those who seriously endeavour to correct their vices."

It is easy to observe that Dacier, in this noble similitude, has confined the praise of his author wholly to the instructive part the commendation turns on this, and so does that which follows:-"In these two books of satire it is the business of Horace to instruct us how to combat our vices, to regulate our passions, to follow nature, to give bounds to our desires, to distinguish betwixt truth and falsehood, and betwixt our conceptions of things and things themselves; to come back from our prejudicate opinions, to understand exactly the principles and motives of all our actions; and to avoid the ridicule into which all men necessarily fall who are intoxicated with those notions which they have received from their masters, and which they obstinately retain without examining whether or no they be founded on right reason.

"In a word, he labours to render us happy in relation to ourselves; agreeable and faithful to our friends; and discreet, serviceable, and well-bred in relation to those with whom we are obliged to live and to converse. To make his figures intelligible, to conduct his readers through the labyrinth of some perplexed sentence or obscure parenthesis, is no great matter; and, as Epictetus says, there is nothing of beauty in all this, or what is worthy of a prudent man. The principal business, and which is of most importance to us, is to show the use, the reason, and the proof of his precepts.

"They who endeavour not to correct themselves according to so exact a model are just like the patients who have open before them a book of admirable receipts for their diseases, and please themselves with reading it without comprehending the nature of the remedies or how to apply them to their cure."

Let Horace go off with these encomiums, which he has so well deserved. To conclude the contention betwixt our three poets I will use the words of Virgil in his fifth AEneid, where AEneas proposes the rewards of the foot-race to the three first who should reach the goal:-

"Tres praemia primi...Accipient, flauaque caput nectentur oliva."Let these three ancients be preferred to all the moderns as first arriving at the goal; let them all be crowned as victors with the wreath that properly belongs to satire. But after that, with this distinction amongst themselves:-"Primus equum phaleris insignem victor habeto."

Let Juvenal ride first in triumph: "Alter Amazoniam pharetram, plenamque sagittis Threiciis, lato quam circumplectitur auro Balteus, et tereti subnectit fibula gemma."

Let Horace, who is the second (and but just the second), carry off the quiver and the arrows as the badges of his satire, and the golden belt and the diamond button: "Tertius Argolico hoc clypeo contentus abito."

And let Persius, the last of the first three worthies, be contented with this Grecian shield, and with victory—not only over all the Grecians, who were ignorant of the Roman satire—but over all the moderns in succeeding ages, excepting Boileau and your lordship.

And thus I have given the history of satire, and derived it as far as from Ennius to your lordship—that is, from its first rudiments of barbarity to its last polishing and perfection; which is, with Virgil, in his address to Augustus-

"Nomen fama tot ferre per annos,...
Tithoni prima quot abest ab origine Caesar."

I said only from Ennius, but I may safely carry it higher, as far as Livius Andronicus, who, as I have said formerly, taught the first play at Rome in the year CCCCCXIV. I have since desired my learned friend Mr. Maidwell to compute the difference of times betwixt Aristophanes and Livius Andronicus; and he assures me from the best chronologers that Plutus, the last of Aristophanes' plays, was represented at Athens in the year of the 97th Olympiad, which agrees with the year urbis conditae CCCLXIV. So that the difference of years betwixt Aristophanes and Andronicus is 150; from whence I have probably deduced that Livius Andronicus, who was a Grecian, had read the plays of the old comedy, which were satirical, and also of the new; for Menander was fifty years before him, which must needs be a great light to him in his own plays that were of the satirical nature. That the Romans had farces before this, it is true; but then they had no communication with Greece; so that Andronicus was the first who wrote after the manner of the old comedy, in his plays: he was imitated by Ennius about thirty years afterwards. Though the former writ fables, the latter, speaking properly, began the Roman satire, according to that description which Juvenal gives of it in his first:-

> *"Quicquid agunt homines, votum, timor, ira voluptas,*
> *Gaudia, discurses, nostri est farrago libelli."*

This is that in which I have made hold to differ from Casaubon, Rigaltius, Dacier, and indeed from all the modern critics—that not Ennius, but Andronicus, was the first who, by the archaea comedia of the Greeks, added many beauties to the first rude and barbarous Roman satire; which sort of poem, though we had not derived from Rome, yet nature teaches it mankind in all ages and in every country.

It is but necessary that, after so much has been said of satire, some definition of it should be given. Heinsius, in his Dissertations on Horace, makes it for me in these words:- "Satire is a kind of poetry, without a series of action, invented for the purging of our minds; in which human vices, ignorance, and errors, and all things besides which are produced from them in every man, are severely reprehended—partly dramatically, partly simply, and sometimes in both kinds of speaking, but for the most part figuratively and occultly; consisting, in a low familiar way, chiefly in a sharp and pungent manner of speech, but partly also in a facetious and civil way of jesting, by which either hatred or laughter or indignation is moved." Where I cannot but observe that this obscure and perplexed definition, or rather description of satire, is wholly accommodated to the Horatian way, and excluding the works of Juvenal and Persius as foreign from that kind of poem. The clause in the beginning of it, "without a series of action," distinguishes satire properly from stage-plays, which are all of one action and one continued series of action. The end or scope of satire is to purge the passions; so far it is common to the satires of Juvenal and Persius.

The rest which follows is also generally belonging to all three, till he comes upon us with the excluding clause, "consisting, in a low familiar way of speech" which is the proper character of Horace, and from which the other two (for their honour be it spoken) are far distant. But how come lowness of style and the familiarity of words to be so much the propriety of satire that without them a poet can be no more a satirist than without risibility he can be a man? Is the fault of Horace to be made the virtue and standing rule of this poem? Is the grande sophos of Persius, and the sublimity of Juvenal, to be circumscribed with the meanness of words and vulgarity of expression?

If Horace refused the pains of numbers and the loftiness of figures are they bound to follow so ill a precedent? Let him walk afoot with his pad in his hand for his own pleasure, but let not them be accounted no poets who choose to mount and show their horsemanship. Holyday is not afraid to say that there was never such a fall as from his odes to his satires, and that he, injuriously to himself, untuned his harp. The majestic way of Persius and Juvenal was new when they began it, but it is old to us; and what poems have not, with time, received an alteration in their fashion?—"which alteration," says Holyday, "is to after-times as good a warrant as the first." Has not Virgil changed the manners of Homer's heroes in his AEneis? Certainly he has, and for the better; for Virgil's age was more civilised and better bred, and he writ according to the politeness of Rome under the reign of Augustus Caesar, not to the rudeness of Agamemnon's age or the times of Homer. Why should we offer to confine free spirits to one form when we cannot so much as confine our bodies to one fashion of apparel? Would not Donne's satires, which abound with so much wit, appear more charming if he had taken care of his words and of his numbers? But he followed Horace so very close that of necessity he must fall with him; and I may safely say it of this present age, that if we are not so great wits as Donne, yet certainly we are better poets.

But I have said enough, and it may be too much, on this subject. Will your lordship be pleased to prolong my audience only so far till I tell you my own trivial thoughts how a modern satire should be made? I will not deviate in the least from the precepts and examples of the ancients, who were always our best masters; I will only illustrate them, and discover some of the hidden beauties in their designs, that we thereby may form our own in imitation of them. Will you please but to observe that Persius, the least in dignity of all the three, has, notwithstanding, been the first who has discovered to us this important secret in the designing of a perfect satire—that it ought only to treat of one subject; to be confined to one particular theme, or, at least, to one principally? If other vices occur in the management of the chief, they should only be transiently lashed, and not be insisted on, so as to make the design double. As in a play of the English fashion which we call a tragicomedy, there is to be but one main design, and though there be an under-plot or second walk of comical characters and adventures, yet they are subservient to the chief fable, carried along under it and helping to it, so that the drama may not seem a monster with two heads.

Thus the Copernican system of the planets makes the moon to be moved by the motion of the earth, and carried about her orb as a dependent of hers. Mascardi, in his discourse of the "Doppia Favola," or double tale in plays, gives an instance of it in the famous pastoral of Guarini, called Il Pastor Fido, where Corisca and the Satyr are the under-parts; yet we may observe that Corisca is brought into the body of the plot and made subservient to it. It is certain that the divine wit of Horace was not ignorant of this rule—that a play, though it consists of many parts, must yet be one in the action, and must drive on the accomplishment of one design—for he gives this very precept, Sit quod vis simplex duntaxat, et unum; yet he seems not much to mind it in his satires, many of them consisting of more arguments than one, and the second without dependence on the first. Casaubon has observed this before me in his preference of Persius to Horace, and will have his own beloved author to be the first who found out and introduced this method of confining himself to one subject.

I know it may be urged in defence of Horace that this unity is not necessary, because the very word satura signifies a dish plentifully stored with all variety of fruits and grains. Yet Juvenal, who calls his poems a farrago (which is a word of the same signification with satura), has chosen to follow the same method of Persius and not of Horace; and Boileau, whose example alone is a sufficient authority, has wholly confined himself in all his satires to this unity of design. That variety which is not to be found in any one satire is at least in many, written on several occasions; and if variety be of absolute necessity in every one of them, according to the etymology of the word, yet it may arise naturally from one subject, as it is diversely treated in the several subordinate branches of it, all relating to the chief. It may be illustrated accordingly with variety of examples in the subdivisions of it, and with as many precepts as there are members of it, which all together may complete that olla or hotch-potch which is properly a satire. Under this unity of theme or subject is comprehended another rule for perfecting the design of true satire.

The poet is bound, and that ex officio, to give his reader some one precept of moral virtue, and to caution him against some one particular vice or folly. Other virtues, subordinate to the first, may be recommended under that chief head, and other vices or follies may be scourged, besides that which he principally intends; but he is chiefly to inculcate one virtue, and insist on that. Thus Juvenal, in every satire excepting the first, ties himself to one principal instructive point, or to the shunning of moral evil. Even in the sixth, which seems only an arraignment of the whole sex of womankind, there is a latent admonition to avoid ill women, by showing how very few who are virtuous and good are to be found amongst them. But this, though the wittiest of all his satires, has yet the least of truth or instruction in it; he has run himself into his old declamatory way, and almost forgotten that he was now setting up for a moral poet.

Persius is never wanting to us in some profitable doctrine, and in exposing the opposite vices to it. His kind of philosophy is one, which is the Stoic, and every satire is a comment on one particular dogma of that sect, unless we will except the first, which is against bad writers; and yet even there he forgets not the precepts of the "porch." In general, all virtues are everywhere to be praised and recommended to practice, and all vices to be reprehended and made either odious or ridiculous, or else there is a fundamental error in the whole design.

I have already declared who are the only persons that are the adequate object of private satire, and who they are that may properly be exposed by name for public examples of vices and follies, and therefore I will trouble your lordship no further with them. Of the best and finest manner of satire, I have said enough in the comparison betwixt Juvenal and Horace; it is that sharp well-mannered way of laughing a folly out of countenance, of which your lordship is the best master in this age. I will proceed to the versification which is most proper for it, and add somewhat to what I have said already on that subject. The sort of verse which is called "burlesque," consisting of eight syllables or four feet, is that which our excellent Hudibras has chosen. I ought to have mentioned him before when I spoke of Donne, but by a slip of an old man's memory he was forgotten. The worth of his poem is too well known to need my commendation, and he is above my censure. His satire is of the Varronian kind, though unmixed with prose.

The choice of his numbers is suitable enough to his design as he has managed it; but in any other hand the shortness of his verse, and the quick returns of rhyme, had debased the dignity of style. And besides, the double rhyme (a necessary companion of burlesque writing) is not so proper for manly satire, for it turns earnest too much to jest, and gives us a boyish kind of pleasure. It tickles awkwardly, with a kind of pain to the best sort of readers; we are pleased ungratefully, and, if I may say so, against our liking. We thank him not for giving us that unseasonable delight, when we know he could have given us a better and more solid. He might have left that task to others who, not being able to put in thought, can only makes us grin with the excrescence of a word of two or three syllables in the close. It is, indeed, below so great a master to make use of such a little instrument. But his good sense is perpetually shining through all he writes; it affords us not the time of finding faults: we pass through the levity of his rhyme, and are immediately carried into some admirable useful thought. After all, he has chosen this kind of verse, and has written the best in it, and had he taken another he would always have excelled; as we say of a court favourite, that whatsoever his office be, he still makes it uppermost and most beneficial to himself. The quickness of your imagination, my lord, has already prevented me; and you know beforehand that I would prefer the verse of ten syllables, which we call the English heroic, to that of eight.

This is truly my opinion, for this sort of number is more roomy; the thought can turn itself with greater ease in a larger compass. When the rhyme comes too thick upon us, it straitens the expression; we are thinking of the close when we should be employed in adorning the thought. It makes a poet giddy with turning in a space too narrow for his imagination; he loses many beauties without gaining one advantage. For a burlesque rhyme I have already concluded to be none; or, if it were, it is more easily purchased in ten syllables than in eight. In both occasions it is as in a tennis-court, when the strokes of greater force are given, when we strike out and play at length. Tassoni and Boileau have left us the best examples of this way in the "Seechia Rapita" and the "Lutrin," and next them Merlin Cocaius in his "Baldus." I will speak only of the two former, because the last is written in Latin verse. The "Secchia Rapita" is an Italian poem, a satire of the Varronian kind. It is written in the stanza of eight, which is their measure for heroic verse. The words are stately, the numbers smooth; the turn both of thoughts and words is happy. The first six lines of the stanza seem majestical and severe, but the two last turn them all into a pleasant ridicule. Boileau, if I am not much deceived, has modelled from hence his famous "Lutrin." He had read the burlesque poetry of Scarron with some kind of indignation, as witty as it was, and found nothing in France that was worthy of his imitation; but he copied the Italian so well that his own may pass for an original. He writes it in the French heroic verse, and calls it an heroic poem; his subject is trivial, but his verse is noble. I doubt not but he had Virgil in his eye, for we find many admirable imitations of him, and some parodies, as particularly this passage in the fourth of the AEneids-

"Nec *tibi diva parens, generis nec Dardanus auctor,*
Perfide; sed duris genuit te cautibus horrens
Caucasus, Hyrrcanaeque admorunt ubera tigres:"

which he thus translates, keeping to the words, but altering the sense:-

"Non, ton pere a Paris, ne fut point boulanger:
Et tu n'es point du sang de Gervais, l'horloger;
Ta mere ne fut point la maitresse d'un coche;
Caucase dans ses flancs te forma d'une roche;
Une tigresse affreuse, en quelque antre ecarte,
Te fit, avec son lait, succer sa cruaute."

And as Virgil in his fourth Georgic of the bees, perpetually raises the lowness of his subject by the loftiness of his words, and ennobles it by comparisons drawn from empires and from monarchs-

"Admiranda tibi levium spectacula rerum,
Magnanimosque duces, totiusque ordine gentis
Mores et studia, et populos, et praelia dicam;"
and again-
"At genus immortale manet, multosque per annos
Stat fortuna domus, et avi numerantur avorum;"

We see Boileau pursuing him in the same flights, and scarcely yielding to his master. This I think, my lord, to be the most beautiful and most noble kind of satire. Here is the majesty of the heroic finely mixed with the venom of the other, and raising the delight, which otherwise would be flat and vulgar, by the sublimity of the expression. I could say somewhat more of the delicacy of this and some other of his satires, but it might turn to his prejudice if it were carried back to France.

I have given your lordship but this bare hint—in what verse and in what manner this sort of satire may be best managed. Had I time I could enlarge on the beautiful turns of words and thoughts which are as requisite in this as in heroic poetry itself, of which the satire is undoubtedly a species. With these beautiful turns I confess myself to have been unacquainted till about twenty years ago. In a conversation which I had with that noble wit of Scotland, Sir George Mackenzie, he asked me why I did not imitate in my verses the turns of Mr. Waller and Sir John Denham, of which he repeated many to me. I had often read with pleasure, and with some profit, those two fathers of our English poetry, but had not seriously enough considered those beauties which give the last perfection to their works. Some sprinklings of this kind I had also formerly in my plays; but they were casual, and not designed. But this hint, thus seasonably given me, first made me sensible of my own wants, and brought me afterwards to seek for the supply of them in other English authors. I looked over the darling of my youth, the famous Cowley; there I found, instead of them, the points of wit and quirks of epigram, even in the "Davideis" (an heroic poem which is of an opposite nature to those puerilities), but no elegant turns, either on the word or on the thought.

Then I consulted a greater genius (without offence to the manes of that noble author)—I mean Milton; but as he endeavours everywhere to express Homer, whose age had not arrived to that fineness, I found in him a true sublimity, lofty thoughts which were clothed with admirable Grecisms and ancient words, which he had been digging from the minds of Chaucer and Spenser, and which, with all their rusticity, had somewhat of venerable in them. But I found not there neither that for which I looked. At last I had recourse to his master, Spenser, the author of that immortal poem called the "Faerie Queen," and there I met with that which I had been looking for so long in vain. Spenser had studied Virgil to as much advantage as Milton had done Homer, and amongst the rest of his excellences had copied that. Looking farther into the Italian, I found Tasso had done the same; nay, more, that all the sonnets in that language are on the turn of the first thought—which Mr. Walsh, in his late ingenious preface to his poems, has observed. In short, Virgil and Ovid are the two principal fountains of them in Latin poetry. And the French at this day are so fond of them that they judge them to be the first beauties; delicate, et bien tourne, are the highest commendations which they bestow on somewhat which they think a masterpiece.

An example of the turn of words, amongst a thousand others, is that in the last book of Ovid's "Metamorphoses":

"Heu! quantum scelus est, in viscera, viscera condi!
Congestoque avidum pinguescere corpore corpus;
Alteriusque animantem animantis vivere leto."

An example on the turn both of thoughts and words is to be found in Catullus in the complaint of Ariadne when she was left by Theseus:-

"Tum jam nulla viro juranti faemina credat;
Nulla viri speret sermones esse fideles;
Qui, dum aliquid cupiens animus praegestit apisci,
Nil metuunt jurare, nihil promittere parcunt:
Sed simul ac cupidae mentis satiata libido est,
Dicta nihil metuere, nihil perjuria curant."

An extraordinary turn upon the words is that in Ovid's "Epistolae Heroidum" of Sappho to Phaon:

"Si, nisi quae forma poterit te digna videri,
Nulla futura tua est, nulla futura tua est."

Lastly a turn, which I cannot say is absolutely on words—for the thought turns with them—is in the fourth Georgic of Virgil, where Orpheus is to receive his wife from hell on express condition not to look on her till she was come on earth:

"Cum subita incautum dementia cepit amantem;
Ignoscenda quidem, scirent si ignoscere Manes."

I will not burthen your lordship with more of them, for I write to a master who understands them better than myself; but I may safely conclude them to be great beauties. I might descend also to the mechanic beauties of heroic verse; but we have yet no English Prosodia, not so much as a tolerable dictionary or a grammar (so that our language is in a manner barbarous); and what Government will encourage any one, or more, who are capable of refining it, I know not: but nothing under a public expense can go through with it. And I rather fear a declination of the language than hope an advancement of it in the present age.

I am still speaking to you, my lord, though in all probability you are already out of hearing. Nothing which my meanness can produce is worthy of this long attention. But I am come to the last petition of Abraham: if there be ten righteous lines in this vast preface, spare it for their sake; and also spare the next city, because it is but a little one.

I would excuse the performance of this translation if it were all my own; but the better, though not the greater, part being the work of some gentlemen who have succeeded very happily in their undertaking, let their excellences atone for my imperfections and those of my sons. I have perused some of the Satires which are done by other hands, and they seem to me as perfect in their kind as anything I have seen in English verse. The common way which we have taken is not a literal translation, but a kind of paraphrase; or somewhat which is yet more loose, betwixt a paraphrase and imitation. It was not possible for us, or any men, to have made it pleasant any other way. If rendering the exact sense of these authors, almost line for line, had been our business, Barten Holyday had done it already to our hands; and by the help of his learned notes and illustrations, not only Juvenal and Persius, but, what yet is more obscure, his own verses might be understood.

But he wrote for fame, and wrote to scholars; we write only for the pleasure and entertainment of those gentlemen and ladies who, though they are not scholars, are not ignorant—persons of understanding and good sense, who, not having been conversant in the original (or, at least, not having made Latin verse so much their business as to be critics in it), would be glad to find if the wit of our two great authors be answerable to their fame and reputation in the world. We have therefore endeavoured to give the public all the satisfaction we are able in this kind.

And if we are not altogether so faithful to our author as our predecessors Holyday and Stapleton, yet we may challenge to ourselves this praise—that we shall be far more pleasing to our readers. We have followed our authors at greater distance, though not step by step as they have done; for oftentimes they have gone so close that they have trod on the heels of Juvenal and Persius, and hurt them by their too near approach. A noble author would not be pursued too close by a translator. We lose his spirit when we think to take his body. The grosser part remains with us, but the soul is flown away in some noble expression, or some delicate turn of words or thought. Thus Holyday, who made this way his choice, seized the meaning of Juvenal, but the poetry has always escaped him. They who will not grant me that pleasure is one of the ends of poetry, but that it is only a means of compassing the only end (which is instruction), must yet allow that without the means of pleasure the instruction is but a bare and dry philosophy, a crude preparation of morals which we may have from Aristotle and Epictetus with more profit than from any poet. Neither Holyday nor Stapleton have imitated Juvenal in the poetical part of him, his diction, and his elocution. Nor, had they been poets (as neither of them were), yet in the way they took, it was impossible for them to have succeeded in the poetic part.

The English verse which we call heroic consists of no more than ten syllables; the Latin hexameter sometimes rises to seventeen; as, for example, this verse in Virgil:

"Pulverulenta putrem sonitu quatit ungula campum."

Here is the difference of no less than seven syllables in a line betwixt the English and the Latin. Now the medium of these is about fourteen syllables, because the dactyl is a more frequent foot in hexameters than the spondee. But Holyday (without considering that he writ with the disadvantage of four syllables less in every verse) endeavours to make one of his lines to comprehend the sense of one of Juvenal's. According to the falsity of the proposition was the success. He was forced to crowd his verse with ill-sounding monosyllables (of which our barbarous language affords him a wild plenty), and by that means he arrived at his pedantic end, which was to make a literal translation. His verses have nothing of verse in them, but only the worst part of it—the rhyme; and that, into the bargain, is far from good. But, which is more intolerable, by cramming his ill-chosen and worse-sounding monosyllables so close together, the very sense which he endeavours to explain is become more obscure than that of his author; so that Holyday himself cannot be understood without as large a commentary as that which he makes on his two authors. For my own part, I can make a shift to find the meaning of Juvenal without his notes, but his translation is more difficult than his author. And I find beauties in the Latin to recompense my pains; but in Holyday and Stapleton my ears, in the first place, are mortally offended, and then their sense is so perplexed that I return to the original as the more pleasing task as well as the more easy.

This must be said for our translation—that if we give not the whole sense of Juvenal, yet we give the most considerable part of it; we give it, in general, so clearly that few notes are sufficient to make us intelligible. We make our author at least appear in a poetic dress. We have actually made him more sounding and more elegant than he was before in English, and have endeavoured to make him speak that kind of English which he would have spoken had he lived in England and had written to this age. If sometimes any of us (and it is but seldom) make him express the customs and manners of our native country rather than of Rome, it is either when there was some kind of analogy betwixt their customs and ours, or when (to make him more easy to vulgar understandings) we gave him those manners which are familiar to us. But I defend not this innovation; it is enough if I can excuse it. For (to speak sincerely) the manners of nations and ages are not to be confounded; we should either make them English or leave them Roman. If this can neither be defended nor excused, let it be pardoned at least, because it is acknowledged; and so much the more easily as being a fault which is never committed without some pleasure to the reader. Thus, my lord, having troubled you with a tedious visit, the best manners will be shown in the least ceremony. I will slip away while your back is turned, and while you are otherwise employed; with great confusion for having entertained you so long with this discourse, and for having no other recompense to make you than the worthy labours of my fellow-undertakers in this work, and the thankful acknowledgments, prayers, and perpetual good wishes of,

My Lord,
Your Lordship's
Most obliged, most humble, and
Most obedient servant,
JOHN DRYDEN.

A DISCOURSE ON EPIC POETRY.
ADDRESSED TO THE MOST HONOURABLE
JOHN, LORD MARQUIS OF NORMANBY,
EARL OF MULGRAVE, ETC., AND KNIGHT OF THE MOST NOBLE ORDER
OF THE GARTER.

An heroic poem (truly such) is undoubtedly the greatest work which the soul of man is capable to perform. The design of it is to form the mind to heroic virtue by example; it is conveyed in verse that it may delight while it instructs. The action of it is always one, entire, and great. The least and most trivial episodes or under-actions which are interwoven in it are parts either necessary or convenient to carry on the main design—either so necessary that without them the poem must be imperfect, or so convenient that no others can be imagined more suitable to the place in which they are. There is nothing to be left void in a firm building; even the cavities ought not to be filled with rubbish which is of a perishable kind—destructive to the strength—but with brick or stone (though of less pieces, yet of the same nature), and fitted to the crannies. Even the least portions of them must be of the epic kind; all things must be grave, majestical, and sublime; nothing of a foreign nature, like the trifling novels which Ariosto and others have inserted in their poems, by which the reader is misled into another sort of pleasure, opposite to that which is designed in an epic poem. One raises the soul and hardens it to virtue; the other softens it again and unbends it into vice. One conduces to the poet's aim (the completing of his work), which he is driving on, labouring, and hastening in every line; the other slackens his pace, diverts him from his way, and locks him up like a knight-errant in an enchanted castle when he should be pursuing his first adventure. Statius (as Bossu has well observed) was ambitions of trying his strength with his master, Virgil, as Virgil had before tried his with Homer. The Grecian gave the two Romans an example in the games which were celebrated at the funerals of Patroclus.

Virgil imitated the invention of Homer, but changed the sports. But both the Greek and Latin poet took their occasions from the subject, though (to confess the truth) they were both ornamental, or, at best, convenient parts of it, rather than of necessity arising from it. Statius (who through his whole poem is noted for want of conduct and judgment), instead of staying, as he might have done, for the death of Capaneus, Hippomedon, Tydeus, or some other of his Seven Champions (who are heroes all alike), or more properly for the tragical end of the two brothers whose exequies the next successor had leisure to perform when the siege was raised, and in the interval betwixt the poet's first action and his second, went out of his way—as it were, on prepense malice—to commit a fault; for he took his opportunity to kill a royal infant by the means of a serpent (that author of all evil) to make way for those funeral honours which he intended for him. Now if this innocent had been of any relation to his Thebais, if he had either farthered or hindered the taking of the town, the poet might have found some sorry excuse at least for detaining the reader from the promised siege. On these terms this Capaneus of a poet engaged his two immortal predecessors, and his success was answerable to his enterprise.

If this economy must be observed in the minutest parts of an epic poem, which to a common reader seem to be detached from the body, and almost independent of it, what soul, though sent into the world with great advantages of nature, cultivated with the liberal arts and sciences, conversant with histories of the dead, and enriched with observations on the living, can be sufficient to inform the whole body of so great a work? I touch here but transiently, without any strict method, on some few of those many rules of imitating nature which Aristotle drew from Homer's "Iliads" and "Odysses," and which he fitted to the drama—furnishing himself also with observations from the practice of the theatre when it flourished under AEschylus, Euripides, and Sophocles (for the original of the stage was from the epic poem).

Narration, doubtless, preceded acting, and gave laws to it. What at first was told artfully was in process of time represented gracefully to the sight and hearing. Those episodes of Homer which were proper for the stage, the poets amplified each into an action. Out of his limbs they formed their bodies; what he had contracted, they enlarged; out of one Hercules were made infinity of pigmies, yet all endued with human souls; for from him, their great creator, they have each of them the divinae particulam aurae. They flowed from him at first, and are at last resolved into him. Nor were they only animated by him, but their measure and symmetry was owing to him. His one, entire, and great action was copied by them, according to the proportions of the drama. If he finished his orb within the year, it sufficed to teach them that their action being less, and being also less diversified with incidents, their orb, of consequence, must be circumscribed in a less compass, which they reduced within the limits either of a natural or an artificial day. So that, as he taught them to amplify what he had shortened, by the same rule applied the contrary way he taught them to shorten what he had amplified.

ragedy is the miniature of human life; an epic poem is the draft at length. Here, my lord, I must contract also, for before I was aware I was almost running into a long digression to prove that there is no such absolute necessity that the time of a stage-action should so strictly be confined to twenty-four hours as never to exceed them (for which Aristotle contends, and the Grecian stage has practised). Some longer space on some occasions, I think, may be allowed, especially for the

English theatre, which requires more variety of incidents than the French. Corneille himself, after long practice, was inclined to think that the time allotted by the ancients was too short to raise and finish a great action; and better a mechanic rule were stretched or broken than a great beauty were omitted. To raise, and afterwards to calm, the passions; to purge the soul from pride by the examples of human miseries which befall the greatest; in few words, to expel arrogance and introduce compassion, are the great effects of tragedy—great, I must confess, if they were altogether as true as they are pompous. But are habits to be introduced at three hours' warning?

Are radical diseases so suddenly removed? A mountebank may promise such a cure, but a skilful physician will not undertake it. An epic poem is not in so much haste; it works leisurely: the changes which it makes are slow, but the cure is likely to be more perfect. The effects of tragedy, as I said, are too violent to be lasting. If it be answered, that for this reason tragedies are often to be seen, and the dose to be repeated, this is tacitly to confess that there is more virtue in one heroic poem than in many tragedies. A man is humbled one day, and his pride returns the next. Chemical medicines are observed to relieve oftener than to cure; for it is the nature of spirits to make swift impressions, but not deep. Galenical decoctions, to which I may properly compare an epic poem, have more of body in them; they work by their substance and their weight.

It is one reason of Aristotle's to prove that tragedy is the more noble, because it turns in a shorter compass—the whole action being circumscribed within the space of four-and-twenty hours. He might prove as well that a mushroom is to be preferred before a peach, because it shoots up in the compass of a night. A chariot may be driven round the pillar in less space than a large machine, because the bulk is not so great. Is the moon a more noble planet than Saturn, because she makes her revolution in less than thirty days, and he in little less than thirty years? Both their orbs are in proportion to their several magnitudes; and consequently the quickness or slowness of their motion, and the time of their circumvolutions, is no argument of the greater or less perfection. And besides, what virtue is there in a tragedy which is not contained in an epic poem, where pride is humbled, virtue rewarded, and vice punished, and those more amply treated than the narrowness of the drama can admit? The shining quality of an epic hero, his magnanimity, his constancy, his patience, his piety, or whatever characteristical virtue his poet gives him, raises first our admiration; we are naturally prone to imitate what we admire, and frequent acts produce a habit. If the hero's chief quality be vicious—as, for example, the choler and obstinate desire of vengeance in Achilles—yet the moral is instructive; and besides, we are informed in the very proposition of the "Iliads" that this anger was pernicious, that it brought a thousand ills on the Grecian camp.

The courage of Achilles is proposed to imitation, not his pride and disobedience to his general; nor his brutal cruelty to his dead enemy, nor the selling his body to his father. We abhor these actions while we read them, and what we abhor we never imitate; the poet only shows them, like rocks or quicksands to be shunned. By this example the critics have concluded that it is not necessary the manners of the hero should be virtuous (they are poetically good if they are of a piece); though where a character of perfect virtue is set before us, it is more lovely; for there the whole hero is to be imitated. This is the AEneas of our author; this is that idea of perfection in an epic poem which painters and statuaries have only in their minds, and which no hands are able to express. These are the beauties of a God in a human body. When the picture of Achilles is drawn in tragedy, he is taken with those warts and moles and hard features by those who represent him on the stage, or he is no more Achilles; for his creator, Homer, has so described him. Yet even thus he appears a perfect hero, though an imperfect character of virtue. Horace paints him after Homer, and delivers him to be copied on the stage with all those imperfections. Therefore they are either not faults in an heroic poem, or faults common to the drama.

After all, on the whole merits of the cause, it must be acknowledged that the epic poem is more for the manners, and tragedy for the passions. The passions, as I have said, are violent; and acute distempers require medicines of a strong and speedy operation. Ill habits of the mind are, like chronical diseases, to be corrected by degrees, and cured by alteratives; wherein, though purges are sometimes necessary, yet diet, good air, and moderate exercise have the greatest part. The matter being thus stated, it will appear that both sorts of poetry are of use for their proper ends. The stage is more active, the epic poem works at greater leisure; yet is active too when need requires, for dialogue is imitated by the drama from the more active parts of it. One puts off a fit, like the quinquina, and relieves us only for a time; the other roots out the distemper, and gives a healthful habit. The sun enlightens and cheers us, dispels fogs, and warms the ground with his daily beams; but the corn is sowed, increases, is ripened, and is reaped for use in process of time and in its proper season.

I proceed from the greatness of the action to the dignity of the actors—I mean, to the persons employed in both poems. There likewise tragedy will be seen to borrow from the epopee; and that which borrows is always of less dignity, because it has not of its own. A subject, it is true, may lend to his sovereign; but the act of borrowing makes the king inferior, because he wants and the subject supplies. And suppose the persons of the drama wholly fabulous, or of the poet's invention, yet heroic poetry gave him the examples of that invention, because it was first, and Homer the common father of the stage. I know not of any one advantage which tragedy can boast above heroic poetry but that it is represented to the view as well as read, and instructs in the closet as well as on the theatre. This is an uncontended excellence, and a chief branch of its prerogative; yet I may be allowed to say without partiality that herein the actors share the poet's praise.

Your lordship knows some modern tragedies which are beautiful on the stage, and yet I am confident you would not read them. Tryphon the stationer complains they are seldom asked for in his shop. The poet who flourished in the scene is damned in the ruelle; nay, more, he is not esteemed a good poet by those who see and hear his extravagances with delight.

They are a sort of stately fustian and lofty childishness. Nothing but nature can give a sincere pleasure; where that is not imitated, it is grotesque painting; the fine woman ends in a fish's tail.

I might also add that many things which not only please, but are real beauties in the reading, would appear absurd upon the stage; and those not only the speciosa miracula, as Horace calls them, of transformations of Scylla, Antiphates, and the Laestrygons (which cannot be represented even in operas), but the prowess of Achilles or AEneas would appear ridiculous in our dwarf-heroes of the theatre. We can believe they routed armies in Homer or in Virgil, but ne Hercules contra duos in the drama. I forbear to instance in many things which the stage cannot or ought not to represent; for I have said already more than I intended on this subject, and should fear it might be turned against me that I plead for the pre-eminence of epic poetry because I have taken some pains in translating Virgil, if this were the first time that I had delivered my opinion in this dispute; but I have more than once already maintained the rights of my two masters against their rivals of the scene, even while I wrote tragedies myself and had no thoughts of this present undertaking.

I submit my opinion to your judgment, who are better qualified than any man I know to decide this controversy. You come, my lord, instructed in the cause, and needed not that I should open it. Your "Essay of Poetry," which was published without a name, and of which I was not honoured with the confidence, I read over and over with much delight and as much instruction, and without flattering you, or making myself more moral than I am, not without some envy. I was loth to be informed how an epic poem should be written, or how a tragedy should be contrived and managed, in better verse and with more judgment than I could teach others. A native of Parnassus, and bred up in the studies of its fundamental laws, may receive new lights from his contemporaries, but it is a grudging kind of praise which he gives his benefactors. He is more obliged than he is willing to acknowledge; there is a tincture of malice in his commendations: for where I own I am taught, I confess my want of knowledge. A judge upon the bench may, out of good nature, or, at least, interest, encourage the pleadings of a puny counsellor, but he does not willingly commend his brother-serjeant at the bar, especially when he controls his law, and exposes that ignorance which is made sacred by his place. I gave the unknown author his due commendation, I must confess; but who can answer for me, and for the rest of the poets who heard me read the poem, whether we should not have been better pleased to have seen our own names at the bottom of the title-page?

Perhaps we commended it the more that we might seem to be above the censure. We are naturally displeased with an unknown critic, as the ladies are with a lampooner, because we are bitten in the dark, and know not where to fasten our revenge; but great excellences will work their way through all sorts of opposition. I applauded rather out of decency than affection; and was ambitious, as some yet can witness, to be acquainted with a man with whom I had the honour to converse, and that almost daily, for so many years together. Heaven knows if I have heartily forgiven you this deceit. You extorted a praise, which I should willingly have given had I known you. Nothing had been more easy than to commend a patron of a long standing. The world would join with me if the encomiums were just, and if unjust would excuse a grateful flatterer. But to come anonymous upon me, and force me to commend you against my interest, was not altogether so fair, give me leave to say, as it was politic; for by concealing your quality you might clearly understand how your work succeeded, and that the general approbation was given to your merit, not your titles.

Thus, like Apelles, you stood unseen behind your own Venus, and received the praises of the passing multitude. The work was commended, not the author; and, I doubt not, this was one of the most pleasing adventures of your life. I have detained your lordship longer than I intended in this dispute of preference betwixt the epic poem and the drama, and yet have not formally answered any of the arguments which are brought by Aristotle on the other side, and set in the fairest light by Dacier. But I suppose without looking on the book, I may have touched on some of the objections; for in this address to your lordship I design not a treatise of heroic poetry, but write in a loose epistolary way somewhat tending to that subject, after the example of Horace in his first epistle of the second book to Augustus Caesar, and of that to the Pisos, which we call his "Art of Poetry," in both of which he observes no method that I can trace, whatever Scaliger the father, or Heinsius may have seen, or rather think they had seen. I have taken up, laid down, and resumed, as often as I pleased, the same subject, and this loose proceeding I shall use through all this prefatory dedication. Yet all this while I have been sailing with some side-wind or other toward the point I proposed in the beginning—the greatness and excellence of an heroic poem, with some of the difficulties which attend that work. The comparison therefore which I made betwixt the epopee and the tragedy was not altogether a digression, for it is concluded on all hands that they are both the masterpieces of human wit. In the meantime I may be bold to draw this corollary from what has been already said—that the file of heroic poets is very short; all are not such who have assumed that lofty title in ancient or modern ages, or have been so esteemed by their partial and ignorant admirers.

There have been but one great "Ilias" and one "AEneis" in so many ages; the next (but the next with a long interval betwixt) was the "Jerusalem"—I mean, not so much in distance of time as in excellence. After these three are entered, some Lord Chamberlain should be appointed, some critic of authority should be set before the door to keep out a crowd of little poets who press for admission, and are not of quality. Maevius would be deafening your lordship's ears with his

"Fortunam Priami cantabo, et nobile bellum."

Mere fustian (as Horace would tell you from behind, without pressing forward), and more smoke than fire. Pulci, Boiardo, and Ariosto would cry out, "Make room for the Italian poets, the descendants of Virgil in a right line." Father Le Moine with his "Saint Louis," and Scudery with his "Alaric" (for a godly king and a Gothic conqueror); and Chapelain would take it ill that his "Maid" should be refused a place with Helen and Lavinia. Spenser has a better plea for his "Faerie Queen," had his action been finished, or had been one; and Milton, if the devil had not been his hero instead of Adam; if the giant had not foiled the knight, and driven him out of his stronghold to wander through the world with his lady-errant; and if there had not been more machining persons than human in his poem. After these the rest of our English poets shall not be mentioned; I have that honour for them which I ought to have; but if they are worthies, they are not to be ranked amongst the three whom I have named, and who are established in their reputation.

Before I quitted the comparison betwixt epic poetry and tragedy I should have acquainted my judge with one advantage of the former over the latter, which I now casually remember out of the preface of Segrais before his translation of the "AEneis," or out of Bossu—no matter which: "The style of the heroic poem is, and ought to be, more lofty than that of the drama." The critic is certainly in the right, for the reason already urged—the work of tragedy is on the passions, and in dialogue; both of them abhor strong metaphors, in which the epopee delights. A poet cannot speak too plainly on the stage, for volat irrevocabile verbum (the sense is lost if it be not taken flying) but what we read alone we have leisure to digest.

There an author may beautify his sense by the boldness of his expression, which if we understand not fully at the first we may dwell upon it till we find the secret force and excellence. That which cures the manners by alterative physic, as I said before, must proceed by insensible degrees; but that which purges the passions must do its business all at once, or wholly fail of its effect—at least, in the present operation—and without repeated doses. We must beat the iron while it is hot, but we may polish it at leisure. Thus, my lord, you pay the fine of my forgetfulness,; and yet the merits of both causes are where they were, and undecided, till you declare whether it be more for the benefit of mankind to have their manners in general corrected, or their pride and hard-heartedness removed. I must now come closer to my present business, and not think of making more invasive wars abroad, when, like Hannibal, I am called back to the defence of my own country. Virgil is attacked by many enemies; he has a whole confederacy against him; and I must endeavour to defend him as well as I am able. But their principal objections being against his moral, the duration or length of time taken up in the action of the poem, and what they have to urge against the manners of his hero, I shall omit the rest as mere cavils of grammarians—at the worst but casual slips of a great man's pen, or inconsiderable faults of an admirable poem, which the author had not leisure to review before his death.

Macrobius has answered what the ancients could urge against him, and some things I have lately read in Tannegui le Febvre, Valois, and another whom I name not, which are scarce worth answering.

They begin with the moral of his poem, which I have elsewhere confessed, and still must own, not to be so noble as that of Homer. But let both be fairly stated, and without contradicting my first opinion I can show that Virgil's was as useful to the Romans of his age as Homer's was to the Grecians of his, in what time soever he may be supposed to have lived and flourished.

Homer's moral was to urge the necessity of union, and of a good understanding betwixt confederate states and princes engaged in a war with a mighty monarch; as also of discipline in an army, and obedience in the several chiefs to the supreme commander of the joint forces. To inculcate this, he sets forth the ruinous effects of discord in the camp of those allies, occasioned by the quarrel betwixt the general and one of the next in office under him. Agamemnon gives the provocation, and Achilles resents the injury.

Both parties are faulty in the quarrel, and accordingly they are both punished; the aggressor is forced to sue for peace to his inferior on dishonourable conditions; the deserter refuses the satisfaction offered, and his obstinacy costs him his best friend. This works the natural effect of choler, and turns his rage against him by whom he was last affronted, and most sensibly. The greater anger expels the less, but his character is still preserved. In the meantime the Grecian army receives loss on loss, and is half destroyed by a pestilence into the bargain:-

"Quicquid delirant reges, plectuntur Achivi."

As the poet in the first part of the example had shown the bad effects of discord, so after the reconcilement he gives the good effects of unity; for Hector is slain, and then Troy must fall. By this it is probable that Homer lived when the Median monarchy was grown formidable to the Grecians, and that the joint endeavours of his countrymen were little enough to preserve their common freedom from an encroaching enemy. Such was his moral, which all critics have allowed to be more noble than that of Virgil, though not adapted to the times in which the Roman poet lived. Had Virgil flourished in the age of Ennius and addressed to Scipio, he had probably taken the same moral, or some other not unlike it; for then the Romans were in as much danger from the Carthaginian commonwealth as the Grecians were from the Assyrian or Median monarchy. But we are to consider him as writing his poem in a time when the old form of government was subverted, and a new one just established by Octavius Caesar—in effect, by force of arms, but seemingly by the consent of the Roman people.

The commonwealth had received a deadly wound in the former civil wars betwixt Marius and Sylla. The commons, while the first prevailed, had almost shaken off the yoke of the nobility; and Marius and Cinna (like the captains of the mob), under the specious pretence of the public good and of doing justice on the oppressors of their liberty, revenged themselves without form of law on their private enemies. Sylla, in his turn, proscribed the heads of the adverse party. He, too, had nothing but liberty and reformation in his mouth; for the cause of religion is but a modern motive to rebellion, invented by the Christian priesthood refining on the heathen. Sylla, to be sure, meant no more good to the Roman people than Marius before him, whatever he declared; but sacrificed the lives and took the estates of all his enemies to gratify those who brought him into power. Such was the reformation of the government by both parties. The senate and the commons were the two bases on which it stood, and the two champions of either faction each destroyed the foundations of the other side; so the fabric, of consequence, must fall betwixt them, and tyranny must be built upon their ruins. This comes of altering fundamental laws and constitutions; like him who, being in good health, lodged himself in a physician's house, and was over-persuaded by his landlord to take physic (of which be died) for the benefit of his doctor. "Stavo ben," was written on his monument, "ma, per star meglio, sto qui." After the death of those two usurpers the commonwealth seemed to recover, and held up its head for a little time, but it was all the while in a deep consumption, which is a flattering disease. Pompey, Crassus, and Caesar had found the sweets of arbitrary power, and each being a check to the other's growth, struck up a false friendship amongst themselves and divided the government betwixt them, which none of them was able to assume alone. These were the public-spirited men of their age—that is, patriots for their own interest.

The commonwealth looked with a florid countenance in their management; spread in bulk, and all the while was wasting in the vitals. Not to trouble your lordship with the repetition of what you know, after the death of Crassus Pompey found himself outwitted by Caesar, broke with him, overpowered him in the senate, and caused many unjust decrees to pass against him. Caesar thus injured, and unable to resist the faction of the nobles which was now uppermost (for he was a Marian), had recourse to arms, and his cause was just against Pompey, but not against his country, whose constitution ought to have been sacred to him, and never to have been violated on the account of any private wrong. But he prevailed, and Heaven declaring for him, he became a providential monarch under the title of Perpetual Dictator. He being murdered by his own son (whom I neither dare commend nor can justly blame, though Dante in his "Inferno" has put him and Cassius, and Judas Iscariot betwixt them, into the great devil's mouth), the commonwealth popped up its head for the third time under Brutus and Cassius, and then sank for ever.

Thus the Roman people were grossly gulled twice or thrice over, and as often enslaved, in one century, and under the same pretence of reformation. At last the two battles of Philippi gave the decisive stroke against liberty, and not long after the commonwealth was turned into a monarchy by the conduct and good fortune of Augustus. It is true that the despotic power could not have fallen into better hands than those of the first and second Caesar. Your lordship well knows what obligations Virgil had to the latter of them. He saw, beside, that the commonwealth was lost without resource; the heads of it destroyed; the senate, new moulded, grown degenerate, and either bought off or thrusting their own necks into the yoke out of fear of being forced. Yet I may safely affirm for our great author (as men of good sense are generally honest) that he was still of republican principles in heart.

"Secretosque pios; his dantem jura Catonem."

I think I need use no other argument to justify my opinion than that of this one line taken from the eighth book of the AEneis. If he had not well studied his patron's temper it might have ruined him with another prince. But Augustus was not discontented (at least, that we can find) that Cato was placed by his own poet in Elysium, and there giving laws to the holy souls who deserved to be separated from the vulgar sort of good spirits; for his conscience could not but whisper to the arbitrary monarch that the kings of Rome were at first elective, and governed not without a senate; that Romulus was no hereditary prince, and though after his death he received divine honours for the good he did on earth, yet he was but a god of their own making; that the last Tarquin was expelled justly for overt acts of tyranny and mal-administration (for such are the conditions of an elective kingdom, and I meddle not with others, being, for my own opinion, of Montange's principles—that an honest man ought to be contented with that form of government, and with those fundamental constitutions of it, which he received from his ancestors, and under which himself was born, though at the same time he confessed freely that if he could have chosen his place of birth it should have been at Venice, which for many reasons I dislike, and am better pleased to have been born an Englishman). But to return from my long rambling; I say that Virgil having maturely weighed the condition of the times in which he lived; that an entire liberty was not to be retrieved; that the present settlement had the prospect of a long continuance in the same family or those adopted into it; that he held his paternal estate from the bounty of the conqueror, by whom he was likewise enriched, esteemed, and cherished; that this conqueror, though of a bad kind, was the very best of it; that the arts of peace flourished under him; that all men might be happy if they would be quiet; that now he was in possession of the whole, yet he shared a great part of his authority with the senate; that he would be chosen into the ancient offices of the commonwealth, and ruled by the power which he derived from them, and prorogued his government from time to time, still, as it were, threatening to dismiss himself from public cares, which he exercised more for the common good than for any delight he took in greatness— these things, I say, being considered by the poet, he concluded it to be the interest of his country to be so governed, to infuse an awful respect into the people towards such a prince, by that respect to confirm their obedience to him, and by that obedience to make them happy. This was the moral of his divine poem; honest in the poet, honourable to the emperor (whom he derives from a divine extraction), and reflecting part of that honour on the Roman people (whom he derives also from the Trojans), and not only profitable, but necessary, to the present age, and likely to be such to their posterity.

That it was the received opinion that the Romans were descended from the Trojans, and Julius Caesar from Iulus, the son of AEneas, was enough for Virgil, though perhaps he thought not so himself, or that AEneas ever was in Italy, which Bochartus manifestly proves. And Homer (where he says that Jupiter hated the house of Priam, and was resolved to transfer the kingdom to the family of AEneas) yet mentions nothing of his leading a colony into a foreign country and settling there. But that the Romans valued themselves on their Trojan ancestry is so undoubted a truth that I need not prove it. Even the seals which we have remaining of Julius Caesar (which we know to be antique) have the star of Venus over them—though they were all graven after his death—as a note that he was deified. I doubt not but one reason why Augustus should be so passionately concerned for the preservation of the "AEneis," which its author had condemned to be burnt as an imperfect poem by his last will and testament, was because it did him a real service as well as an honour; that a work should not be lost where his divine original was celebrated in verse which had the character of immortality stamped upon it.

Neither were the great Roman families which flourished in his time less obliged by him than the emperor. Your lordship knows with what address he makes mention of them as captains of ships or leaders in the war; and even some of Italian extraction are not forgotten. These are the single stars which are sprinkled through the "AEneis," but there are whole constellations of them in the fifth book; and I could not but take notice, when I translated it, of some favourite families to which he gives the victory and awards the prizes, in the person of his hero, at the funeral games which were celebrated in honour of Anchises. I insist not on their names, but am pleased to find the Memmii amongst them, derived from Mnestheus, because Lucretius dedicates to one of that family, a branch of which destroyed Corinth.

I likewise either found or formed an image to myself of the contrary kind—that those who lost the prizes were such as had disobliged the poet, or were in disgrace with Augustus, or enemies to Maecenas; and this was the poetical revenge he took, for genus irritabile vatum, as Horace says. When a poet is thoroughly provoked, he will do himself justice, how ever dear it cost him, animamque in vulnere ponit. I think these are not bare imaginations of my own, though I find no trace of them in the commentators; but one poet may judge of another by himself. The vengeance we defer is not forgotten. I hinted before that the whole Roman people were obliged by Virgil in deriving them from Troy, an ancestry which they affected. We and the French are of the same humour: they would be thought to descend from a son, I think, of Hector; and we would have our Britain both named and planted by a descendant of AEneas. Spenser favours this opinion what he can. His Prince Arthur, or whoever he intends by him, is a Trojan. Thus the hero of Homer was a Grecian; of Virgil, a Roman; of Tasso, an Italian.

I have transgressed my bounds and gone farther than the moral led me; but if your lordship is not tired, I am safe enough. Thus far, I think, my author is defended. But as Augustus is still shadowed in the person of AEneas (of which I shall say more when I come to the manners which the poet gives his hero), I must prepare that subject by showing how dexterously he managed both the prince and people, so as to displease neither, and to do good to both— which is the part of a wise and an honest man, and proves that it is possible for a courtier not to be a knave. I shall continue still to speak my thoughts like a free-born subject, as I am, though such things perhaps as no Dutch commentator could, and I am sure no Frenchman durst. I have already told your lordship my opinion of Virgil—that he was no arbitrary man.

Obliged he was to his master for his bounty, and he repays him with good counsel how to behave himself in his new monarchy so as to gain the affections of his subjects, and deserve to be called the "Father of His Country." From this consideration it is that he chose for the groundwork of his poem one empire destroyed, and another raised from the ruins of it. This was just the parallel. AEneas could not pretend to be Priam's heir in a lineal succession, for Anchises, the hero's father, was only of the second branch of the royal family, and Helenus, a son of Priam, was yet surviving, and might lawfully claim before him. It may be, Virgil mentions him on that account.

Neither has he forgotten Priamus, in the fifth of his "AEneis," the son of Polites, youngest son to Priam, who was slain by Pyrrhus in the second book. AEneas had only married Creusa, Priam's daughter, and by her could have no title while any of the male issue were remaining. In this case the poet gave him the next title, which is that of an Elective King. The remaining Trojans chose him to lead them forth and settle them in some foreign country. Ilioneus in his speech to Dido calls him expressly by the name of king. Our poet, who all this while had Augustus in his eye, had no desire he should seem to succeed by any right of inheritance derived from Julius Caesar, such a title being but one degree removed from conquest: for what was introduced by force, by force may be removed. It was better for the people that they should give than he should take, since that gift was indeed no more at bottom than a trust.

Virgil gives us an example of this in the person of Mezentius. He governed arbitrarily; he was expelled and came to the deserved end of all tyrants. Our author shows us another sort of kingship in the person of Latinus. He was descended from Saturn, and, as I remember, in the third degree. He is described a just and a gracious prince, solicitous for the welfare of his people, always consulting with his senate to promote the common good. We find him at the head of them when he enters into the council-hall—speaking first, but still demanding their advice, and steering by it, as far as the iniquity of the times would suffer him. And this is the proper character of a king by inheritance, who is born a father of his country. AEneas, though he married the heiress of the crown, yet claimed no title to it during the life of his father-in-law.

Socer arma Latinus hebeto, &c., are Virgil's words. As for himself, he was contented to take care of his country gods, who were not those of Latium; wherein our divine author seems to relate to the after-practice of the Romans, which was to adopt the gods of those they conquered or received as members of their commonwealth. Yet, withal, he plainly touches at the office of the high-priesthood, with which Augustus was invested and which made his person more sacred and inviolable than even the tribunitial power. It was not therefore for nothing that the most judicious of all poets made that office vacant by the death of Pantheus, in the second book of the "AEneis," for his hero to succeed in it, and consequently for Augustus to enjoy. I know not that any of the commentators have taken notice of that passage. If they have not, I am sure they ought; and if they have, I am not indebted to them for the observation. The words of Virgil are very plain:

"Sacra suosque tibi commendat Troja Penates."

As for Augustus or his uncle Julius claiming by descent from AEneas, that title is already out of doors. AEneas succeeded not, but was elected. Troy was fore-doomed to fall for ever:

"Postquam res Asiae, Priamique evertere gentem,
Immeritam visum superis."—AENEIS, I. iii., line 1.

Augustus, it is true, had once resolved to rebuild that city, and there to make the seat of the Empire; but Horace writes an ode on purpose to deter him from that thought, declaring the place to be accursed, and that the gods would as often destroy it as it should be raised. Hereupon the emperor laid aside a project so ungrateful to the Roman people. But by this, my lord, we may conclude that he had still his pedigree in his head, and had an itch of being thought a divine king if his poets had not given him better counsel. I will pass by many less material objections for want of room to answer them. What follows next is of great importance, if the critics can make out their charge, for it is levelled at the manners which our poet gives his hero, and which are the same which were eminently seen in his Augustus.

Those manners were piety to the gods and a dutiful affection to his father, love to his relations, care of his people, courage and conduct in the wars, gratitude to those who had obliged him, and justice in general to mankind. Piety, as your lordship sees, takes place of all as the chief part of his character; and the word in Latin is more full than it can possibly be expressed in any modern language, for there it comprehends not only devotion to the gods, but filial love and tender affection to relations of all sorts. As instances of this the deities of Troy and his own Penates are made the companions of his flight; they appear to him in his voyage and advise him, and at last he replaces them in Italy, their native country. For his father, he takes him on his back.

He leads his little son, his wife follows him; but losing his footsteps through fear or ignorance he goes back into the midst of his enemies to find her, and leaves not his pursuit till her ghost appears to forbid his farther search. I will say nothing of his duty to his father while he lived, his sorrow for his death, of the games instituted in honour of his memory, or seeking him by his command even after death in the Elysian fields. I will not mention his tenderness for his son, which everywhere is visible; of his raising a tomb for Polydorus; the obsequies for Misenus; his pious remembrance of Deiphobus; the funerals of his nurse; his grief for Pallas, and his revenge taken on his murderer, whom otherwise, by his natural compassion, he had forgiven: and then the poem had been left imperfect, for we could have had no certain prospect of his happiness while the last obstacle to it was unremoved.

Of the other parts which compose his character as a king or as a general I need say nothing; the whole "AEneis" is one continued instance of some one or other of them; and where I find anything of them taxed, it shall suffice me (as briefly as I can) to vindicate my divine master to your lordship, and by you to the reader. But herein Segrais, in his admirable preface to his translation of the "AEneis," as the author of the Dauphin's "Virgil" justly calls it, has prevented me. Him I follow, and what I borrow from him am ready to acknowledge to him, for, impartially speaking, the French are as much better critics than the English as they are worse poets. Thus we generally allow that they better understand the management of a war than our islanders, but we know we are superior to them in the day of battle; they value themselves on their generals, we on our soldiers.

But this is not the proper place to decide that question, if they make it one. I shall say perhaps as much of other nations and their poets (excepting only Tasso), and hope to make my assertion good, which is but doing justice to my country—part of which honour will reflect on your lordship, whose thoughts are always just, your numbers harmonious, your words chosen, your expressions strong and manly, your verse flowing, and your turns as happy as they are easy. If you would set us more copies, your example would make all precepts needless. In the meantime that little you have written is owned, and that particularly by the poets (who are a nation not over-lavish of praise to their contemporaries), as a principal ornament of our language; but the sweetest essences are always confined in the smallest glasses. When I speak of your lordship, it is never a digression, and therefore I need beg no pardon for it, but take up Segrais where I left him, and shall use him less often than I have occasion for him. For his preface is a perfect piece of criticism, full and clear, and digested into an exact method; mine is loose and, as I intended it, epistolary. Yet I dwell on many things which he durst not touch, for it is dangerous to offend an arbitrary master, and every patron who has the power of Augustus has not his clemency.

In short, my lord, I would not translate him because I would bring you somewhat of my own. His notes and observations on every book are of the same excellency, and for the same reason I omit the greater part. He takes no notice that Virgil is arraigned for placing piety before valour, and making that piety the chief character of his hero. I have said already from Bossu, that a poet is not obliged to make his hero a virtuous man; therefore neither Homer nor Tasso are to be blamed for giving what predominant quality they pleased to their first character. But Virgil, who designed to form a perfect prince, and would insinuate that Augustus (whom he calls AEneas in his poem) was truly such, found himself obliged to make him without blemish— thoroughly virtuous; and a thorough virtue both begins and ends in piety. Tasso without question observed this before me, and therefore split his hero in two; he gave Godfrey piety, and Rinaldo fortitude, for their chief qualities or manners. Homer, who had chosen another moral, makes both Agamemnon and Achilles vicious; for his design was to instruct in virtue by showing the deformity of vice. I avoid repetition of that I have said above. What follows is translated literally from Segrais:-

"Virgil had considered that the greatest virtues of Augustus consisted in the perfect art of governing his people, which caused him to reign for more than forty years in great felicity. He considered that his emperor was valiant, civil, popular, eloquent, politic, and religious; he has given all these qualities to AEneas. But knowing that piety alone comprehends the whole duty of man towards the gods, towards his country, and towards his relations, he judged that this ought to be his first character whom he would set for a pattern of perfection. In reality, they who believe that the praises which arise from valour are superior to those which proceed from any other virtues, have not considered, as they ought, that valour, destitute of other virtues, cannot render a man worthy of any true esteem.

That quality, which signifies no more than an intrepid courage, may he separated from many others which are good, and accompanied with many which are ill. A man may be very valiant, and yet impious and vicious; but the same cannot be said of piety, which excludes all ill qualities, and comprehends even valour itself, with all other qualities which are good. Can we, for example, give the praise of valour to a man who should see his gods profaned, and should want the courage to defend them? to a man who should abandon his father, or desert his king, in his last necessity?" Thus far Segrais, in giving the preference to piety before valour; I will now follow him where he considers this valour or intrepid courage singly in itself; and this also Virgil gives to his AEneas, and that in a heroical degree.

Having first concluded that our poet did for the best in taking the first character of his hero from that essential virtue on which the rest depend, he proceeds to tell us that in the ten years' war of Troy he was considered as the second champion of his country, allowing Hector the first place; and this even by the confession of Homer, who took all occasions of setting up his own countrymen the Grecians, and of undervaluing the Trojan chiefs. But Virgil (whom Segrais forgot to cite) makes Diomede give him a higher character for strength and courage. His testimony is this, in the eleventh book:-

"Stetimus tela aspera contra,
Contulimusque manus: experto credite, quantus
In clypeum adsurgat, quo turbine torqueat hastam.
Si duo praeterea tales Inachias venisset ad urbes

Dardanus, et versis lugeret Graecia fatis.
Quicquid apud durae cessatum est maenia Trojae,
Hectoris AEneaeque manu victoria Grajum
Haesit, et in decumum vestigia retulit annum.
Ambo animis, ambo insignes praestantibus armis:
Hic pietate prior."

I give not here my translation of these verses, though I think I have not ill succeeded in them, because your lordship is so great a master of the original that I have no reason to desire you should see Virgil and me so near together. But you may please, my lord, to take notice that the Latin author refines upon the Greek, and insinuates that Homer had done his hero wrong in giving the advantage of the duel to his own countryman, though Diomedes was manifestly the second champion of the Grecians; and Ulysses preferred him before Ajax when he chose him for the companion of his nightly expedition, for he had a headpiece of his own, and wanted only the fortitude of another to bring him off with safety, and that he might compass his design with honour. The French translator thus proceeds:-"They who accuse AEneas for want of courage, either understand not Virgil or have read him slightly; otherwise they would not raise an objection so easy to be answered."

Hereupon he gives so many instances of the hero's valour that to repeat them after him would tire your lordship, and put me to the unnecessary trouble of transcribing the greatest part of the three last AEneids. In short, more could not be expected from an Amadis, a Sir Lancelot, or the whole Round Table than he performs. Proxima quaeque metit galdio is the perfect account of a knight-errant. If it be replied, continues Segrais, that it was not difficult for him to undertake and achieve such hardy enterprises because he wore enchanted arms, that accusation in the first place must fall on Homer ere it can reach Virgil. Achilles was as well provided with them as AEneas, though he was invulnerable without them; and Ariosto, the two Tassos (Bernardo and Torquato), even our own Spenser—in a word, all modern poets—have copied Homer, as well as Virgil; he is neither the first nor last, but in the midst of them, and therefore is safe if they are so. Who knows, says Segrais, but that his fated armour was only an allegorical defence, and signified no more than that he was under the peculiar protection of the gods? born, as the astrologers will tell us out of Virgil (who was well versed in the Chaldean mysteries), under the favourable influence of Jupiter, Venus, and thc Sun? But I insist not on this because I know you believe not there is such an art; though not only Horace and Persius, but Augustus himself, thought otherwise. But in defence of Virgil, I dare positively say that he has been more cautious in this particular than either his predecessor or his descendants; for AEneas was actually wounded in the twelfth of the "AEneis," though he had the same godsmith to forge his arms as had Achilles.

It seems he was no "war-luck," as the Scots commonly call such men, who, they say, are iron-free or lead-free. Yet after this experiment that his arms were not impenetrable (when he was cured indeed by his mother's help, because he was that day to conclude the war by the death of Turnus), the poet durst not carry the miracle too far and restore him wholly to his former vigour; he was still too weak to overtake his enemy, yet we see with what courage he attacks Turnus when he faces and renews the combat. I need say no more, for Virgil defends himself without needing my assistance, and proves his hero truly to deserve that name. He was not, then, a second-rate champion, as they would have him who think fortitude the first virtue in a hero. But being beaten from this hold, they will not yet allow him to be valiant, because he wept more often, as they think, than well becomes a man of courage.

In the first place, if tears are arguments of cowardice, what shall I say of Homer's hero? Shall Achilles pass for timorous because he wept, and wept on less occasions than AEneas? Herein Virgil must be granted to have excelled his master; for once both heroes are described lamenting their lost loves: Briseis was taken away by force from the Grecians, Creusa was lost for ever to her husband. But Achilles went roaring along the salt sea-shore, and, like a booby, was complaining to his mother when he should have revenged his injury by arms:

AEneas took a nobler course; for, having secured his father and his son, he repeated all his former dangers to have found his wife, if she had been above ground. And here your lordship may observe the address of Virgil; it was not for nothing that this passage was related, with all these tender circumstances. AEneas told it, Dido heard it. That he had been so affectionate a husband was no ill argument to the coming dowager that he might prove as kind to her. Virgil has a thousand secret beauties, though I have not leisure to remark them.

Segrais, on this subject of a hero's shedding tears, observes that historians commend Alexander for weeping when he read the mighty actions of Achilles; and Julius Caesar is likewise praised when out of the same noble envy, he wept at the victories of Alexander. But if we observe more closely, we shall find that the tears of AEneas were always on a laudable occasion. Thus he weeps out of compassion and tenderness of nature when in the temple of Carthage he beholds the pictures of his friends who sacrificed their lives in defence of their country. He deplores the lamentable end of his pilot Palinurus, the untimely death of young Pallas his confederate, and the rest which I omit. Yet even for these tears his wretched critics dare condemn him; they make AEneas little better than a kind of St. Swithin hero, always raining. One of these censors was bold enough to argue him of cowardice, when in the beginning of the first book he not only weeps, but trembles, at an approaching storm:-

"Extemplo AEneae solvuntur frigore membra:
Ingemit, et duplices tendens ad sidera palmas," &c.

But to this I have answered formerly that his fear was not for himself, but for his people. And who can give a sovereign a better commendation, or recommend a hero more to the affection of the reader? They were threatened with a tempest, and he wept; he was promised Italy, and therefore he prayed for the accomplishment of that promise;—all this in the beginning of a storm; therefore he showed the more early piety and the quicker sense of compassion. Thus much I have urged elsewhere in the defence of Virgil: and since, I have been informed by Mr.

Moyle, a young gentleman whom I can never sufficiently commend, that the ancients accounted drowning an accursed death. So that if we grant him to have been afraid, he had just occasion for that fear, both in relation to himself and to his subjects. I think our adversaries can carry this argument no farther, unless they tell us that he ought to have had more confidence in the promise of the gods. But how was he assured that he had understood their oracles aright? Helenus might be mistaken; Phoebus might speak doubtfully; even his mother might flatter him that he might prosecute his voyage, which if it succeeded happily he should be the founder of an empire: for that she herself was doubtful of his fortune is apparent by the address she made to Jupiter on his behalf; to which the god makes answer in these words:-

"Parce metu, Cytherea, manent immota tuorum Fata tibi," &c. Notwithstanding which the goddess, though comforted, was not assured; for even after this, through the course of the whole "AEneis," she still apprehends the interest which Juno might make with Jupiter against her son. For it was a moot point in heaven whether he could alter fate or not; and indeed some passages in Virgil would make us suspect that he was of opinion Jupiter might defer fate, though he could not alter it; for in the latter end of the tenth book he introduces Juno begging for the life of Turnus, and flattering her husband with the power of changing destiny, tua, qui potes, orsa reflectas! To which he graciously answers—

"Si mora praesentis leti, tempusque caduco
Oratur juveni, meque hoc ita ponere sentis,
Tolle fuga Turnum, atquc instantibus eripe fatis.
Hactenus indulsisse vacat. Sin altior istis
Sub precibus venia ulla latet, totumque moveri
Mutarive putas bellum, spes pascis inanis."

But that he could not alter those decrees the king of gods himself confesses in the book above cited, when he comforts Hercules for the death of Pallas, who had invoked his aid before he threw his lance at Turnus:-

"Trojae sub maenibus altis
Tot nati cecidere deum; quin occidit una

Sarpedon, mea progenies; etiam sua Turnum
Fata vocant, metasque dati pervenit ad aevi."

Where he plainly acknowledges that he could not save his own son, or prevent the death which he foresaw. Of his power to defer the blow, I once occasionally discoursed with that excellent person Sir Robert Howard, who is better conversant than any man that I know in the doctrine of the Stoics, and he set me right, from the concurrent testimony of philosophers and poets, that Jupiter could not retard the effects of fate, even for a moment; for when I cited Virgil as favouring the contrary opinion in that verse:

"Tolle fuga Turnum, atque instantibus eripe fatis"

he replied, and I think with exact judgment, that when Jupiter gave Juno leave to withdraw Turnus from the present danger, it was because he certainly foreknew that his fatal hour was not come, that it was in destiny for Juno at that time to save him, and that himself obeyed destiny in giving her that leave. I need say no more in justification of our hero's courage, and am much deceived if he ever be attacked on this side of his character again. But he is arraigned with more show of reason by the ladies, who will make a numerous party against him, for being false to love in forsaking Dido; and I cannot much blame them, for, to say the truth, it is an ill precedent for their gallants to follow.

Yet if I can bring him off with flying colours, they may learn experience at her cost; and for her sake avoid a cave as the worse shelter they can choose from a shower of rain, especially when they have a lover in their company. In the first place, Segrais observes with much acuteness that they who blame AEneas for his insensibility of love when he left Carthage, contradict their former accusation of him for being always crying, compassionate, and effeminately sensible of those misfortunes which befell others. They give him two contrary characters; but Virgil makes him of a piece, always grateful, always tender-hearted. But they are impudent enough to discharge themselves of this blunder by haying the contradiction at Virgil's door.

He, they say, has shown his hero with these inconsistent

characters—acknowledging and ungrateful, compassionate and hard-hearted, but at the bottom fickle and self-interested; for Dido had not only received his weather-beaten troops before she saw him, and given them her protection, but had also offered them an equal share in her dominion:

"Vultis et his mecum pariter considere regnis?
Urbem quam statuo, vesra est."

This was an obligement never to be forgotten, and the more to be considered because antecedent to her love. That passion, it is true, produced the usual effects of generosity, gallantry, and care to please, and thither we refer them; but when she had made all these advances, it was still in his power to have refused them. After the intrigue of the cave—call it marriage, or enjoyment only--he was no longer free to take or leave; he had accepted the favour, and was obliged to be constant, if he would be grateful. My lord, I have set this argument in the best light I can, that the ladies may not think I write booty; and perhaps it may happen to me, as it did to Doctor Cudworth, who has raised such strong objections against the being of a God and Providence, that many think he has not answered them.

You may please at least to hear the adverse party. Segrais pleads for Virgil that no less than an absolute command from Jupiter could excuse this insensibility of the hero, and this abrupt departure, which looks so like extreme ingratitude; but at the same time he does wisely to remember you that Virgil had made piety the first character of AEneas; and this being allowed, as I am afraid it must, he was obliged, antecedent to all other considerations, to search an asylum for his gods in Italy—for those very gods, I say, who had promised to his race the universal empire. Could a pious man dispense with the commands of Jupiter to satisfy his passion, or—take it in the strongest sense—to comply with the obligations of his gratitude? Religion, it is true, must have moral honesty for its groundwork, or we shall be apt to suspect its truth; but an immediate revelation dispenses with all duties of morality.

All casuists agree that theft is a breach of the moral law; yet if I might presume to mingle things sacred with profane, the Israelites only spoiled the Egyptians, not robbed them, because the propriety was transferred by a revelation to their lawgiver. I confess Dido was a very infidel in this point; for she would not believe, as Virgil makes her say, that ever Jupiter would send Mercury on such an immoral errand. But this needs no answer—at least, no more than Virgil gives it:-

"Fata obstant, placidasque viri Deus obstruit aures."

This notwithstanding, as Segrais confesses, he might have shown a little more sensibility when he left her, for that had been according to his character. But let Virgil answer for himself. He still loved her, and

struggled with his inclinations to obey the gods:

"Curam sub corde premebat,
Multa gemens, magnoque animum labefactus amore."

Upon the whole matter, and humanly speaking, I doubt there was a fault somewhere, and Jupiter is better able to bear the blame than either Virgil or AEneas. The poet, it seems, had found it out, and therefore brings the deserting hero and the forsaken lady to meet together in the lower regions, where he excuses himself when it is too late, and accordingly she will take no satisfaction, nor so much as hear him. Now Segrais is forced to abandon his defence, and excuses his author by saying that the "AEneis" is an imperfect work, and that death prevented the divine poet from reviewing it, and for that reason he had condemned it to the fire, though at the same time his two translators must acknowledge that the sixth book is the most correct of the whole "AEneis."

Oh, how convenient is a machine sometimes in a heroic poem! This of Mercury is plainly one; and Virgil was constrained to use it here, or the honesty of his hero would be ill defended; and the fair sex, however, if they had the deserter in their power, would certainly have shown him no more mercy than the Bacchanals did Orpheus: for if too much constancy may be a fault sometimes, then want of constancy, and ingratitude after the last favour, is a crime that never will be forgiven. But of machines, more in their proper place, where I shall show with how much judgment they have been used by Virgil; and in the meantime pass to another article of his defence on the present subject, where, if I cannot clear the hero, I hope at least to bring off the poet, for here I must divide their causes. Let AEneas trust to his machine, which will only help to break his fall; but the address is incomparable. Plato, who borrowed so much from Homer, and yet concluded for the banishment of all poets, would at least have rewarded Virgil before he sent him into exile; but I go farther, and say that he ought to be acquitted, and deserved, beside, the bounty of Augustus and the gratitude of the Roman people.

If after this the ladies will stand out, let them remember that the jury is not all agreed; for Octavia was of his party, and was of the first quality in Rome: she was also present at the reading of the sixth AEneid, and we know not that she condemned AEneas, but we are sure she presented the poet for his admirable elegy on her son Marcellus. But let us consider the secret reasons which Virgil had for thus framing this noble episode, wherein the whole passion of love is more exactly described than in any other poet. Love was the theme of his fourth book; and though it is the shortest of the whole "AEneis," yet there he has given its beginning, its progress, its traverses, and its conclusion; and had exhausted so entirely this subject that he could resume it but very slightly in the eight ensuing books.

She was warmed with the graceful appearance of the hero; she smothered those sparkles out of decency, but conversation blew them up into a flame. Then she was forced to make a confidante of her whom she best might trust, her own sister, who approves the passion, and thereby augments it; then succeeds her public owning it; and after that the consummation. Of Venus and Juno, Jupiter and Mercury, I say nothing (for they were all machining work); but possession having cooled his love, as it increased hers, she soon perceived the change, or at least grew suspicious of a change. This suspicion soon turned to jealousy, and jealousy to rage; then she disdains and threatens, and again is humble and entreats: and, nothing availing, despairs, curses, and at last becomes her own executioner. See here the whole process of that passion, to which nothing can be added. I dare go no farther, lest I should lose the connection of my discourse. To love our native country, and to study its benefit and its glory; to be interested in its concerns, is natural to all men, and is indeed our common duty. A poet makes a farther step for endeavouring to do honour to it. It is allowable in him even to be partial in its cause; for he is not tied to truth, or fettered by the laws of history. Homer and Tasso are justly praised for choosing their heroes out of Greece and Italy; Virgil, indeed, made his a Trojan, but it was to derive the Romans and his own Augustus from him; but all the three poets are manifestly partial to their heroes in favour of their country. For Dares Phrygius reports of Hector that he was slain cowardly; AEneas, according to the best account, slew not Mezentius, but was slain by him; and the chronicles of Italy tell us little of that Rinaldo d'Este who conquers Jerusalem in Tasso.

He might be a champion of the Church, but we know not that he was so much as present at the siege. To apply this to Virgil, he thought himself engaged in honour to espouse the cause and quarrel of his country against Carthage. He knew he could not please the Romans better, or oblige them more to patronise his poem, than by disgracing the foundress of that city. He shows her ungrateful to the memory of her first husband, doting on a stranger, enjoyed and afterwards forsaken by him. This was the original, says he, of the immortal hatred betwixt the two rival nations.

It is true, he colours the falsehood of AEneas by an express command from Jupiter to forsake the queen who had obliged him; but he knew the Romans were to be his readers, and them he bribed—perhaps at the expense of his hero's honesty; but he gained his cause, however, as pleading before corrupt judges. They were content to see their founder false to love, for still he had the advantage of the amour. It was their enemy whom he forsook, and she might have forsaken him if he had not got the start of her. She had already forgotten her vows to her Sichaeus, and varium et nutabile semper femina is the sharpest satire in the fewest words that ever was made on womankind; for both the adjectives are neuter, and animal must be understood to make them grammar. Virgil does well to put those words into the mouth of Mercury. If a god had not spoken them, neither durst he have written them, nor I translated them. Yet the deity was forced to come twice on the same errand; and the second time, as much a hero as AEneas was, he frighted him. It seems he feared not Jupiter so much as Dido; for your lordship may observe that, as much intent as he was upon his voyage, yet he still delayed it, till the messenger was obliged to tell him plainly that if he weighed not anchor in the night the queen would be with him in the morning, notumque furens quid femina possit: she was injured, she was revengeful, she was powerful. The poet had likewise before hinted that the people were naturally perfidious, for he gives their character in the queen, and makes a proverb of Punica fides many ages before it was invented.

Thus I hope, my lord, that I have made good my promise, and justified the poet, whatever becomes of the false knight. And, sure, a poet is as much privileged to lie as an ambassador for the honour and interest of his country—at least, as Sir Henry Wotton has defined. This naturally leads me to the defence of the famous anachronism in making AEneas and Dido contemporaries, for it is certain that the hero lived almost two hundred years before the building of Carthage. One who imitates Boccalini says that Virgil was accused before Apollo for this error. The god soon found that he was not able to defend his favourite by reason, for the case was clear; he therefore gave this middle sentence: that anything might be allowed to his son Virgil on the account of his other merits; that, being a monarch, he had a dispensing power, and pardoned him.

But that this special act of grace might never be drawn into example, or pleaded by his puny successors in justification of their ignorance, he decreed for the future—no poet should presume to make a lady die for love two hundred years before her birth. To moralise this story, Virgil is the Apollo who has this dispensing power. His great judgment made the laws of poetry, but he never made himself a slave to them; chronology at best is but a cobweb law, and he broke through it with his weight. They who will imitate him wisely must choose, as he did, an obscure and a remote era, where they may invent at pleasure, and not be easily contradicted. Neither he nor the Romans had ever read the Bible, by which only his false computation of times can be made out against him. This Segrais says in his defence, and proves it from his learned friend Bochartus, whose letter on this subject he has printed at the end of the fourth AEneid, to which I refer your lordship and the reader. Yet the credit of Virgil was so great that he made this fable of his own invention pass for an authentic history, or at least as credible as anything in Homer.

Ovid takes it up after him even in the same age, and makes an ancient heroine of Virgil's new-created Dido; dictates a letter for her, just before her death, to the ingrateful fugitive; and, very unluckily for himself, is for measuring a sword with a man so much superior in force to him on the same subject. I think I may be judge of this, because I have translated both. The famous author of "The Art of Love" has nothing of his own; he borrows all from a greater master in his own profession, and, which is worse, improves nothing which he finds. Nature fails him; and, being forced to his old shift, he has recourse to witticism. This passes, indeed, with his soft admirers, and gives him the preference to Virgil in their esteem; but let them like for themselves, and not prescribe to others, for our author needs not their admiration. The motive that induced Virgil to coin this fable I have showed already, and have also begun to show that he might make this anachronism, by superseding the mechanic rules of poetry, for the same reason that a monarch may dispense with or suspend his own laws when he finds it necessary so to do, especially if those laws are not altogether fundamental.

Nothing is to be called a fault in poetry, says Aristotle, but what is against the art; therefore a man may be an admirable poet without being an exact chronologer. Shall we dare, continues Segrais, to condemn Virgil for having made a fiction against the order of time, when we commend Ovid and other poets who have made many of their fictions against the order of nature? For what else are the splendid miracles of the "Metamorphoses?" Yet these are beautiful as they are related, and have also deep learning and instructive mythologies couched under them. But to give, as Virgil does in this episode, the original cause of the long wars betwixt Rome and Carthage; to draw truth out of fiction after so probable a manner, with so much beauty, and so much for the honour of his country, was proper only to the divine wit of Maro; and Tasso, in one of his discourses, admires him for this particularly. It is not lawful indeed to contradict a point of history which is known to all the world—as, for example, to make Hannibal and Scipio contemporaries with Alexander—but in the dark recesses of antiquity a great poet may and ought to feign such things as he finds not there, if they can be brought to embellish that subject which he treats.

On the other side, the pains and diligence of ill poets is but thrown away when they want the genius to invent and feign agreeably. But if the fictions be delightful (which they always are if they be natural) if they be of a piece; if the beginning, the middle, and the end be in their due places, and artfully united to each other, such works can never fail of their deserved success. And such is Virgil's episode of Dido and AEneas, where the sourest critic must acknowledge that if he had deprived his "AEneis" of so great an ornament, because he found no traces of it in antiquity, he had avoided their unjust censure, but had wanted one of the greatest beauties of his poem.

I shall say more of this in the next article of their charge against him, which is—want of invention. In the meantime I may affirm, in honour of this episode, that it is not only now esteemed the most pleasing entertainment of the "AEneis," but was so accounted in his own age, and before it was mellowed into that reputation which time has given it; for which I need produce no other testimony than that of Ovid, his contemporary:

"Nec pars ulla magis legitur de corpore toto,
Quam non legitimo faedere junctus amor."

Where, by the way, you may observe, my lord, that Ovid in those words, non legitimo faedere junctus amor, will by no means allow it to be a lawful marriage betwixt Dido and

AEneas. He was in banishment when he wrote those verses, which I cite from his letter to Augustus. "You, sir," saith he, "have sent me into exile for writing my 'Art of Love' and my wanton elegies; yet your own poet was happy in your good graces, though he brought Dido and AEneas into a cave, and left them there not over-honestly together: may I be so bold to ask your majesty is it a greater fault to teach the art of unlawful love than to show it in the action?" But was Ovid the court-poet so bad a courtier as to find no other plea to excuse himself than by a plain accusation of his master? Virgil confessed it was a lawful marriage betwixt the lovers; that Juno, the goddess of matrimony, had ratified it by her presence (for it was her business to bring matters to that issue): that the ceremonies were short we may believe, for Dido was not only amorous, but a widow.

Mercury himself, though employed on a quite contrary errand, yet owns it a marriage by an innuendo—pulchramque uxorius urbem extruis. He calls AEneas not only a husband, but upbraids him for being a fond husband, as the word uxorius implies. Now mark a little, if your lordship pleases, why Virgil is so much concerned to make this marriage (for he seems to be the father of the bride himself, and to give her to the bridegroom); it was to make way for the divorce which he intended afterwards, for he was a finer flatterer than Ovid, and I more than conjecture that he had in his eye the divorce which not long before had passed betwixt the emperor and Scribonia. He drew this dimple in the cheek of AEneas to prove Augustus of the same family by so remarkable a feature in the same place. Thus, as we say in our home-spun English proverb, he killed two birds with one stone—pleased the emperor by giving him the resemblance of his ancestor, and gave him such a resemblance as was not scandalous in that age (for to leave one wife and take another was but a matter of gallantry at that time of day among the Romans).

Neque haec in faedera veni is the very excuse which AEneas makes when he leaves his lady. "I made no such bargain with you at our marriage to live always drudging on at Carthage; my business was Italy, and I never made a secret of it. If I took my pleasure, had not you your share of it? I leave you free at my departure to comfort yourself with the next stranger who happens to be shipwrecked on your coast; be as kind an hostess as you have been to me, and you can never fail of another husband. In the meantime I call the gods to witness that I leave your shore unwillingly; for though Juno made the marriage, yet Jupiter commands me to forsake you." This is the effect of what he saith when it is dishonoured out of Latin verse into English prose. If the poet argued not aright, we must pardon him for a poor blind heathen, who knew no better morals.

I have detained your lordship longer than I intended on this objection, which would indeed weigh something in a Spiritual Court;--but I am not to defend our poet there. The next, I think, is but a cavil, though the cry is great against him, and hath continued from the time of Macrobius to this present age; I hinted it before. They lay no less than want of invention to his charge—a capital charge, I must acknowledge; for a poet is a maker, as the word signifies; and who cannot make—that is, invent—hath his name for nothing. That which makes this accusation look so strong at the first sight is that he has borrowed so many things from Homer, Apollonius Rhodius, and others who preceded him. But in the first place, if invention is to be taken in so strict a sense that the matter of a poem must be wholly new, and that in all its parts, then Scaliger hath made out, saith Segrais, that the history of Troy was no more the invention of Homer than of Virgil.

There was not an old woman or almost a child, but had it in their mouths before the Greek poet or his friends digested it into this admirable order in which we read it. At this rate, as Solomon hath told us, there is nothing new beneath the sun. Who, then, can pass for an inventor if Homer as well as Virgil must be deprived of that glory! Is Versailles the less a new building because the architect of that palace hath imitated others which were built before it? Walls, doors and windows, apartments, offices, rooms of convenience and magnificence, are in all great houses. So descriptions, figures, fables, and the rest, must be in all heroic poems; they are the common materials of poetry, furnished from the magazine of nature: every poet hath as much right to them as every man hath to air or water

"Quid prohibetis aquas? Usus communis aquarum est."

But the argument of the work (that is to say, its principal action), the economy and disposition of it—these are the things which distinguish copies from originals. The Poet who borrows nothing from others is yet to be born; he and the Jews' Messias will come together. There are parts of the "AEneis" which resemble some parts both of the "Ilias" and of the "Odysses;" as, for example, AEneas descended into hell, and Ulysses had been there before him; AEneas loved Dido, and Ulysses loved Calypso: in few words, Virgil hath imitated Homer's "Odysses" in his first six books, and in his six last the "Ilias." But from hence can we infer that the two poets write the same history? Is there no invention in some other parts of Virgil's "AEneis?" The disposition of so many various matters, is not that his own? From what book of Homer had Virgil his episode of Nysus and Euryalus, of Mezentius and Lausus?

From whence did he borrow his design of bringing AEneas into Italy? of establishing the Roman Empire on the foundations of a Trojan colony? to say nothing of the honour he did his patron, not only in his descent from Venus, but in making him so like her in his best features that the goddess might have mistaken Augustus for her son. He had indeed the story from common fame, as Homer had his from the Egyptian priestess. AEneadum genetrix was no more unknown to Lucretius than to him; but Lucretius taught him not to form his hero, to give him piety or valour for his manners—and both in so eminent a degree that, having done what was possible for man to save his king and country, his mother was forced to appear to him and restrain his fury, which hurried him to death in their revenge.

But the poet made his piety more successful; he brought off his father and his son; and his gods witnessed to his devotion by putting themselves under his protection, to be replaced by him in their promised Italy. Neither the invention nor the conduct of this great action were owing to Homer or any other poet; it is one thing to copy, and another thing to imitate from nature. The copier is that servile imitator to whom Horace gives no better a name than that of animal; he will not so much as allow him to be a man. Raffaelle imitated nature; they who copy one of Raffaelle's pieces, imitate but him, for his work is their original. They translate him, as I do Virgil; and fall as short of him as I of Virgil. There is a kind of invention in the imitation of Raffaelle; for though the thing was in nature, yet the idea of it was his own. Ulysses travelled, so did AEneas; but neither of them were the first travellers: for Cain went into the land of Nod before they were born, and neither of the poets ever heard of such a man. If Ulysses had been killed at Troy, yet AEneas must have gone to sea, or he could never have arrived in Italy; but the designs of the two poets were as different as the courses of their heroes—one went home, and the other sought a home.

To return to my first similitude. Suppose Apelles and Raffaelle had each of them painted a burning Troy, might not the modern painter have succeeded as well as the ancient, though neither of them had seen the town on fire? For the drafts of both were taken from the ideas which they had of nature. Cities have been burnt before either of them were in being. But to close the simile as I began it: they would not have designed it after the same manner; Apelles would have distinguished Pyrrhus from the rest of all the Grecians, and showed him forcing his entrance into Priam's palace; there he had set him in the fairest light, and given him the chief place of all his figures, because he was a Grecian and he would do honour to his country. Raffaelle, who was an Italian, and descended from the Trojans, would have made AEneas the hero of his piece, and perhaps not with his father on his back, his son in one hand, his bundle of gods in the other, and his wife following (for an act of piety is not half so graceful in a picture as an act of courage); he would rather have drawn him killing Androgeus or some other hand to hand, and the blaze of the fires should have darted full upon his face, to make him conspicuous amongst his Trojans.

This, I think, is a just comparison betwixt the two poets

in the conduct of their several designs. Virgil cannot be said to copy Homer; the Grecian had only the advantage of writing first. If it be urged that I have granted a resemblance in some parts, yet therein Virgil has excelled him; for what are the tears of Calypso for being left, to the fury and death of Dido? Where is there the whole process of her passion and all its violent effects to be found in the languishing episode of the "Odysses"? If this be to copy, let the critics show us the same disposition, features, or colouring in their original. The like may be said of the descent to hell, which was not of Homer's invention either; he had it from the story of Orpheus and Eurydice. But to what end did Ulysses make that journey? AEneas undertook it by the express commandment of his father's ghost. There he was to show him all the succeeding heroes of his race, and next to Romulus (mark, if you please the address of Virgil) his own patron, Augustus Caesar. Anchises was likewise to instruct him how to manage the Italian war, and how to conclude it with his honour—that is, in other words, to lay the foundations of that empire which Augustus was to govern. This is the noble invention of our author, but it hath been copied by so many sign-post daubers that now it is grown fulsome, rather by their want of skill than by the commonness.

In the last place. I may safely grant that by reading Homer, Virgil was taught to imitate his invention—that is to imitate like him (which is no more than if a painter studied Raffaelle that he might learn to design after his manner). And thus I might imitate Virgil if I were capable of writing an heroic poem, and yet the invention be my own; but I should endeavour to avoid a servile copying. I would not give the same story under other names, with the same characters, in the same order, and with the same sequel, for every common reader to find me out at the first sight for a plagiary, and cry, "This I read before in Virgil in a better language and in better verse." This is like Merry-Andrew on the low rope copying lubberly the same tricks which his master is so dexterously performing on the high.

I will trouble your lordship but with one objection more,

which I know not whether I found in Le Febvre or Valois, but I am sure I have read it in another French critic, whom I will not name because I think it is not much for his reputation. Virgil in the heat of action—suppose, for example, in describing the fury of his hero in a battle (when he is endeavouring to raise our concernments to the highest pitch)—turns short on the sudden into some similitude which diverts, say they, your attention from the main subject, and misspends it on some trivial image. He pours cold water into the caldron when his business is to make it boil.

This accusation is general against all who would be thought heroic poets, but I think it touches Virgil less than any; he is too great a master of his art to make a blot which may so easily be hit. Similitudes (as I have said) are not for tragedy, which is all violent, and where the passions are in a perpetual ferment; for there they deaden, where they should animate; they are not of the nature of dialogue unless in comedy. A metaphor is almost all the stage can suffer, which is a kind of similitude comprehended in a word. But this figure has a contrary effect in heroic poetry; there it is employed to raise the admiration, which is its proper business; and admiration is not of so violent a nature as fear or hope, compassion or horror, or any concernment we can have for such or such a person on the stage. Not but I confess that similitudes and descriptions when drawn into an unreasonable length must needs nauseate the reader. Once I remember (and but once) Virgil makes a similitude of fourteen lines, and his description of Fame is about the same number. He is blamed for both, and I doubt not but he would have contracted them had be lived to have reviewed his work; but faults are no precedents. This I have observed of his similitudes in general—that they are not placed (as our unobserving critics tell us) in the heat of any action, but commonly in its declining; when he has warmed us in his description as much as possibly he can, then (lest that warmth should languish) he renews it by some apt similitude which illustrates his subject and yet palls not his audience. I need give your lordship but one example of this kind, and leave the rest to your observation when next you review the whole "AEneis" in the original, unblemished by my rude translation; it is in the first hook, where the poet describes Neptune composing the ocean, on which AEolus had raised a tempest without his permission. He had already chidden the rebellious winds for obeying the commands of their usurping master; he had warned them from the seas; he had beaten down the billows with his mace; dispelled the clouds, restored the sunshine, while Triton and Cymothoe were heaving the ships from off the quicksands, before the poet would offer at a similitude for illustration

"Ac, veluti magno in populo cum saepe coorta est
Seditio, saevitque animis ignobile vulgus;
Jamque faces, et saxa volant; furor arma ministrat;
Tum, pietate gravem ac meritis si forte virum quem
Conspexere, silent, arrectisque auribus adstant:
Ille regit dictis animos, et pectora mulcet:
Sic cunctus pelagi cecidit fragor, aequora postquam
Prospiciens genitor, coeloque invectus aperto
Flectit equos, curruque volans dat lora secundo."

This is the first similitude which Virgil makes in this poem, and one of the longest in the whole, for which reason I the rather cite it. While the storm was in its fury, any allusion had been improper; for the poet could have compared it to nothing more impetuous than itself; consequently he could have made no illustration. If he could have illustrated, it had been an ambitious ornament out of season, and would have diverted our concernment (nunc non erat his locus), and therefore he deferred it to its proper place.

These are the criticisms of most moment which have been made against the "AEneis" by the ancients or moderns. As for the particular exceptions against this or that passage, Macrobius and Pontanus have answered them already. If I desired to appear more learned than I am, it had been as easy for me to have taken their objections and solutions as it is for a country parson to take the expositions of the Fathers out of Junius and Tremellius, or not to have named the authors from whence I had them; for so Ruaeus (otherwise a most judicious commentator on Virgil's works) has used Pontanus, his greatest benefactor, of whom he is very silent, and I do not remember that he once cites him.

What follows next is no objection; for that implies a fault, and it had been none in Virgil if he had extended the time of his action beyond a year—at least, Aristotle has set no precise limits to it. Homer's, we know, was within two months; Tasso; I am sure, exceeds not a summer, and if I examined him perhaps he might be reduced into a much less compass. Bossu leaves it doubtful whether Virgil's action were within the year, or took up some months beyond it. Indeed, the whole dispute is of no more concernment to the common reader than it is to a ploughman whether February this year had twenty-eight or twenty-nine days in it; but for the satisfaction of the more curious (of which number I am sure your lordship is one) I will translate what I think convenient out of Segrais, whom perhaps you have not read, for he has made it highly probable that the action of the "AEneis" began in the spring, and was not extended beyond the autumn; and we have known campaigns that have begun sooner and have ended later.

Ronsard and the rest whom Segrais names, who are of opinion that the action of this poem takes up almost a year and half, ground their calculation thus:-Anchises died in Sicily at the end of winter or beginning of the spring. AEneas, immediately after the interment of his father, puts to sea for Italy; he is surprised by the tempest described in the beginning of the first book; and there it is that the scene of the poem opens, and where the action must commence. He is driven by this storm on the coasts of Africa; he stays at Carthage all that summer, and almost all the winter following; sets sail again for Italy just before the beginning of the spring; meets with contrary winds, and makes Sicily the second time. This part of the action completes the year.

Then he celebrates the anniversary of his father's funerals, and shortly after arrives at Cumes. And from thence his time is taken up in his first treaty with Latinus; the overture of the war; the siege of his camp by Turnus; his going for succours to relieve it; his return; the raising of the siege by the first battle; the twelve days' truce; the second battle; the assault of

Laurentum, and the single fight with Turnus—all which, they say, cannot take up less than four or five months more, by which account we cannot suppose the entire action to be contained in a much less compass than a year and half. Segrais reckons another way, and his computation is not condemned by the learned Ruaeus, who compiled and published the commentaries on our poet which we call the "Dauphin's Virgil." He allows the time of year when Anchises died to be in the latter end of winter or the beginning of the spring; he acknowledges that when AEneas is first seen at sea afterwards, and is driven by the tempest on the coast of Africa, is the time when the action is naturally to begin; he confesses farther, that AEneas left Carthage in the latter end of winter, for Dido tells him in express terms, as an argument for his longer stay-

"Quin etiam hiberno moliris sidere classem."

But whereas Ronsard's followers suppose that when AEneas had buried his father he set sail immediately for Italy (though the tempest drove him on the coast of Carthage), Segrais will by no means allow that supposition, but thinks it much more probable that he remained in Sicily till the midst of July or the beginning of August, at which time he places the first appearance of his hero on the sea, and there opens the action of the poem. From which beginning, to the death of Turnus, which concludes the action, there need not be supposed above ten months of intermediate time; for arriving at Carthage in the latter end of summer, staying there the winter following, departing thence in the very beginning of the spring, making a short abode in Sicily the second time, landing in Italy, and making the war, may be reasonably judged the business but of ten months.

To this the Ronsardians reply that, having been for seven years before in quest of Italy, and having no more to do in Sicily than to inter his father—after that office was performed, what remained for him but without delay to pursue his first adventure? To which Segrais answers that the obsequies of his father, according to the rites of the Greeks and Romans, would detain him for many days; that a longer time must be taken up in the re-fitting of his ships after so tedious a voyage, and in refreshing his weather-beaten soldiers on a friendly coast. These indeed are but suppositions on both sides, yet those of Segrais seem better grounded; for the feast of Dido, when she entertained AEneas first, has the appearance of a summer's night, which seems already almost ended, when he begins his story. Therefore the love was made in autumn; the hunting followed properly, when the heats of that scorching country were declining. The winter was passed in jollity, as the season and their love required; and he left her in the latter end of winter, as is already proved. This opinion is fortified by the arrival of AEneas at the mouth of Tiber, which marks the season of the spring, that season being perfectly described by the singing of the birds saluting the dawn, and by the beauty of the place, which the poet seems to have painted expressly in the seventh AEneid:-

> *"Aurora in roseis fulgebat lutea bigis,*
> *Cum venti posuere...*
> *... variae circumque supraque*
> *Assuetae ripis volucres, et fluminis alveo,*
> *AEthera mulcebant cantu."*

The remainder of the action required but three months more; for when AEneas went for succour to the Tuscans, he found their army in a readiness to march and wanting only a commander: so that, according to this calculation, the "AEneas" takes not up above a year complete, and may be comprehended in less compass.

This, amongst other circumstances treated more at large by Segrais, agrees with the rising of Orion, which caused the tempest described in the beginning of the first book. By some passages in the "Pastorals," but more particularly in the "Georgics," our poet is found to be an exact astronomer, according to the knowledge of that age. Now Ilioneus, whom Virgil twice employs in embassies as the best speaker of the Trojans, attributes that tempest to Orion in his speech to Dido:-

"Cum subito assurgens fluctu nimbosus Orion."

He must mean either the heliacal or achronical rising of that sign. The heliacal rising of a constellation is when it comes from under the rays of the sun, and begins to appear before daylight. The achronical rising, on the contrary, is when it appears at the close of day, and in opposition of the sun's diurnal course. The heliacal rising of Orion is at present computed to be about the 6th of July; and about that time it is that he either causes or presages tempests on the seas. Segrais has observed farther, that when Anna counsels Dido to stay AEneas during the winter, she speaks also of Orion:

"Dum pelago desaevit hiems, et aquosus Orion."

If therefore Ilioneus, according to our supposition, understand the heliacal rising of Orion, Anna must mean the achronical, which the different epithets given to that constellation seem to manifest. Ilioneus calls him nimbosus, Anna, aquosus. He is tempestuous in the summer, when he rises heliacally; and rainy in the winter, when he rises achronically. Your lordship will pardon me for the frequent repetition of these cant words, which I could not avoid in this abbreviation of Segrais, who, I think, deserves no little commendation in this new criticism.

I have yet a word or two to say of Virgil's machines, from my own observation of them. He has imitated those of Homer, but not copied them. It was established long before this time, in the Roman religion as well as in the Greek, that there were gods, and both nations for the most part worshipped the same deities, as did also the Trojans (from whom the Romans, I suppose, would rather be thought to derive the rites of their religion than from the Grecians, because they thought themselves descended from them). Each of those gods had his proper office, and the chief of them their particular attendants. Thus Jupiter had in propriety Ganymede and Mercury, and Juno had Iris. It was not for Virgil, then, to Create new ministers; he must take what he found in his religion. It cannot therefore be said that he borrowed them from Homer, any more than from Apollo, Diana, and the rest, whom he uses as he finds occasion for them, as the Grecian poet did; but he invents the occasions for which he uses them.

Venus, after the destruction of Troy, had gained Neptune entirely to her party; therefore we find him busy in the beginning of the "AEneis" to calm the tempest raised by

AEolus, and afterwards conducting the Trojan fleet to Cumes in safety, with the loss only of their pilot, for whom he bargains. I name those two examples—amongst a hundred which I omit—to prove that Virgil, generally speaking, employed his machines in performing those things which might possibly have been done without them. What more frequent than a storm at sea upon the rising of Orion? What wonder if amongst so many ships there should one be overset, which was commanded by Orontes, though half the winds had not been there which AEolus employed? Might not Palinurus, without a miracle, fall asleep and drop into the sea, having been over-wearied with watching, and secure of a quiet passage by his observation of the skies? At least AEneas, who knew nothing of the machine of Somnus, takes it plainly in this sense:

"O nimium coelo et pelago confise sereno,
Nudus in ignota, Palinure, jacebis arena."

But machines sometimes are specious things to amuse the reader, and give a colour of probability to things otherwise incredible; and, besides, it soothed the vanity of the Romans to find the gods so visibly concerned in all the actions of their predecessors. We who are better taught by our religion, yet own every wonderful accident which befalls us for the best, to be brought to pass by some special providence of Almighty God, and by the care of guardian angels; and from hence I might infer that no heroic poem can be writ on the Epicurean principles, which I could easily demonstrate if there were need to prove it or I had leisure. When Venus opens the eyes of her son AEneas to behold the gods who combated against Troy in that fatal night when it was surprised, we share the pleasure of that glorious vision (which Tasso has not ill copied in the sacking of Jerusalem).

But the Greeks had done their business though neither Neptune, Juno, or Pallas had given them their divine assistance. The most crude machine which Virgil uses is in the episode of Camilla, where Opis by the command of her mistress kills Aruns. The next is in the twelfth AEneid, where Venus cures her son AEneas. But in the last of these the poet was driven to a necessity, for Turnus was to be slain that very day; and AEneas, wounded as he was, could not have engaged him in single combat unless his hurt had been miraculously healed and the poet had considered that the dittany which she brought from Crete could not have wrought so speedy an effect without the juice of ambrosia which she mingled with it. After all, that his machine might not seem too violent, we see the hero limping after Turnus; the wound was skinned, but the strength of his thigh was not restored. But what reason had our author to wound AEneas at so critical a time?

And how came the cuishes to be worse tempered than the rest of his armour, which was all wrought by Vulcan and his journeymen? These difficulties are not easily to be solved without confessing that Virgil had not life enough to correct his work, though he had reviewed it and found those errors, which he resolved to mend; but being prevented by death, and not willing to leave an imperfect work behind him, he ordained by his last testament that his "AEneis" should be burned. As for the death of Aruns, who was shot by a goddess, the machine was not altogether so outrageous as the wounding Mars and Venus by the sword of Diomede. Two divinities, one would have thought, might have pleaded their prerogative of impassibility, or at least not have been wounded by any mortal hand. Beside that, the [Greek text which cannot be reproduced] which they shed was so very like our common blood that it was not to be distinguished from it but only by the name and colour. As for what Horace says in his "Art of Poetry," that no machines are to be used unless on some extraordinary occasion:

"Nec deus intersit, nisi dignus vindice nodus"

That rule is to be applied to the theatre, of which he is then speaking, and means no more than this—that when the knot of the play is to be untied, and no other way is left for making the discovery, then, and not otherwise, let a god descend upon a rope, and clear the business to the audience. But this has no relation to the machines which are used in an epic poem.

In the last place, for the dira, or flying pest which,

flapping on the shield of Turnus and fluttering about his head, disheartened him in the duel, and presaged to him his approaching death—I might have placed it more properly amongst the objections, for the critics who lay want of courage to the charge of Virgil's hero quote this passage as a main proof of their assertion. They say our author had not only secured him before the duel, but also in the beginning of it had given him the advantage in impenetrable arms and in his sword; for that of Turnus was not his own (which was forged by Vulcan for his father), but a weapon which he had snatched in haste, and by mistake, belonging to his charioteer Metiscus. That after all this Jupiter, who was partial to the Trojan, and distrustful of the event, though he had hung the balance and given it a jog of his hand to weigh down Turnus, thought convenient to give the Fates a collateral security by sending the screech-owl to discourage him; for which they quote these words of Virgil:

"Non me tua turbida virtus
Terret, ait; dii me terrent, et Jupiter hostis."

In answer to which, I say that this machine is one of those which the poet uses only for ornament, and not out of necessity. Nothing can be more beautiful or more poetical than his description of the three Dirae, or the setting of the balance, which our Milton has borrowed from him, but employed to a different end; for, first, he makes God Almighty set the scales for St. Gabriel and Satan, when he knew no combat was to follow; then he makes the good angel's scale descend, and the devil's mount—quite contrary to Virgil, if I have translated the three verses according to my author's sense:

"Jupiter ipse duas aequota examine lances
Sustinet, et fata imponit diversa duorum;
Quem damnet labour, et quo vergat pondere letum."

For I have taken these words Quem damnet labour in the sense which Virgil gives them in another place (Damnabis tu quoque votis), to signify a prosperous event. Yet I dare not condemn so great a genius as Milton; for I am much mistaken if he alludes not to the text in Daniel where Belshazzar was put into the balance and found too light. This is digression, and I return to my subject. I said above that these two machines of the balance and the Dira were only ornamental, and that the success of the duel had been the same without them; for when AEneas and Turnus stood fronting each other before the altar, Turnus looked dejected, and his colour faded in his face, as if he desponded of the victory before the fight; and not only he, but all his party, when the strength of the two champions was judged by the proportion of their limbs, concluded it was impar pugna, and that their chief was overmatched. Whereupon Juturna, who was of the same opinion, took this opportunity to break the treaty and renew the war. Juno herself had plainly told the nymph beforehand that her brother was to fight "Imparibus fatis; nec diis, nec viribus aequis;" so that there was no need of an apparition to fright Turnus, he had the presage within himself of his impending destiny. The Dira only served to confirm him in his first opinion, that it was his destiny to die in the ensuing combat. And in this sense are those words of Virgil to be taken:

"Non me tua turbida virtus
Terret, ait; dii me terrent, et Jupiter hostis."

I doubt not but the adverb solum is to be understood ("It is not your valour only that gives me this concernment, but I find also by this portent that Jupiter is my enemy"); for Turnus fled before, when his first sword was broken, till his sister supplied him with a better, which indeed he could not use because AEneas kept him at a distance with his spear. I wonder Ruaeus saw not this, where he charges his author so unjustly for giving Turnus a second sword to no purpose. How could he fasten a blow or make a thrust, when he was not suffered to approach? Besides, the chief errand of the Dira was to warn Juturna from the field, for she could have brought the chariot again when she saw her brother worsted in the duel. I might farther add that AEneas was so eager of the fight that he left the city, now almost in his possession, to decide his quarrel with Turnus by the sword; whereas Turnus had manifestly declined the combat, and suffered his sister to convey him as far from the reach of his enemy as she could. I say, not only suffered her, but consented to it; for it is plain he knew her by these words:

"O soror, et dudum agnovi, cum prima per artem
Faedera turbasti, teque haec in bella dedisti;
Et tunc necquicquam fallis dea."

I have dwelt so long on this subject that I must contract what I have to say in reference to my translation, unless I would swell my preface into a volume, and make it formidable to your lordship, when you see so many pages yet behind. And, indeed, what I have already written, either in justification or praise of Virgil, is against myself for presuming to copy in my coarse English the thoughts and beautiful expressions of this inimitable poet, who flourished in an age when his language was brought to its last perfection, for which it was particularly owing to him and Horace. I will give your lordship my opinion that those two friends had consulted each other's judgment wherein they should endeavour to excel; and they seem to have pitched on propriety of thought, elegance of words, and harmony of numbers. According to this model, Horace wrote his odes and epodes; for his satires and epistles, being intended wholly for instruction, required another style- "Ornari res ipsa negat, contenta doceri"-and therefore, as he himself professes, are sermoni propriora (nearer prose than verse). But Virgil, who never attempted the lyric verse, is everywhere elegant, sweet, and flowing in his hexameters. His words are not only chosen, but the places in which he ranks them for the sound; he who removes them from the station wherein their master sets them spoils the harmony. What he says of the Sibyl's prophecies may be as properly applied to every word of his—they must be read in order as they lie; the least breath discomposes them, and somewhat of their divinity is lost. I cannot boast that I have been thus exact in my verses; but I have endeavoured to follow the example of my master, and am the first Englishman perhaps who made it his design to copy him in his numbers, his choice of words, and his placing them for the sweetness of the sound.

On this last consideration I have shunned the caesura as much as possibly I could; for wherever that is used, it gives a roughness to the verse, of which we can have little need in a language which is overstocked with consonants. Such is not the Latin where the vowels and consonants are mixed in proportion to each other; yet Virgil judged the vowels to have somewhat of an over-balance, and therefore tempers their sweetness with caesuras. Such difference there is in tongues that the same figure which roughens one, gives majesty to another; and that was it which Virgil studied in his verses. Ovid uses it but rarely; and hence it is that his versification cannot so properly be called sweet as luscious. The Italians are forced upon it once or twice in every line, because they have a redundancy of vowels in their language; their metal is so soft that it will not coin without alloy to harden it.

On the other side, for the reason already named, it is all we can do to give sufficient sweetness to our language; we must not only choose our words for elegance, but for sound—to perform which a mastery in the language is required; the poet must have a magazine of words, and have the art to manage his few vowels to the best advantage, that they may go the farther. He must also know the nature of the vowels—which are more sonorous, and which more soft and sweet—and so dispose them as his present occasions require; all which, and a thousand secrets of versification beside, he may learn from Virgil, if he will take him for his guide. If he be above Virgil, and is resolved to follow his own verve (as the French call it), the proverb will fall heavily upon him: "Who teaches himself has a fool for his master."

Virgil employed eleven years upon his "AEneis," yet he left it, as he thought himself, imperfect; which, when I seriously consider, I wish that, instead of three years which I have spent in the translation of his works, I had four years more allowed me to correct my errors, that I might make my version somewhat more tolerable than it is; for a poet cannot have too great a reverence for his readers if he expects his labours should survive him.

Yet I will neither plead my age nor sickness in excuse of the faults which I have made. That I wanted time is all I have to say; for some of my subscribers grew so clamorous that I could no longer defer the publication. I hope, from the candour of your lordship, and your often-experienced goodness to me, that if the faults are not too many you will make allowances, with Horace:

"Si plura nitent in carmine, non ego paucis
Offendar maculis, quas aut incuria fudit,
Aut humana parum cavit natura."

You may please also to observe that there is not, to the best of my remembrance, one vowel gaping on another for want of a caesura in this whole poem. But where a vowel ends a word the next begins either with a consonant or what is its equivalent; for our w and h aspirate, and our diphthongs, are plainly such. The greatest latitude I take is in the letter y when it concludes a word and the first syllable of the next begins with a vowel. Neither need I have called this a latitude, which is only an explanation of this general rule—that no vowel can be cut off before another when we cannot sink the pronunciation of it, as he, she, me, I, &c. Virgil thinks it sometimes a beauty to imitate the licence of the Greeks, and leave two vowels opening on each other, as in that verse of the third pastoral:

"Et succus pecori, et lac subducitur agnis."

But nobis non licet esse tam disertis—at least, if we study to refine our numbers. I have long had by me the materials of an English "Prosodia," containing all the mechanical rules of versification, wherein I have treated with some exactness of the feet, the quantities, and the pauses. The French and Italians know nothing of the two first—at least, their best poets have not practised them. As for the pauses, Malherbe first brought them into France within this last century, and we see how they adorn their Alexandrines. But as Virgil propounds a riddle which he leaves unsolved:

"Dic quibus in terris, inscripti nomina regum
Nascantur flores, et Phyllida solus habeto"

so I will give your lordship another, and leave the exposition of it to your acute judgment. I am sure there are few who make verses have observed the sweetness of these two lines in "Cooper's Hill":

"Though deep, yet clear; though gentle, yet not dull;
Strong without rage; without o'erflowing, full".

and there are yet fewer who can find the reason of that sweetness. I have given it to some of my friends in conversation, and they have allowed the criticism to be just. But since the evil of false quantities is difficult to be cured in any modern language; since the French and the Italians, as well as we, are yet ignorant what feet are to be used in heroic poetry; since I have not strictly observed those rules myself which I can teach others; since I pretend to no dictatorship among my fellow-poets; since, if I should instruct some of them to make well-running verses, they want genius to give them strength as well as sweetness; and, above all, since your lordship has advised me not to publish that little which I know, I look on your counsel as your command, which I shall observe inviolably till you shall please to revoke it and leave me at liberty to make my thoughts public.

In the meantime, that I may arrogate nothing to myself, I must acknowledge that Virgil in Latin and Spenser in English have been my masters. Spenser has also given me the boldness to make use sometimes of his Alexandrine line, which we call, though improperly, the Pindaric, because Mr. Cowley has often employed it in his odes. It adds a certain majesty to the verse when it is used with judgment, and stops the sense from overflowing into another line.

Formerly the French, like us and the Italians, had but five feet or ten syllables in their heroic verse; but since Ronsard's time, as I suppose, they found their tongue too weak to support their epic poetry without the addition of another foot. That indeed has given it somewhat of the run and measure of a trimetre, but it runs with more activity than strength. Their language is not strong with sinews, like our English; it has the nimbleness of a greyhound, but not the bulk and body of a mastiff.

Our men and our verses overbear them by their weight; and pondere, non numero is the British motto. The French have set up purity for the standard of their language; and a masculine vigour is that of ours. Like their tongue is the genius of their poets, light and trifling in comparison of the English—more proper for sonnets, madrigals, and elegies than heroic poetry. The turn on thoughts and words is their chief talent: but the epic poem is too stately to receive those little ornaments. The painters draw their nymphs in thin and airy habits, but the weight of gold and of embroideries is reserved for queens and goddesses. Virgil is never frequent in those turns, like Ovid, but much more sparing of them in his "AEneis" than in his Pastorals and Georgics:

"Ignoscenda quidem, scirent si ignoscere manes."

That turn is beautiful indeed; but he employs it in the story of Orpheus and Eurydice, not in his great poem. I have used that licence in his "AEneis" sometimes, but I own it as my fault; it was given to those who understand no better. It is like Ovid's:

"Semivirumque bovem, semibovemque virum."

The poet found it before his critics, but it was a darling sin which he would not be persuaded to reform. The want of genius, of which I have accused the French, is laid to their charge by one of their own great authors, though I have forgotten his name, and where I read it. If rewards could make good poets, their great master has not been wanting on his part in his bountiful encouragements; for he is wise enough to imitate Augustus if he had a Maro. The Triumvir and Proscriber had descended to us in a more hideous form than they now appear, if the emperor had not taken care to make friends of him and Horace. I confess the banishment of Ovid was a blot in his escutcheon; yet he was only banished, and who knows but his crime was capital? And then his exile was a favour. Ariosto, who, with all his faults, must be acknowledged a great poet, has put these words into the mouth of an Evangelist; but whether they will pass for gospel now I cannot tell:

"Non fu si santo ni benigno Augusto,
Come la tuba di Virgilio suona;
L'haver havuto in poesia buon gusto,
La proscrittione iniqua gli pardona."

But heroic poetry is not of the growth of France, as it might be of England if it were cultivated. Spenser wanted only to have read the rules of Bossu, for no man was ever born with a greater genius or had more knowledge to support it. But the performance of the French is not equal to their skill; and hitherto we have wanted skill to perform better. Segrais, whose preface is so wonderfully good, yet is wholly destitute of elevation; though his version is much better than that of the two brothers, or any of the rest who have attempted Virgil. Annibale Caro is a great name amongst the Italians, yet his translation of the "AEneis" is most scandalously mean, though he has taken the advantage of writing in blank verse, and freed himself from the shackles of modern rhyme—if it be modern; for Le Clerc has told us lately, and I believe has made it out, that David's Psalms were written in as errant rhyme as they are translated. Now if a Muse cannot run when she is unfettered, it is a sign she has but little speed.

I will not make a digression here, though I am strangely tempted to it, but will only say that he who can write well in rhyme may write better in blank verse. Rhyme is certainly a constraint even to the best poets, and those who make it with most ease; though perhaps I have as little reason to complain of that hardship as any man, excepting Quarles and Withers. What it adds to sweetness, it takes away from sense; and he who loses the least by it may be called a gainer; it often makes us swerve from an author's meaning.

As if a mark he set up for an archer at a great distance, let him aim as exactly as he can, the least wind will take his arrow and divert it from the white. I return to our Italian translator of the "AEneis;" he is a foot-poet; he lackeys by the side of Virgil at the best, but never mounts behind him. Doctor Morelli, who is no mean critic in our poetry, and therefore may be presumed to be a better in his own language, has confirmed me in this opinion by his judgment, and thinks withal that he has often mistaken his master's sense. I would say so if I durst, but am afraid I have committed the same fault more often and more grossly; for I have forsaken Ruaeus (whom generally I follow) in many places, and made expositions of my own in some, quite contrary to him, of which I will give but two examples, because they are so near each other in the tenth AEneid:

"Sorti pater aequus utrique."

Pallas says it to Turnus just before they fight. Ruaeus thinks that the word pater is to be referred to Evander, the father of Pallas; but how could he imagine that it was the same thing to Evander if his son were slain, or if he overcame? The poet certainly intended Jupiter, the common father of mankind, who, as Pallas hoped, would stand an impartial spectator of the combat, and not be more favourable to Turnus than to him. The second is not long after it, and both before the duel is begun. They are the words of Jupiter, who comforts Hercules for the death of Pallas, which was immediately to ensue, and which Hercules could not hinder, though the young hero had addressed his prayers to him for his assistance, because the gods cannot control destiny. The verse follows-

"Sic ait; atque oculos Rutulorum rejicit arvis"-which the same Ruaeus thus construes: "Jupiter, after he had said this, immediately turns his eyes to the Rutulian fields and beholds the duel." I have given this place another exposition—that he turned his eyes from the field of combat that he might not behold a sight so unpleasing to him. The word rejicit, I know, will admit of both senses; but Jupiter having confessed that he could not alter fate, and being grieved he could not in consideration of Hercules, it seems to me that he should avert his eyes rather than take pleasure in the spectacle. But of this I am not so confident as the other, though I think I have followed Virgil's sense.

What I have said, though it has the face of arrogance, yet is intended for the honour of my country, and therefore I will boldly own that this English translation has more of Virgil's spirit in it than either the French or the Italian. Some of our countrymen have translated episodes and other parts of Virgil with great success; as particularly your lordship, whose version of Orpheus and Eurydice is eminently good. Amongst the dead authors, the Silenus of my Lord Rescommon cannot be too much commended. I say nothing of Sir John Denham, Mr. Waller, and Mr. Cowley; it is the utmost of my ambition to be thought their equal, or not to be much inferior to them and some others of the living. But it is one thing to take pains on a fragment and translate it perfectly, and another thing to have the weight of a whole author on my shoulders. They who believe the burden light, let them attempt the fourth, sixth, or eighth Pastoral; the first or fourth Georgic; and, amongst the AEneids, the fourth, the fifth, the seventh, the ninth, the tenth, the eleventh, or the twelfth, for in these I think I have succeeded best. Long before I undertook this work I was no stranger to the original. I had also studied Virgil's design, his disposition of it, his manners, his judicious management of the figures, the sobre retrenchments of his sense, which always leaves somewhat to gratify our imagination, on which it may enlarge at pleasure; but, above all, the elegance of his expressions and the harmony of his numbers. For, as I have said in a former dissertation, the words are in poetry what the colours are in painting. If the design be good, and the draft be true, the colouring is the first beauty that strikes the eye. Spenser and Milton are the nearest in English to Virgil and Horace in the Latin, and I have endeavoured to form my style by imitating their masters.

I will farther own to you, my lord, that my chief ambition is to please those readers who have discernment enough to prefer Virgil before any other poet in the Latin tongue. Such spirits as he desired to please, such would I choose for my judges, and would stand or fall by them alone. Segrais has distinguished the readers of poetry, according to their capacity of judging, into three classes (he might have said the same of writers, too, if he had pleased). In the lowest form he places those whom he calls les petits esprits—such things as are our upper-gallery audience in a playhouse, who like nothing but the husk and rind of wit; prefer a quibble, a conceit, an epigram, before solid sense and elegant expression. These are mob-readers. If Virgil and Martial steed for Parliament-men, we know already who would carry it. But though they make the greatest appearance in the field, and cry the loudest, the best of it is they are but a sort of French Huguenots, or Dutch boors, brought ever in herds, but not naturalised, who have not land of two pounds per annum in Parnassus, and therefore are not privileged to poll.

Their authors are of the same level; fit to represent them on a mountebank's stage, or to be masters of the ceremonies in a bear-garden. Yet these are they who have the most admirers. But it often happens, to their mortification, that as their readers improve their stock of sense (as they may by reading better books, and by conversation with men of judgment), they soon forsake them; and when the torrent from the mountains falls no more, the swelling writer is reduced into his shallow bed, like the Mancanares at Madrid, with scarce water to moisten his own pebbles. There are a middle sort of readers (as we held there is a middle state of souls), such as have a farther insight than the former, yet have not the capacity of judging right; for I speak not of those who are bribed by a party, and knew better if they were not corrupted, but I mean a company of warm young men, who are not yet arrived so far as to discern the difference betwixt fustian or ostentations sentences and the true sublime. These are above liking Martial or Owen's epigrams, but they would certainly set Virgil below Statius or Lucan.

I need not say their poets are of the same paste with their admirers. They affect greatness in all they write, but it is a bladdered greatness, like that of the vain man whom Seneca describes an ill habit of body, full of humours, and swelled with dropsy. Even these, too, desert their authors as their judgment ripens. The young gentlemen themselves are commonly misled by their pedagogue at school, their tutor at the university, or their governor in their travels, and many of these three sorts are the most positive blockheads in the world. How many of these flatulent writers have I known who have sunk in their reputation after seven or eight editions of their works! for indeed they are poets only for young men. They had great success at their first appearance, but not being of God, as a wit said formerly, they could not stand.

I have already named two sorts of judges, but Virgil wrote for neither of them, and by his example I am not ambitious of pleasing the lowest or the middle form of readers. He chose to please the most judicious souls, of the highest rank and truest understanding. These are few in number; but whoever is so happy as to gain their approbation can never lose it, because they never give it blindly. Then they have a certain magnetism in their judgment which attracts others to their sense. Every day they gain some new proselyte, and in time become the Church. For this reason a well-weighed judicious poem, which at its first appearance gains no more upon the world than to be just received, and rather not blamed than much applauded, insinuates itself by insensible degrees into the liking of the reader; the more he studies it, the more it grows upon him, every time he takes it up he discovers some new graces in it. And whereas poems which are produced by the vigour of imagination only have a gloss upon them at the first (which time wears off), the works of judgment are like the diamond, the more they are polished the more lustre they receive. Such is the difference betwixt Virgil's "AEneis" and Marini's "Adone." And if I may be allowed to change the metaphor, I would say that Virgil is like the Fame which he describes:

"Mobilitate viget, viresque acquirit eundo."

Such a sort of reputation is my aim, though in a far inferior degree, according to my motto in the title-page—sequiturque patrem non passibus aequis—and therefore I appeal to the highest court of judicature, like that of the peers, of which your lordship is so great an ornament. Without this ambition which I own, of desiring to please the judices natos, I could never have been able to have done anything at this age, when the fire of poetry is commonly extinguished in other men. Yet Virgil has given me the example of Entellus for my encouragement; when he was well heated, the younger champion could not stand before him. And we find the elder contended not for the gift, but for the honour (nec dona moror); for Dampier has informed us in his "Voyages" that the air of the country which produces gold is never wholesome.

I had long since considered that the way to please the best judges is not to translate a poet literally, and Virgil least of any other; for his peculiar beauty lying in his choice of words,

I am excluded from it by the narrow compass of our heroic verse, unless I would make use of monosyllables only, and these clogged with consonants, which are the dead weight of our mother tongue. It is possible, I confess, though it rarely happens, that a verse of monosyllables may sound harmoniously; and some examples of it I have seen. My first line of the "AEneis" is not harsh:

"Arms, and the man I sing, who forced by Fate," &c.

But a much better instance may be given from the last line of Manilius, made English by our learned and judicious Mr. Creech:

"Nor could the world have borne so fierce a flame"

where the many liquid consonants are placed so artfully that they give a pleasing sound to the words, though they are all of one syllable. It is true, I have been sometimes forced upon it in other places of this work, but I never did it out of choice: I was either in haste, or Virgil gave me no occasion for the ornament of words; for it seldom happens but a monosyllable line turns verse to prose, and even that prose is rugged and unharmonious. Philarchus, I remember, taxes Balzac for placing twenty monosyllables in file without one dissyllable betwixt them.

The way I have taken is not so strait as metaphrase, nor so loose as paraphrase; some things, too, I have omitted, and sometimes have added of my own. Yet the omissions, I hope, are but of circumstances, and such as would have no grace in English; and the additions, I also hope, are easily deduced from Virgil's sense. They will seem (at least, I have the vanity to think so), not stuck into him, but growing out of him. He studies brevity more than any other poet; but he had the advantage of a language wherein much may be comprehended in a little space. We and all the modern tongues have more articles and pronouns, besides signs of tenses and cases, and other barbarities on which our speech is built, by the faults of our forefathers. The Romans founded theirs upon the Greek; and the Greeks, we know, were labouring many hundred years upon their language before they brought it to perfection. They rejected all those signs, and cut off as many articles as they could spare, comprehending in one word what we are constrained to express in two; which is one reason why we cannot write so concisely as they have done. The word pater, for example, signifies not only "a father," but "your father," "my father," "his or her father"—all included in a word.

This inconvenience is common to all modern tongues, and this alone constrains us to employ more words than the ancients needed. But having before observed that Virgil endeavours to be short, and at the same time elegant, I pursue the excellence and forsake the brevity. For there he is like ambergris, a rich perfume, but of so close and glutinous a body that it must be opened with inferior scents of musk or civet, or the sweetness will not be drawn out into another language.

On the whole matter I thought fit to steer betwixt the two extremes of paraphrase and literal translation; to keep as near my author as I could without losing all his graces, the most eminent of which are in the beauty of his words: and those words, I must add, are always figurative. Such of these as would retain their elegance in our tongue, I have endeavoured to graff on it; but most of them are of necessity to be lest, because they will not shine in any but their own. Virgil has sometimes two of them in a line; but the scantiness of our heroic verse is not capable of receiving more than one; and that, too, must expiate for many others which have none. Such is the difference of the languages, or such my want of skill in choosing words. Yet I may presume to say, and I hope with as much reason as the French translator, that, taking all the materials of this divine author, I have endeavoured to make Virgil speak such English as he would himself have spoken if he had been born in England and in this present age. I acknowledge, with Segrais, that I have not succeeded in this attempt according to my desire; yet I shall not be wholly without praise, if in some sort I may be allowed to have copied the clearness, the purity, the easiness, and the magnificence of his style. But I shall have occasion to speak farther on this subject before I end the preface.

When I mentioned the Pindaric line, I should have added

that I take another licence in my verses; for I frequently make use of triplet rhymes, and for the same reason—because they bound the sense. And therefore I generally join these two licences together, and make the last verse of the triplet a Pindaric; for besides the majesty which it gives, it confines the sense within the barriers of three lines, which would languish if it were lengthened into four. Spenser is my example for both these privileges of English verses; and Chapman has followed him in his translation of Homer. Mr. Cowley has given in to them after both; and all succeeding writers after him. I regard them now as the Magna Charta of heroic poetry; and am too much an Englishman to lose what my ancestors have gained for me. Let the French and Italians value themselves on their regularity; strength and elevation are our standard. I said before, and I repeat it, that the affected purity of the French has unsinewed their heroic verse. The language of an epic poem is almost wholly figurative; yet they are so fearful of a metaphor that no example of Virgil can encourage them to be bold with safety. Sure, they might warm themselves by that sprightly blaze, without approaching it so close as to singe their wings; they may come as near it as their master.

Not that I would discourage that purity of diction in which he excels all other poets; but he knows how far to extend his franchises, and advances to the verge without venturing a foot beyond it. On the other side, without being injurious to the memory of our English Pindar, I will presume to say that his metaphors are sometimes too violent, and his language is not always pure. But at the same time I must excuse him, for through the iniquity of the times he was forced to travel at an age when, instead of learning foreign languages, he should have studied the beauties of his mother tongue, which, like all other speeches, is to be cultivated early, or we shall never write it with any kind of elegance. Thus by gaining abroad he lost at home, like the painter in the "Arcadia," who, going to see a skirmish, had his arms lopped off, and returned, says Sir Philip Sidney, well instructed how to draw a battle, but without a hand to perform his work.

There is another thing in which I have presumed to

deviate from him and Spenser. They both make hemistichs, or half-verses, breaking off in the middle of a line. I confess there are not many such in the "Faerie Queen," and even those few might be occasioned by his unhappy choice of so long a stanza. Mr. Cowley had found out that no kind of staff is proper for an heroic poem, as being all too lyrical; yet though he wrote in couplets, where rhyme is freer from constraint, he frequently affects half-verses, of which we find not one in Homer, and I think not in any of the Greek poets or the Latin, excepting only Virgil and there is no question but he thought he had Virgil's authority for that licence.

But I am confident our poet never meant to leave him or any other such a precedent; and I ground my opinion on these two reasons: first, we find no example of a hemistich in any of his Pastorals or Georgics, for he had given the last finishing strokes to both these poems; but his "AEneis" he left so incorrect, at least so short of that perfection at which he aimed, that we know how hard a sentence he passed upon it. And, in the second place, I reasonably presume that he intended to have filled up all these hemistichs, because in one of them we find the sense imperfect:

"Quem tibi jam Troja; which some foolish grammarian has ended for him with a half-line of nonsense:-

"Peperit fumante Creusa."

For Ascanius must have been born some years before the burning of that city, which I need not prove. On the other side we find also that he himself filled up one line in the sixth AEneid, the enthusiasm seizing him while he was reading to Augustus:- *"Misenum AEolidem, quo non praestantior alter AEre ciere viros,..."* to which he added in that transport, Martemque accendare cantu, and never was any line more nobly finished, for the reasons which I have given in the *"Book of Painting."*

On these considerations I have shunned hemistichs, not being willing to imitate Virgil to a fault, like Alexander's courtiers, who affected to hold their necks awry because he could not help it. I am confident your lordship is by this time of my opinion, and that you will look on those half-lines hereafter as the imperfect products of a hasty muse, like the frogs and serpents in the Nile, part of them kindled into life, and part a lump of unformed, unanimated mud.

I am sensible that many of my whole verses are as imperfect as those halves, for want of time to digest them better. But give me leave to make the excuse of Boccace, who, when he was upbraided that some of his novels had not the spirit of the rest, returned this answer: that Charlemagne, who made the Paladins, was never able to raise an army of them. The leaders may be heroes, but the multitude must consist of common men.

I am also bound to tell your lordship, in my own defence, that from the beginning of the first Georgic to the end of the last AEneid, I found the difficulty of translation growing on me in every succeeding book. For Virgil, above all poets, had a stock which I may call almost inexhaustible, of figurative, elegant, and sounding words. I, who inherit but a small portion of his genius, and write in a language so much inferior to the Latin, have found it very painful to vary phrases when the same sense returns upon me.

Even he himself, whether out of necessity or choice, has often expressed the same thing in the same words, and often repeated two or three whole verses which he had used before. Words are not so easily coined as money; and yet we see that the credit not only of banks, but of exchequers, cracks when little comes in and much goes out. Virgil called upon me in every line for some new word, and I paid so long that I was almost bankrupt; so that the latter end must needs be more burthensome than the beginning or the middle; and consequently the twelfth AEneid cost me double the time of the first and second.

What had become of me, if Virgil had taxed me with another book? I had certainly been reduced to pay the public in hammered money for want of milled; that is, in the same old words which I had used before; and the receivers must have been forced to have taken anything, where there was so little to be had.

Besides this difficulty with which I have struggled and made a shift to pass it ever, there is one remaining, which is insuperable to all translators. We are bound to our author's sense, though with the latitudes already mentioned; for I think it not so sacred as that one iota must not be added or diminished, on pain of an anathema. But slaves we are, and labour on another man's plantation; we dress the vineyard, but the wine is the owner's.

If the soil be sometimes barren, then we are sure of being scourged; if it be fruitful, and our care succeeds, we are not thanked; for the proud reader will only say—the poor drudge has done his duty. But this is nothing to what follows; for being obliged to make his sense intelligible, we are forced to untune our own verses that we may give his meaning to the reader. He who invents is master of his thoughts and words: he can turn and vary them as he pleases, till he renders them harmonious. But the wretched translator has no such privilege, for being tied to the thoughts, he must make what music he can in the expression; and for this reason it cannot always be so sweet as that of the original. There is a beauty of sound, as Segrais has observed, in some Latin words, which is wholly lost in any modern language. He instances in that mollis amaracus, on which Venus lays Cupid in the first AEneid.

If I should translate it sweet-marjoram, as the word signifies, the reader would think I had mistaken Virgil; for these village-words, as I may call them, give us a mean idea of the thing; but the sound of the Latin is so much more pleasing, by the just mixture of the vowels with the consonants, that it raises our fancies to conceive somewhat more noble than a common herb, and to spread roses under him, and strew lilies over him—a bed not unworthy the grandson of the goddess.

If I cannot copy his harmonious numbers, how shall I imitate his noble flights, where his thoughts and words are equally sublime? Quem

Quisquis studet aemulari,
Caeratis ope Dedalea
Nititur pennis, vitreo daturus
Nomina ponto."

What modern language or what poet can express the majestic beauty of this one verse, amongst a thousand others?

"Aude, hospes, contemnere opes, et te quoque dignum
Finge Deo..."

For my part, I am lost in the admiration of it. I contemn the world when I think on it, and myself when I translate it. Lay by Virgil, I beseech your lordship and all my better sort of judges, when you take up my version, and it will appear a passable beauty when the original muse is absent; but like Spenser's false Florimel, made of snow, it melts and vanishes when the true one comes in sight. I will not excuse, but justify, myself for one pretended crime with which I am liable to be charged by false critics, not only in this translation, but in many of my original poems—that I Latinise too much. It is true, that when I find an English word significant and sounding, I neither borrow from the Latin nor any other language; but when I want at home, I must seek abroad. If sounding words are not of our growth and manufacture, who shall hinder me to import them from a foreign country? I carry not out the treasure of the nation which is never to return, but what I bring from Italy I spend in England. Here it remains and here it circulates, for if the coin be good it will pass from one hand to another.

I trade both with the living and the dead for the enrichment of our native language. We have enough in England to supply our necessity; but if we will have things of magnificence and splendour, we must get them by commerce. Poetry requires ornament, and that is not to be had from our old Teuton monosyllables; therefore, if I find any elegant word in a classic author, I propose it to be naturalised by using it myself; and if the public approves of it, the bill passes. But every man cannot distinguish betwixt pedantry and poetry; every man, therefore, is not fit to innovate. Upon the whole matter, a poet must first be certain that the word he would introduce is beautiful in the Latin; and is to consider, in the next place, whether it will agree with the English idiom. After this he ought to take the opinion of judicious friends, such as are learned in both languages; and lastly, since no man is infallible, let him use this licence very sparingly; for if too many foreign words are poured in upon us, it looks as if they were designed not to assist the natives, but to conquer them. I am now drawing towards a conclusion, and suspect your lordship is very glad of it. But permit me first to own what helps I have had in this undertaking. The late Earl of Lauderdale sent me over his new translation of the "AEneis," which he had ended before I engaged in the same design. Neither did I then intend it; but some proposals being afterwards made me by my bookseller, I desired his lordship's leave that I might accept them, which he freely granted, and I have his letter yet to show for that permission.

He resolved to have printed his work, which he might have done two years before I could publish mine; and had performed it, if death had not prevented him. But having his manuscript in my hands, I consulted it as often as I doubted of my author's sense, for no man understood Virgil better than that learned nobleman. His friends, I hear, have yet another and more correct copy of that translation by them, which had they pleased to have given the public, the judges must have been convinced that I have not flattered him.

Besides this help, which was not inconsiderable, Mr. Congreve has done me the favour to review the "AEneis," and compare my version with the original. I shall never be ashamed to own that this excellent young man has shown me many faults, which I have endeavoured to correct. It is true he might have easily found more, and then my translation had been more perfect.

Two other worthy friends of mine, who desire to have their names concealed, seeing me straitened in my time, took pity on me and gave me the life of Virgil, the two prefaces—to the Pastorals and the Georgics—and all the arguments in prose to the whole translation; which perhaps has caused a report that the two first poems are not mine. If it had been true that I had taken their verses for my own, I might have gloried in their aid; and like Terence, have farthered the opinion that Scipio and Laelius joined with me. But the same style being continued through the whole, and the same laws of versification observed, are proofs sufficient that this is one man's work; and your lordship is too well acquainted with my manner to doubt that any part of it is another's. That your lordship may see I was in earnest when I premised to hasten to an end, I will not give the reasons why I writ not always in the proper terms of navigation, land-service, or in the cant of any profession. I will only say that Virgil has avoided these proprieties, because he writ not to mariners, soldiers, astronomers, gardeners, peasants, &c., but to all in general, and in particular to men and ladies of the first quality, who have been better bred than to be too nicely knowing in the terms. In such cases, it is enough for a poet to write so plainly that he may be understood by his readers; to avoid impropriety, and not affect to be thought learned in all things. I have emitted the four preliminary lines of the first AEneid, because I think them inferior to any four others in the whole poem; and consequently believe they are not Virgil's. There is too great a gap betwixt the adjective vicina in the second line, and the substantive arva in the latter end of the third; which keeps his meaning in obscurity too long, and is contrary to the clearness of his style. Ut quamvis avido is too ambitious an ornament to be his, and gratum opus agricolis are all words unnecessary, and independent of what he had said before.

Horrentia Martis arma is worse than any of the rest. Horrentia is such a flat epithet as Tully would have given us in his verses. It is a mere filler to stop a vacancy in the hexameter, and connect the preface to the work of Virgil. Our author seems to sound a charge, and begins like the clangour of a trumpet:-"Arma, virumque cano, Trojae qui primus ab oris,"-Scarce a word without an r, and the vowels for the greater part sonorous. The prefacer began with Ille ego, which he was constrained to patch up in the fourth line with at nunc to make the sense cohere; and if both those words are not notorious botches I am much deceived, though the French translator thinks otherwise. For my own part, I am rather of the opinion that they were added by Tucca and Varius, than retrenched.

I know it may be answered by such as think Virgil the author of the four lines—that he asserts his title to the "AEneis" in the beginning of this work, as he did to the two former, in the last lines of the fourth Georgic. I will not reply otherwise to this, than by desiring them to compare these four lines with the four others, which we know are his, because no poet but he alone could write them. If they cannot distinguish creeping from flying, let them lay down Virgil, and take up Ovid de Ponto in his stead. My master needed not the assistance of that preliminary poet to prove his claim: his own majestic mien discovers him to be the king amidst a thousand courtiers. It was a superfluous office, and therefore I would not set those verses in the front of Virgil; but have rejected them to my own preface:

"I, who before, with shepherds in the groves,
Sung to my oaten pipe their rural loves,
And issuing thence, compelled the neighb'ring field
A plenteous crop of rising corn to yield;
Manured the glebe, and stocked the fruitful plain
(A poem grateful to the greedy swain)," &c.

If there be not a tolerable line in all these six, the prefacer gave me no occasion to write better. This is a just apology in this place; but I have done great wrong to Virgil in the whole translation. Want of time, the inferiority of our language, the inconvenience of rhyme, and all the other excuses I have made, may alleviate my fault, but cannot justify the boldness of my undertaking. What avails it me to acknowledge freely that I have not been able to do him right in any line? For even my own confession makes against me; and it will always be returned upon me, "Why, then, did you attempt it?" To which no other answer can be made, than that I have done him less injury than any of his former libellers.

What they called his picture had been drawn at length so many times by the daubers of almost all nations, and still so unlike him, that I snatched up the pencil with disdain, being satisfied beforehand that I could make some small resemblance of him, though I must be content with a worse likeness. A sixth Pastoral, a Pharmaceutria, a single Orpheus, and some other features have been exactly taken. But those holiday authors writ for pleasure, and only showed us what they could have done if they would have taken pains to perform the whole.

Be pleased, my lord, to accept with your wonted goodness this unworthy present which I make you. I have taken off one trouble from you, of defending it, by acknowledging its imperfections; and though some part of them are covered in the verse (as Ericthonius rode always in a chariot to hide his lameness), such of them as cannot be concealed you will please to connive at, though in the strictness of your judgment you cannot pardon.

If Homer was allowed to nod sometimes, in so long a work it will be no wonder if I often fall asleep. You took my "Aurengzebe" into your protection with all his faults; and I hope here cannot be so many, because I translate an author who gives me such examples of correctness. What my jury may be I know not; but it is good for a criminal to plead before a favourable judge: if I had said partial, would your lordship have forgiven me? Or will you give me leave to acquaint the world that I have many times been obliged to your bounty since the Revolution? Though I never was reduced to beg a charity, nor ever had the impudence to ask one, either of your lordship or your noble kinsman the Earl of Dorset, much less of any other, yet when I least expected it you have both remembered me, so inherent it is in your family not to forget an old servant. It looks rather like ingratitude on my part, that where I have been so often obliged, I have appeared so seldom to return my thanks, and where I was also so sure of being well received.

Somewhat of laziness was in the case, and somewhat too of modesty; but nothing of disrespect or of unthankfulness. I will not say that your lordship has encouraged me to this presumption, lest, if my labours meet with no success in public, I may expose your judgment to be censured. As for my own enemies, I shall never think them worth an answer; and if your lordship has any, they will not dare to arraign you for want of knowledge in this art till they can produce somewhat better of their own than your "Essay on Poetry." It was on this consideration that I have drawn out my preface to so great a length. Had I not addressed to a poet and a critic of the first magnitude, I had myself been taxed for want of judgment, and shamed my patron for want of understanding. But neither will you, my lord, so soon be tired as any other, because the discourse is on your art; neither will the learned reader think it tedious, because it is ad Clerum: at least, when he begins to be weary, the church doors are open. That I may pursue the allegory with a short prayer after a long sermon. May you live happily and long for the service of your country, the encouragement of good letters and the ornament of poetry, which cannot be wished more earnestly by any man than by

Your Lordship's most humble,
Most obliged and most
Obedient servant,
JOHN DRYDEN.

POSTSCRIPT.

What Virgil wrote in the vigour of his age (in plenty and at ease) I have undertaken to translate in my declining years; struggling with wants, oppressed by sickness, curbed in my genius, liable to be misconstrued in all I write; and my judges, if they are not very equitable, already prejudiced against me by the lying character which has been given them of my morals. Yet steady to my principles, and not dispirited with my afflictions, I have, by the blessing of God on my endeavours, overcome all difficulties; and, in some measure, acquitted myself of the debt which I owed the public when I undertook this work.

In the first place, therefore, I thankfully acknowledge to the Almighty Power the assistance He has given me in the beginning, the prosecution, and conclusion of my present studies, which are more happily performed than I could have promised to myself when I laboured under such discouragements. For what I have done, imperfect as it is for want of health and leisure to correct it, will be judged in after-ages, and possibly in the present, to be no dishonour to my native country, whose language and poetry would be more esteemed abroad if they were better understood.

Somewhat (give me leave to say) I have added to both of them in the choice of words and harmony of numbers, which were wanting, especially the last, in all our poets; even in those who being endued with genius yet have not cultivated their mother-tongue with sufficient care, or, relying on the beauty of their thoughts, have judged the ornament of words and sweetness of sound unnecessary. One is for raking in Chaucer (our English Ennius) for antiquated words, which are never to be revived but when sound or significancy is wanting in the present language.

But many of his deserve not this redemption any more than the crowds of men who daily die, or are slain for sixpence in a battle, merit to be restored to life if a wish could revive them. Others have no ear for verse, nor choice of words, nor distinction of thoughts, but mingle farthings with their gold to make up the sum. Here is a field of satire opened to me, but since the Revolution I have wholly renounced that talent. For who would give physic to the great, when he is uncalled, to do his patient no good and endanger himself for his prescription? Neither am I ignorant but I may justly be condemned for many of these faults of which I have too liberally arraigned others:

"Cynthius aurem
Vellit, et admonuit."

It is enough for me if the government will let me pass unquestioned. In the meantime I am obliged in gratitude to return my thanks to many of them, who have not only distinguished me from others of the same party by a particular exception of grace, but without considering the man have been bountiful to the poet, have encouraged Virgil to speak such English as I could teach him, and rewarded his interpreter for the pains he has taken in bringing him over into Britain by defraying the charges of his voyage. Even Cerberus, when he had received the sop, permitted AEneas to pass freely to Elysium.

Had it been offered me and I had refused it, yet still some gratitude is due to such who were willing to oblige me. But how much more to those from whom I have received the favours which they have offered to one of a different persuasion; amongst whom I cannot omit naming the Earls of Derby and of Peterborough.

To the first of these I have not the honour to be known, and therefore his liberality as much unexpected as it was undeserved. The present Earl of Peterborough has been pleased long since to accept the tenders of my service: his favours are so frequent to me that I receive them almost by prescription. No difference of interests or opinion has been able to withdraw his protection from me, and I might justly be condemned for the most unthankful of mankind if I did not always preserve for him a most profound respect and inviolable gratitude.

I must also add that if the last AEneid shine amongst its fellows, it is owing to the commands of Sir William Trumbull, one of the principal Secretaries of State, who recommended it, as his favourite, to my care; and for his sake particularly I have made it mine. For who would confess weariness when he enjoined a fresh labour? I could not but invoke the assistance of a muse for this last office:-

"Extremum hunc, Arethusa;...
... neget quis carmina Gallo?"

Neither am I to forget the noble present which was made me by Gilbert Dolben, Esq., the worthy son of the late Archbishop of York, who (when I began this work) enriched me with all the several editions of Virgil and all the commentaries of those editions in Latin, amongst which I could not but prefer the Dauphin's as the last, the shortest, and the most judicious. Fabrini I had also sent me from Italy, but either he understands Virgil very imperfectly or I have no knowledge of my author.

Being invited by that worthy gentleman, Sir William Bowyer, to Denham Court, I translated the first Georgic at his house and the greatest part of the last AEneid. A more friendly entertainment no man ever found. No wonder, therefore, if both these versions surpass the rest; and own the satisfaction I received in his converse, with whom I had the honour to be bred in Cambridge, and in the same college.

The seventh AEneid was made English at Burghley, the magnificent abode of the Earl of Exeter. In a village belonging to his family I was born, and under his roof I endeavoured to make that AEneid appear in English with as much lustre as I could, though my author has not given the finishing strokes either to it or to the eleventh, as I perhaps could prove in both if I durst presume to criticise my master. By a letter from William Walsh, Esq., of Abberley (who has so long honoured me with his friendship, and who, without flattery, is the best critic of our nation), I have been informed that his Grace the Duke of Shrewsbury has procured a printed copy of the Pastorals, Georgics, and six first AEneids from my bookseller, and has read them in the country together with my friend.

This noble person (having been pleased to give them a commendation which I presume not to insert) has made me vain enough to boast of so great a favour, and to think I have succeeded beyond my hopes; the character of his excellent judgment, the acuteness of his wit, and his general knowledge of good letters, being known as well to all the world as the sweetness of his disposition, his humanity, his easiness of access, and desire of obliging those who stand in need of his protection are known to all who have approached him, and to me in particular, who have formerly had the honour of his conversation.

Whoever has given the world the translation of part of the third Georgic (which he calls "The Power of Love") has put me to sufficient pains to make my own not inferior to his; as my Lord Roscommon's "Silenus" had formerly given me the same trouble.

The most ingenious Mr. Addison, of Oxford, has also been as troublesome to me as the other two, and on the same account; after his bees my latter swarm is scarcely worth the hiving. Mr. Cowley's praise of a country life is excellent, but it is rather an imitation of Virgil than a version.

That I have recovered in some measure the health which I had lost by too much application to this work, is owing (next to God's mercy) to the skill and care of Dr. Guibbons and Dr. Hobbs (the two ornaments of their profession), whom I can only pay by this acknowledgment. The whole faculty has always been ready to oblige me, and the only one of them who endeavoured to defame me had it not in his power.

I desire pardon from my readers for saying so much in relation to myself which concerns not them; and with my acknowledgments to all my subscribers, have only to add that the few notes which follow are par maniere d'acquit, because I had obliged myself by articles to do somewhat of that kind. These scattering observations are rather guesses at my author's meaning in some passages than proofs that so he meant. The unlearned may have recourse to any poetical dictionary in English for the names of persons, places, or fables, which the learned need not, but that little which I say is either new or necessary, and the first of these qualifications never fails to invite a reader, if not to please him.

Bibliography

The Cambridge Companion to John Dryden. Ed. Steven N. Zwicker. (Cambridge University Press, 2004).

John Dryden 1631-1700: His Politics, His Plays, and IIis Poets. Claude Julien Rawson & Aaron Santesso. Univ of Delaware Press, 2004).

John Dryden: Tercentenary Essays. Paul Hammond & David Hopkins. (Oxford Univ Press, 2000).

John Dryden: Selected Criticism. G.A. Parfitt & James Kinsley. (Oxford University Press, 1999).

Ancient Faith and Modern Freedom in John Dryden's the Hind and the Panther. Anne Barbeau Gardiner. (Catholic Univ of Amer Press, 1998).

"*When Beauty Fires the Blood*": Love and the Arts in the Age of Dryden. James Anderson Winn. (University of Michigan Press, 1998).

Dryden and the Problem of Freedom: The Republican Aftermath 1649-1680. David B. Haley. (Yale Univ Press, 1997).

Critical Essays on John Dryden. Ed. James Anderson Winn. (G K Hall, 1997).

Dryden in Revolutionary England. David A. Bywaters. (University of California Press, 1991).

John Dryden and His World. James Anderson Winn. (Yale Univ Press, 1988).

John Dryden (Modern Critical Views). Ed. Harold Bloom. (Chelsea House Publishing, 1987).

Dryden: The Poetics of Translation. Judith Sloman. (Univ of Toronto Press, 1985).

Dryden: The Public Writer. George McFadden. (Princeton Univ Press, 1978).

Dryden As an Adapter of Shakespeare. Allardyce Nicoll. (AMS Press, 1978).

Contexts of Dryden's Thought. John Phillip Harth. (University of Chicago Press, 1978).

A Preface to Dryden. David Wykes. (Longman Group, 1977).

Politics and Poetry in Restoration England: The Case of Dryden's Annus Mirabilis. Michael McKeon. (Harvard Univ Press, 1975).

Tragic Theory in the Critical Works of Thomas Rymer, John Dennis, and John Dryden. Joan C. Grace. (Associated Univ Press, 1975).

Dryden's Classical Theory of Literature. E. Pechter. (Cambridge University Press, 1975).

Dryden's Political Poetry: Typology of King and Nation. Steven Zwicker. (University Press of New England, 1972).

The Intellectual Design of John Dryden's Heroic Plays. Anne T. Barbeau. (Yale Univ Press, 1970).

John Dryden and the Poetry of Statement. K. G. Hamilton. (Michigan State Univ Press, 1969).

Art of John Dryden. Paul Ramsey. (University Press of Kentucky, 1969).

Twentieth Century Interpretations of All for Love: A Collection of Critical Essays. Bruce Alvin King. (Prentice Hall, 1968).

Dryden's Poetry. Earl Roy Miner. (Indiana University Press, 1967).

Dryden's Heroic Drama. Arthur C Kirsch. (Gordian Press, 1965).

John Dryden's Imagery. A. W. Hoffman. (University Press of Florida, 1962).

Life of John Dryden. C.E. Ward. (Univ of North Carolina Press, 1961).

John Dryden: A Study of His Poetry. Mark Van Doren. (Indiana University Press, 1960).

Homage to John Dryden. T. S. Eliot. (Hogarth Press, 1924).